SIMUL 2022

The Fourteenth International Conference on Advances in System Simulation

October 16 - 20, 2022

Lisbon, Portugal

SIMUL 2022 Editors

Frank Herrmann, OTH Regensburg, Germany

Printed from e-media with permission by:

Curran Associates, Inc.
57 Morehouse Lane
Red Hook, NY 12571

Some format issues inherent in the e-media version may also appear in this print version.

Printed with permission by Curran Associates, Inc. (2023)

International Academy, Research, and Industry Association (IARIA)
412 Derby Way
Wilmington, DE 19810

Phone: (408) 893-6407
Fax: (408) 527-6351

petre@iaria.org

Additional copies of this publication are available from:

Curran Associates, Inc.
57 Morehouse Lane
Red Hook, NY 12571 USA
Phone: 845-758-0400
Fax: 845-758-2633
Email: curran@proceedings.com
Web: www.proceedings.com

Table of Contents

SIMUL 2022

Forward

The Fourteenth International Conference on Advances in System Simulation (SIMUL 2022), held between October 16th and October 20th, 2022, continued a series of events focusing on advances in simulation techniques and systems providing new simulation capabilities. While different simulation events are already scheduled for years, SIMUL 2022 identified specific needs for ontology of models, mechanisms, and methodologies in order to facilitate an appropriate tool selection. With the advent of Web Services and WEB 3.0, social simulation and human-in simulations bring new challenging situations along with the more classical process simulations and distributed and parallel simulations.

The conference provided a forum where researchers were able to present recent research results and new research problems and directions related to them. The conference sought contributions to stress-out large changes in scale system simulation, and advanced mechanisms and methodologies to deal with them.

We take here the opportunity to warmly thank all the members of the SIMUL 2022 technical program committee, as well as all the reviewers. The creation of such a high-quality conference program would not have been possible without their involvement. We also kindly thank all the authors who dedicated much of their time and effort to contribute to SIMUL 2022. We truly believe that, thanks to all these efforts, the final conference program consisted of top-quality contributions. We also thank the members of the SIMUL 2022 organizing committee for their help in handling the logistics of this event.

We hope that SIMUL 2022 was a successful international forum for the exchange of ideas and results between academia and industry and for the promotion of progress in the field of system simulation.

SIMUL 2022 Chairs

SIMUL 2022 Steering Committee

Carlo Simon, Hochschule Worms - University of Applied Sciences, Germany
Frank Herrmann, University of Applied Sciences Regensburg, Germany

SIMUL 2022 Publicity Chairs

Sandra Viciano Tudela, Universitat Politecnica de Valencia, Spain
Jose Luis García, Universitat Politecnica de Valencia, Spain

SIMUL 2022
Committee

SIMUL 2022 Steering Committee

Carlo Simon, Hochschule Worms - University of Applied Sciences, Germany
Frank Herrmann, University of Applied Sciences Regensburg, Germany

SIMUL 2022 Publicity Chairs

Sandra Viciano Tudela, Universitat Politecnica de Valencia, Spain
Jose Luis García, Universitat Politecnica de Valencia, Spain

SIMUL 2022 Technical Program Committee

Petra Ahrweiler, Johannes Gutenberg University Mainz, Germany
Chrissanthi Angeli, University of West Attica, Greece
Alfonso Ariza Quintana, University of Malaga, Spain
Natesh B. Arunachalam, The University of Texas at Austin, USA
Michel Audette, Old Dominion University, USA
Ana Paula Barbosa Póvoa, Universidade de Lisboa, Portugal
Marek Bauer, Politechnika Krakowska, Poland
John Betts, Monash University, Australia
Patrick Biemelt, University of Paderborn, Germany
Maria Julia Blas, Instituto de Desarrollo y Diseño (INGAR) | UTN-CONICET, Argentina
Paolo Bocciarelli, University of Rome Tor Vergata, Italy
Stefan Bosse, University of Bremen, Germany
Jalil Boudjadar, Aarhus University, Denmark
Christos Bouras, University of Patras, Greece
Lelio Campanile, Università degli Studi della Campania "L. Vanvitelli", Italy
Enrique Chirivella, University of the West of Scotland, UK
Franco Cicirelli, ICAR-CNR, Italy
Fábio Coelho, CEG-IST Instituto Superior Técnico | University of Lisbon, Portugal
Federico Concone, University of Palermo, Italy
Duilio Curcio, University of Calabria, Italy
Andrea D'Ambrogio, University of Roma TorVergata, Italy
Gabriele D'Angelo, University of Bologna, Italy
Luis Antonio de Santa-Eulalia, Business School | Université de Sherbrooke, Canada
Daniel Delahaye, ENAC LAB, Toulouse, France
Alexander Ditter, Friedrich-Alexander University Erlangen-Nürnberg (FAU), Germany
Anatoli Djanatliev, University of Erlangen-Nuremberg, Germany
Julie Dugdale, University Grenoble Alps, France
Mahmoud Elbattah, Université de Picardie Jules Verne, France
Sabeur Elkosantini, University of Carthage, Tunisia
Amr Eltawil, School of Innovative Design Engineering / Japan University of Science and Technology, Egypt
Diego Encinas, Informatics Research Institute LIDI - CIC - UNLP, Argentina

Eda Marchetti, ISTI-CNR, Pisa, Italy
Romolo Marotta, University of Rome "Sapienza", Italy
Niels Martin, Research Foundation Flanders (FWO) - Hasselt University, Belgium
Omar Masmali, The University of Texas, El Paso, USA
Michele Mastroianni, Università degli Studi della Campania "Luigi Vanvitelli", Italy
Andrea Matta, Politecnico di Milano, Italy
Roger McHaney, Kansas State University, USA
Nuno Melão, Polytechnic Institute of Viseu, Portugal
Roderick Melnik, MS2Discovery Interdisciplinary Research Institute | Wilfrid *Laurier* University, Canada
Adel Mhamdi, RWTH Aachen University, Germany
Owen Molloy, National University of Ireland, Galway, Ireland
Sébastien Monnet, LISTIC / Savoie Mont Blanc University, France
Federico Montori, University of Bologna, Italy
Jérôme Morio, ONERA (the French Aerospace Lab), France
Paulo Moura Oliveira, Universidade de Trás-os-Montes e Alto Douro (UTAD) / INESC-TEC Porto, Portugal
Nazmun Nahar, University of Jyvaskyla, Finland
Luis Gustavo Nardin, National College of Ireland, Ireland
Alessandro Pellegrini, Sapienza University of Rome, Italy
Tomas Potuzak, University of West Bohemia, Czech Republic
Dipak Pudasaini, Tribhuvan University, Nepal / Ryerson University, Canada
Francesco Quaglia, University of Rome Tor Vergata, Italy
Patrick Reinwald, University of Klagenfurt, Austria
Marco Remondino, Università degli Studi di Genova, Italy
Dupas Rémy, University of Bordeaux, France
Oscar Rodríguez Polo, University of Alcala, Spain
Kristin Yvonne Rozier, Iowa State University, USA
Julio Sahuquillo, Universitat Politecnica de Valencia, Spain
Ignacio Sanchez-Navarro, University of the West of Scotland, UK
Nandakishore Santhi, Los Alamos National Laboratory, USA
Victorino Sanz, ETSI Informática | UNED, Spain
Paulo Jorge Sequeira Goncalves, Instituto Politecnico de Castelo Branco, Portugal
Li Shi, Snap Inc., USA
Alireza Shojaei, Mississippi State University, USA
Patrick Siarry, Université Paris-Est Créteil (UPEC), France
Carlo Simon, Hochschule Worms - University of Applied Sciences, Germany
Leszek Siwik, AGH-UST University of Science and Technology, Krakow, Poland
Yuri N. Skiba, Universidad Nacional Autónoma de México, Mexico
Azeddien M. Sllame, University of Tripoli, Libya
Giandomenico Spezzano, CNR-ICAR, Italy
Sven Spieckermann, SimPlan AG, Germany
Renata Spolon Lobato, UNESP - São Paulo State University, Brazil
Mu-Chun Su, National Central University, Taiwan
Grażyna Suchacka, University of Opole, Poland
Violet R. Syrotiuk, Arizona State University, USA
János Száz, Corvinus University, Hungary
Kumar Tamma, University of Minnesota, USA
Ingo J. Timm, Trier University, Germany
Klaus G. Troitzsch, University of Koblenz-Landau, Germany

Copyright Information

A Validation Study of Simulated Illuminance Levels of an Office Space in Gurgaon, India under actual CIE Sky Conditions

Ankit Bhalla
GRIHA Council, TERI
New Delhi, India
Email: ankit.bhalla@grihaindia.org

Riya Malhotra
Sustainable Habitat Division, TERI
New Delhi, India
Email: riya.malhotra@teri.res.in

Rohit Thakur
Sustainable Habitat Division, TERI
New Delhi, India
Email: rohit.thakur@teri.res.in

Sanjay Seth
Sustainable Habitat Division, TERI
New Delhi, India
Email: Sanjay.seth@teri.res.in

Abstract — **In the past decade, numerous daylighting practitioners, architects, engineers, and researchers have progressively used daylighting simulation tools to estimate the daylight areas of building design. Most of these tools employ overcast sky conditions for daylight simulations. However, the accuracy and pertinence of such simulation tools for the tropical sky are uncertain. This study aimed to validate the computer-simulated result of overcast and actual sky models with physical test bed results measured under a real tropical sky. The considered space is modelled as per the constructed test bed space (Mahindra-TERI Centre of Excellence (MTCoE), Gurgaon, India) model to be tested under a real sky measurement. The same model was configured in VELUX Daylight visualizer 3.0 to perform daylighting simulation for March 21st, 2022, from 8:00hrs to 18:00hrs. All the illuminance measurements in the test bed were carried out under prevailing sky conditions in Gurgram, India. In contrast, related CIE sky conditions and overcast sky conditions were used for simulations to compare the results using the agreement of the index method. The International Commission on Illumination (CIE) sky conditions are very dissimilar from the actual tropical sky; simulated absolute value results such as external illuminance, absolute work plane illuminance and surface luminance recorded moderate mean differences from the measured results. Results indicate that the accuracy of illuminance levels increased by almost 24% through daylight simulations under actual sky conditions on March 21st (equinox day). Aimed at imminent research, other parameters can be validated, such as orientations, angle of the overhang, glazing, window sizes, colours, environment settings, and electric lighting.**

Keywords- Illuminance; daylight; validation; office; CIE.

I. Introduction

Daylight is an essential and effective aspect of the sustainable development approach for reducing energy consumption [1], the impact of climate change [2], and for improving well-being and productivity [3], visual comfort [4], and the built environment development [5]. For colour rendering, daylight is the best available light source, and its high quality makes it the only light source suitable for human visuals. The internal spaces are brightened by natural daylight, which mainly enters the space via window openings and establishes a visual link between the area of interest and exterior environments. An important stage in daylighting designs is calculating the daylight illuminance for a specific location in a building [6]-[9].

For daylighting, several guidelines and conceptual design strategies are available; the most common way to predict daylight illuminance is to use the Daylight Factor (DF). The method is simple, and analysis can be carried out analytically or derived via particular design aids. The DF calculation is based on overcast sky conditions and does not account for direct sunlight [10]. DF is frequently described in daylight design guidelines and is an extensively used technique for practitioners in many countries [11]. The DF method has effectively established the connection between the daylight controls and efficiency; as per the split-flux theory, the Average Daylight Factor (AFD) required for any area of interest is directly proportional to the window area and involves a smaller amount of data than DF [12][13].

The sky luminance varies as the distance from the sun changes (both in azimuth and altitude), according to recorded sky luminance data from other tropical nations and accepted sky luminance prediction models [14][15]. Aside from that, the Indian design sky does not consider the changes in sky circumstances when climatic zones shift. As detailed above, azimuthal uniformity, climatic invariance, and insufficiency for calculating annual energy savings owing to daylight are among the limitations of the present Indian design sky model. Because of these flaws, the designers had no choice but to use different sky luminance forecast models for window design and annual building energy load estimates. The sky models of Perez [16] and the International Commission on Illumination (CIE) [17] are commonly used for predicting sky brightness distribution.

The daylight availability is primarily determined by the sky's luminance levels and patterns [18]. In 2003, the CIE approved a set of 15 sky types illustrated in Table I, which presents an overall practical framework for representing the skies in various environments, including different climates such as tropical humid and temperate maritime [19][20]. The respective standard sky characterizes a distinct pattern of sky illuminance. However, the mathematical equations can be rather complicated, particularly for the non-overcast sky, which depends on the various sun positions [21]. The shading properties of nearby buildings can dramatically reduce the amount of sunshine entering the interior of the buildings, specifically in densely populated zones [22][23]. With the advancement in computer technology, computer simulation tools can be utilized to evaluate the building's daylight requirement. On the other hand, full-scale computer simulation programs can be highly complex, costly, and time-consuming, particularly during the early stages of design when numerous architectural possibilities and design schemes are studied and evaluated [24]. Simple simulation tools provide insight into the interdependency of numerous daylight variables for building professionals. In earlier investigations, many researchers have used simulation techniques to accurately validate the light environment in the tropics under an overcast sky with no external obstruction [25], however the studies were not performed under real sky conditions. Once the design schemes have been finalized, the practitioner performs computer simulations, and the calculation results will be used to verify the simulated findings.

The provisions, standards, and criteria for adequate natural light in buildings are specified in several regulations, codes of practice and design handbooks. A measuring station at the TERI Gram, Gurugram, Haryana, India, took solar irradiance and sky luminance measurements. All instruments were placed on the roof in a reasonably free of external impediments and easily accessible for examination, cleaning, and maintenance. Every day, data collection for sky luminance begins at 600hrs and ends at 1800hrs; on the other hand, data for solar irradiance is recorded every minute. All of the data was collected roughly simultaneously in true solar time, which aided in the computation of solar geometry and subsequent data comparison at other places.

TABLE I. A SET OF 15 STANDARD SKY TYPES AND THEIR PARAMETRIZATION (CIE, 2003)

Sky Type	Type of Sky	Standard gradation parameters	Standard indicatrix parameters
1	Overcast with the steep gradation and azimuthal uniformity	I: a=4 b=-0.7	1.c=0 d=-1 e=0
2	Overcast with the steep gradation and slight brightening toward sun	I : a=4 b=-0.7	2.c=2 d=-1.5 e=0.15
3	Overcast moderately graded with azimuthal uniformity	II : a=1.1 b=-0.8	1.c=0 d=-1 e=0
4	Overcast moderately graded and slight brightening toward sun	II : a=1.1 b=-0.8	2.c=2 d=-1.5 e=0.15
5	Overcast, foggy or cloudy with overall uniformity	III : a=0 b=-1	1.c=0 d=-1 e=0
6	Partly cloudy with a uniform gradation and slight brightening toward sun	III : a=0 b=-1	2.c=2 d=-1.5 e=0.15
7	Partly cloudy with a brighter circumsolar effect and uniform gradation	III : a=0 b=-1	3.c=5 d=-2.5 e=0.3
8	Partly cloudy, rather uniform with a clear solar corona	III : a=0 b=-1	4.c=10 d=-3 e=0.45
9	Partly cloudy with a shaded sun position	IV : a=-1 b=-0.55	2.c=2 d=-1.5 e=0.15
10	Partly cloudy with brighter circumsolar effect	IV : a=-1 b=-0.55	3.c=5 d=-2.5 e=0.3
11	White-blue sky with a clear solar corona	IV : a=-1 b=-0.55	4.c=10 d=-3 e=0.45
12	Very clear / unturbid with a clear solar corona	V : a=-1 b=-0.32	4.c=10 d=-3 e=0.45
13	Cloudless polluted with a broader solar corona	V : a=-1 b=-0.32	5.c=16 d=-3 e=0.3
14	Cloudless turbid with a broader solar corona	VI : a=-1 b=-0.15	5.c=16 d=-3 e=0.3
15	White-blue turbid sky with a wide solar corona effect	VI : a=-1 b=-0.15	6.c=24 d=-2.8 e=0.15

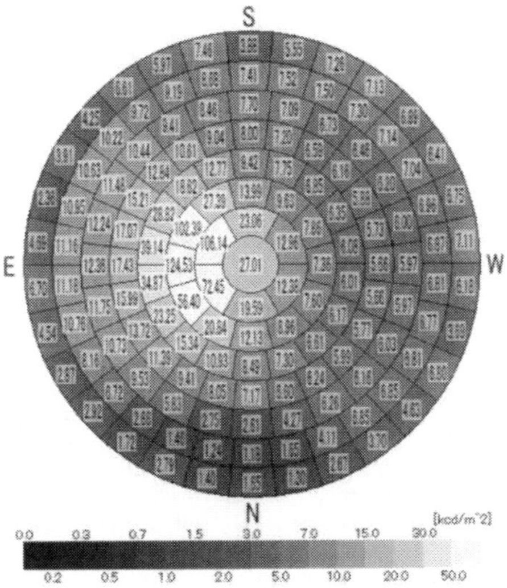

Figure 1. Measurement points for the sky scanner

The EKO MS321LR sky scanner is used to scan the luminance distributions in the sky that presents the sky grid pattern for the sky dome; it records the luminance at 145 sky patches, as shown in Figure 1. The scanner's full view angle is 11 degrees, which allows each sky patch to be regarded as a point source with minimal inaccuracy. This study looks at luminance data measurements and validation of the recorded data by utilizing the VELUX software.

II. METHODOLOGY

The study is divided into four sub-activities where the first activity (see Figure 2) focuses on the CIE analysis of the raw luminance data obtained from the installed sky scanner instrument at the MTCoE lab, Gurugram, India. For the second activity (see Figure 4) of the study, a room was selected in the vicinity of the sky scanner instrument to measure the actual daylight illuminance levels of the space. The considered space is further modelled as per the constructed test bed space as a part of the third activity of the study (see Figure 7). The model was configured in VELUX Daylight Visualizer 3.0 to perform daylighting simulation for equinox day that is 21st March from 800hrs to 1800hrs. All the illuminance measurements in the test bed were carried out under prevailing sky conditions in Gurugram, India. In contrast, related CIE sky conditions and overcast sky conditions were used for simulations to compare the results using the agreement of the index method (see Figure 10).

A. *Activity-1 CIE Analysis of Luminance Distribution Data*

The performance of each CIE standard sky luminance model was evaluated for 21st March 2022 using the Root Mean-Square Errors (RMSE) adapted from ISO 15469:2004 that defines a set of outdoor daylight conditions linking sunlight and skylight for theoretical and practical purposes [18] for the extracted luminance distribution data from the sky scanner instrument. The analyzed measured CIE sky-type for half-hourly data from 800hrs to 1800hrs as mentioned in Table II which is further used as an input for sky type consideration for CIE measured sky simulations as described in Activity-3.

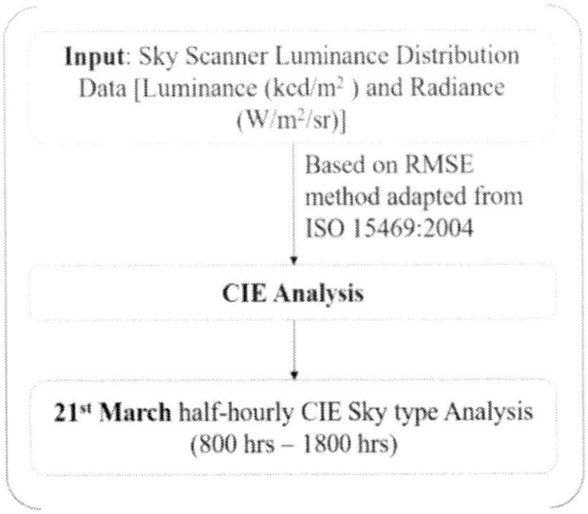

Figure 2. CIE Analysis of Luminance Distribution Data

TABLE II. CIE ANALYSIS MEASURED SKY TYPE FOR 21ST MARCH

Date	Time (hrs)	CIE Analysis Measured Sky-type	CIE Overcast sky-type
21st Mar 2022	800	14	1
	830	14	1
	900	14	1
	930	14	1
	1000	14	1
	1030	14	1
	1100	12	1
	1130	12	1
	1200	12	1
	1230	12	1
	1300	14	1
	1330	14	1
	1400	14	1
	1430	14	1
	1500	14	1
	1530	14	1
	1600	14	1
	1630	15	1
	1700	14	1
	1730	14	1
	1800	14	1

B. *Activity-2 Measurements of Daylight Iluminance levels*

For the second activity of the study, a room was selected in the 100m vicinity of the sky scanner instrument, as shown in Figure 3.

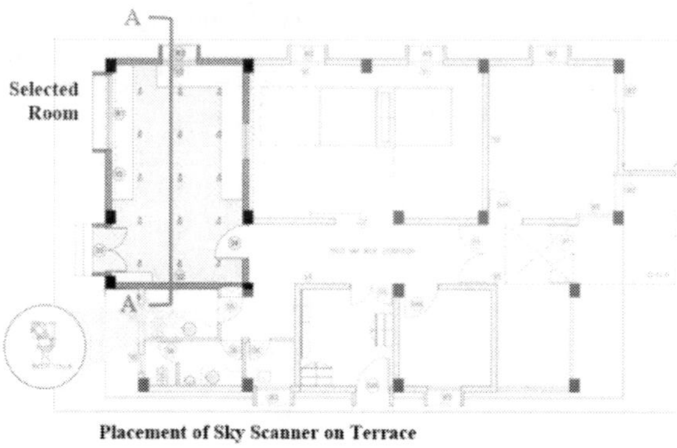

(a) Plan

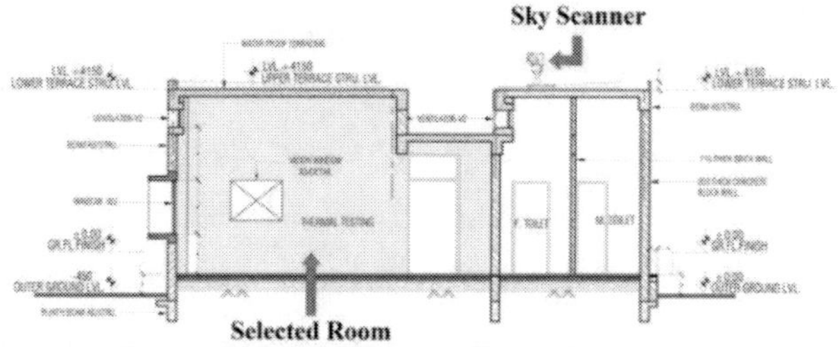

(b) Section A-A'

Figure 3. Placement of the Sky Scanner instrument and the selected room;

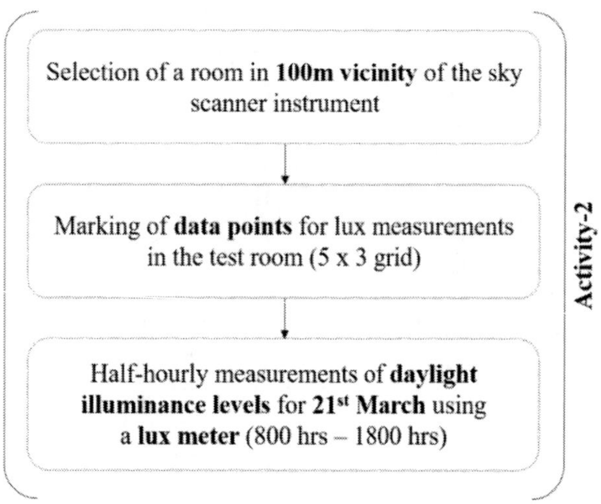

Figure 4. Daylight Illuminance Measurements

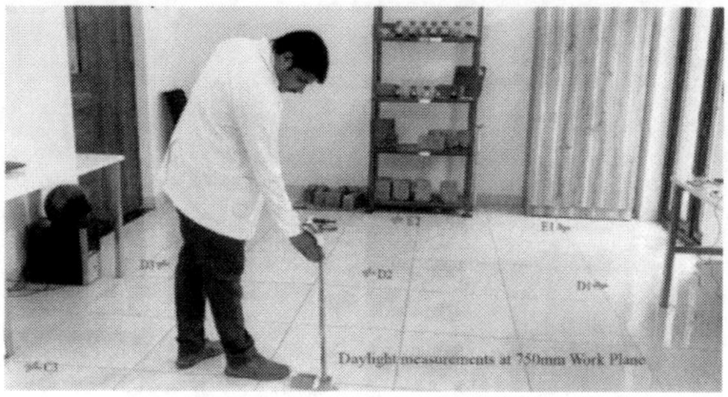

Figure 5. Measurements of illuminance levels using a Lux Meter at the MTCoE lab test bed

A set of 15 grid points (see Figure 6) is marked in the selected room and spatially distributed for data set points to measure the daylight illuminance levels for 21st March (800 hrs -1800 hrs) using testo 540 - Light meter, the light sensor is modelled on the spectral sensitivity of the human eye and is ideal for measuring lighting conditions in the workplace at 750mm work plane as shown in Figure 5.

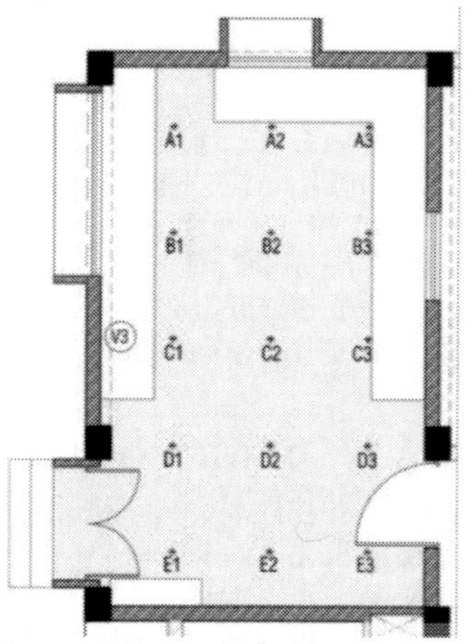

Figure 6. Data points in the selected room

C. *Activity-3 Daylight Simulations*

A 3D Model of the selected room (MTCoE test bed) was developed to perform the daylight simulations under CIE overcast sky type and CIE measured sky type (see Table II). The simulation results in illuminance (lux) for the same data points as shown in Figure 6 grid as the measured case. Under the scope of the study, the simulations were performed for the 21st of March using VELUX Daylight Visualizer 3.0 software that allows the user to perform daylight simulations considering any sky condition out of the CIE 15 general sky type (see Table I) only for the 21st day of each month.

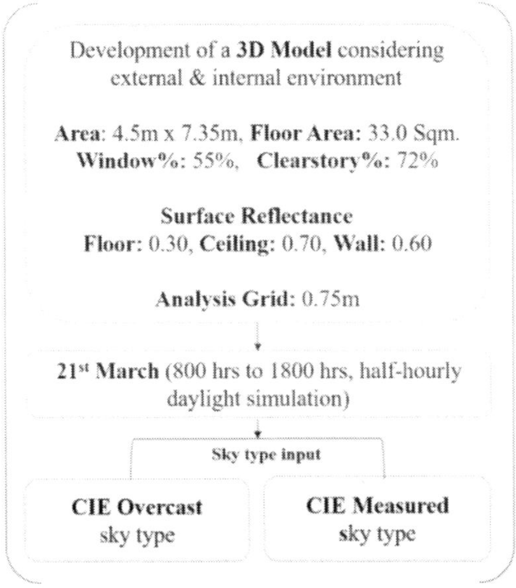

Figure 7. Run Chart for the daylight simulations

Figure 8. CIE Overcast Sky type daylight simulation for 21st March, 800 hrs with input sky type-1 described as 'Overcast with a steep gradation and azimuthal uniform'

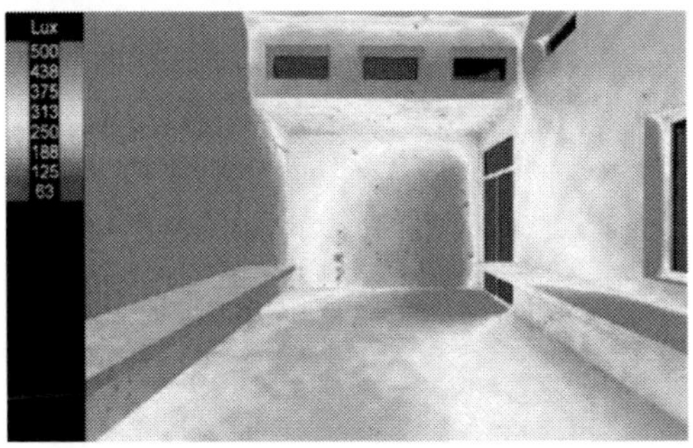

Figure 9. CIE Measured Sky type daylight simulation for 21st March, 800 hrs with input sky type-12 (see Table II) described as 'Very clear/unturbid with a clear solar corona'

D. *Activity-4 Index of Agreement*

The daylight illuminance levels obtained from the second activity for actual measurements were compared with the simulated lux levels from the third activity. The index of Agreement method is used to assess the differences between the two cases as shown in Figure 10.

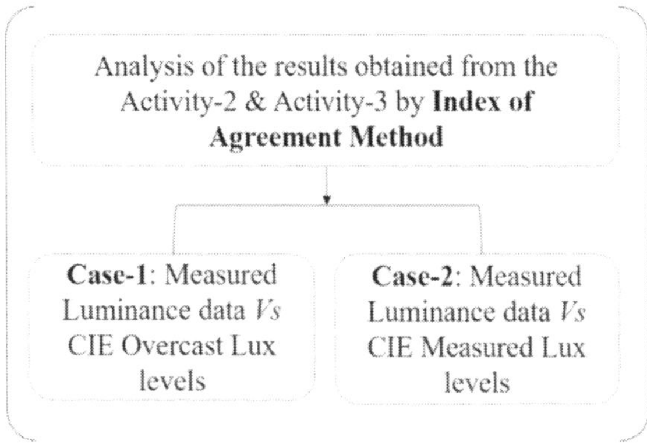

Figure 10. Analysis of the results

The comparison of model-produced estimates with observed/reliable data is an important stage in any modelling investigation. The index of agreement is used to validate this study (also known as the Willmott index); Willmott (1981) recommended a standardized measure of model forecast error called the index of agreement (d), which ranges from 0 to 1 [26]. The index of the agreement represents the ratio of the mean square error and the potential error. A value of one indicates a perfect match, while a value of zero indicates no agreement at all. The index of agreement can identify additive and proportional differences between observed and simulated means and variances; however, due to squared differences, d is susceptible to extreme values.

$$d = 1 - \frac{\sum_{i=1}^{n}(O_i - P_i)^2}{\sum_{i=1}^{n}(|P_i - \bar{O}| + |O_i - \bar{O}|)^2}\ , \quad 0 \leq d \leq 1$$

where O_i is the observed value and P_i is the predicted value and O_{bar} is the average observed value.

III. Observations

Results from the index of agreement method (see Table III and Figure 11) reveal that under overcast sky type illuminance levels were 79% closer to the measured lux levels at 800hrs whereas illuminance levels were only 71% closer to the measured lux level under real sky type, however, at 830hrs the lux levels were calculated to be 80% and 60% closer to the measured illuminance results under overcast sky type and measured CIE sky type. At 900hrs, a decrease in the percentage was observed as the illuminance level was 73% closer to the measured data under measured CIE type as compared to overcast sky type data measurement which was 79% closer to the measured data. Further at 930hrs the illuminance level was 85% and 91% closer to the measured lux level under overcast sky type and measured CIE sky type, it is at this time of the day where the percentage difference between overcast sky type and measured CIE type data was just one percent. At 1000hrs the illuminance level under overcast sky type and measured sky type were observed to be 88% and 91% closer to the measured data readings. At 1030hrs the illuminance levels under overcast sky type and measure sky type were observed to be 82% and 91% closer to the measure data reading however at 1100hrs there was a dip in percentage observed where the illuminance level was 93% closer to measure data under overcast sky type and 60% closer to the measure data under CIE measured sky type which is the maximum percentage closer to the measure readings and at 1130hrs the percentage dropped to 89% and 91%.

As observed during the noon, the illuminance level under overcast sky type and measured sky type were observed to be 68% and 84% closer to the measured illuminance levels and at 1230hrs the levels further dropped to 62% and 26%. At 1300hrs the illuminance level under overcast and CIE measure sky type were observed to be 75% and 95% closer to the measured data readings. Analysis indicates that at 1330hrs the luminance levels under the overcast and CIE Measured sky type were observed to be 39% and 89% during this hour of the day the difference between CIE measured sky type and overcast sky type was 50%. At 1400hrs the illuminance level under overcast and CIE measured sky type was observed to be 43% and 89% closer to the measured illuminance data, however a decrease in the percentage was observed at 1430hrs as the luminance levels under overcast sky type and CIE measured sky type was 24% and 87% closer to the measured illuminance data.

At 1500hrs the illuminance level under overcast and CIE measured sky type were analyzed to be the lowest, as they were just 3% and 73% close to the measured data, moreover by 1530hrs the percentage increase was observed to be 4% and 66%. The percentage increase continued for the next hour and the illuminance level was under overcast and CIE measured sky type were analyzed to be 6% and 73% at 1600hrs and 6% and 83% at 1630hrs closer to the measured illuminance level. By 1700hrs the illuminance level under overcast and CIE measured sky type were analyzed to be 3% and 23% closer to the measured illuminance data, which was lower than the previous hour this percentage, however, increased to 5% and 85% by 1730hrs.

The last reading of the day at 1800hrs demonstrated that the illuminance level was under overcast and CIE measured sky type were zero percent closer to the measured illuminance data.

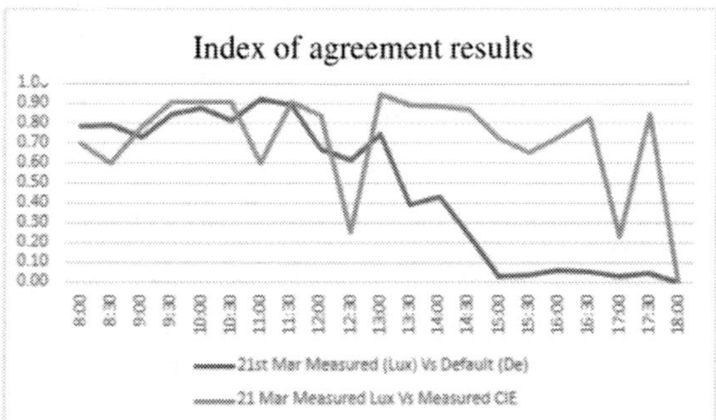

Figure 11. Index of agreement results

TABLE III. EX OF AGREEMENT RESULTS MEASURED LUX LEVEL V/S OVERCAST SKY TYPE (DE) & MEASURED LUX V/S MEASURED CIE SKY TYPE (DA).

Time	Measured (Lux) V/s Overcast sky type (D_e)	Measured Lux V/s Measured CIE sky type (D_a)
0800	0.79	0.71
0830	0.80	0.60
0900	0.73	0.79
0930	0.85	0.91
1000	0.88	0.91
1030	0.82	0.91
1100	0.93	0.60
1130	0.89	0.91
1200	0.68	0.84
1230	0.62	0.26
1300	0.75	0.95
1330	0.39	0.89
1400	0.43	0.89
1430	0.24	0.87
1500	0.03	0.73
1530	0.04	0.66
1600	0.06	0.73
1630	0.06	0.83
1700	0.03	0.23
1730	0.05	0.85
1800	0.00	0.00
Average	0.48	0.72
Standard Deviation	0.34	0.20
Median	0.68	0.83

For the 21st of March 2022 under overcast sky type the daily average of the illuminance level was 48% closer to the measured illuminance level and under CIE sky type data the illuminance level was 72% closer to the measured illuminance data with a standard deviation of 0.34 and 0.2 was observed for overcast sky type and CIE sky type with respect to measured data.

IV. CONCLUSION

The actual set of CIE design skies given in Table II can be selected for daylight simulation analysis for Gurgaon and Delhi NCR region to get 24% more accurate results than the current practice of analyzing under a worst-case scenario of overcast sky conditions. This would help architects and designers to select the glass with optimum visual light transmission and consider the optimum window-wall ratio of the project.

ACKNOWLEDGEMENT

The authors would like to thank Mahindra Lifespace for supporting and providing finical assistance for the study, Ms. Shabnam Bassi, Dy. CEO, GRIHA Council and Dr. Rana Veer Singh, Research Associate, TERI for their valuable suggestions, Dr. Mahua Mukherjee, Associate Professor, IIT Roorkee and Dr. E. Rajasekhar, Assistant Professor, IIT

Roorkee for technical guidance, IUSSTF for international exposure and Mr. Bhushan Sharma, Technical Assistant, TERI for data accumulation.

REFERENCES

[1] S. Karasu, "The effect of daylight saving time options on electricity consumption of Turkey", Energy vol. 35, no. 9, pp. 3773-3782, 2010.

[2] M.T. Markou, A. Bartzokas, and H.D. Kambezidis, "Generation of daylight reference years for two European cities with different climate" : Athens, Greece and Bratislava, Slovakia, Atmos. Res., vol. 86, no. 3-4, pp. 315-329, 2007.

[3] C. Garnier, T. Muneer and L. McCauley, Super insulated aerogel windows: impact on daylighting and thermal performance, Build. Environ. Vol. 94, pp. 231-238, 2015.

[4] M.S. Alrubaih, M.F.M. Zain, M.A. Alghoul, N.L.N. Ibrahim, M.A. Shameri and O. Elayeb, "Research and development on aspects of daylighting fundamentals", Renew. Sustain. Energy Rev. 21, 2013, 494-505.

[5] T. Hwang and T.K. Jeong, "Effects of indoor lighting on occupants' visual comfort and eye health in a green building", Indoor Built Environ. Vol. 20, no. 1, pp. 75-90, 2011.

[6] D.H.W. Li, "A review of daylight illuminance determinations and energy implications", Appl. Energy vol. 87, no. 7, pp. 2109-2118, 2010.

[7] T. Muneer, N. Abodahab and J. Kubie, "Windows in Buildings: Thermal, Acoustic, Visual and Solar Performance", Architectural Press, Oxford, 2000.

[8] X. Yu and Y. Su, "Daylight availability assessment and its potential energy saving estimation - A literature review", Renew. Sustain. Energy Rev. vol. 52, pp. 494-503, 2015.

[9] A. Das and S. K. Paul, "Artificial illumination during daytime in residential buildings: factors, energy implications and future predictions", Appl. Energy vol. 158, pp. 65-85, 2015.

[10] R. G. Hopkinson, P. Petherbridge and J. Longmore, "Daylighting", Heinemann, London UK, 1966.

[11] J. Hraska, "Criteria of daylighting and sunlight access in sustainable construction evaluation systems, in: Proceedings of the 5th International Conference on Solar Radiation and Daylighting", 10e11 Aug, Brno University of Technology, Czech Republic, pp. 98-103, 2011.

[12] P. J. Littlefair, "Average Daylight Factor: A Simple Basis for Daylight Design", November. BRE Information paper, IP 15/88, 1988.

[13] J. Lynes and P. Littlefair, "Lighting energy savings from daylight: estimation at the sketch design stage", Light Res. Technol. Vol. 22, no. 3, pp. 129-137, 1990.

[14] K. P. Lam, A. Mahdawi, M.B. Ullah, E. Ng, and E. Pal, "Comparative study of sky luminance models in the tropical context" Proceedings, Building Simulation 1997, International Building Performance Simulation Association (eds Spilter, J. D. and Hensen, J. L. M.), CVUT-Czech Technical University, Prague, Czechoslovakia, vol. 1, pp. 339–345, 1997.

[15] S. Janjai, "A satellite-based sky luminance model for the tropics". Int. J. Photoenergy, 2013.

[16] R. Perez, R. Seals, and J. Michalsky, "All-weather model for sky luminance distribution preliminary configuration and validation". Sol. Energy, Vol. 50, no. 3, pp. 235–245, 1993.

[17] S. Darula, and R. Kittler, "CIE general sky standard defining luminance distributions", Proc. Conf. eSim, The Canadian conference on building energy simulation. Montreal, Canada, 2002.

[18] International Standardisation Organisation, "CIE S 011/E:2003, Spatial Distribution Daylight-CIE Standard General Sky", 2004. ISO Standard 15469: 2004, Geneva.

[19] P. R. Tregenza, "Standard skies for maritime climates", Light Res. Technol. Vol. 31, no. 3, pp. 97-106, 1999.

[20] D.H.W. Li, C.C.S. Lau, J.C. Lam, "A study of 15 sky luminance patterns against Hong Kong data", Archit. Sci. Rev. vol. 46, no. 1, pp. 61-68, 2003.

[21] R. Kittler, S. Darula and R. Perez, "A set of standard skies", Polygr. Bratisl., 1998.

[22] D. H. W. Li, S. L. Wong, C. L. Tsang and G. H. W. Cheung, "A study of the daylighting performance and energy use in heavily obstructed residential buildings via computer simulation techniques", Energy Build. Vol. 38, no. 11, pp. 1343-1348, 2006.

[23] D. H. W. Li and S. L. Wong, "Daylighting and energy implications due to shading effects from nearby buildings", Appl. Energy vol. 84, no. 12, pp. 1199-1209, 2007.

[24] M. E. Aizlewood and P.J. Littlefair, "Daylight prediction methods: a survey of their use", in: Proceedings of the CIBSE National Lighting Conference. Bath, UK, pp. 126-140, 1996.

[25] Edward Yan-Yung Ng, Lam Khee Poh, Wu Wei and Takehiko Nagakura, "Advanced lighting simulation in architectural design in the tropics", Automation in Construction, Vol. 10, no. 3, pp. 365-379, 2001.

[26] C. J. Willmott, "On the validation of models". Physical Geography, no. 2, pp. 184-194, 1981.

Experimental Comparison of Some Multiple Imputation Methods from the R Package mice

Wim De Mulder
Centre for the Law of Obligations and Property
University of Ghent
Ghent, Belgium
Email: wim.demulder@ugent.be

***Abstract*—Missing values is an annoying, but common, artifact of many real-world data sets. The most convenient solution is to simply discard the variables with missing values. This is, however, not a risk-free operation, as it may entail the elimination of useful information, while under certain circumstances ignoring missing data may even introduce bias in downstream statistical inferences. A more statistically valid approach is to employ multiple imputation to impute plausible values at locations where values are missing. This paper provides an experimental comparison of some multiple imputation methods from the R package `mice` on two real-world data sets. Our analysis suggests some interesting hypotheses, e.g., that the absolute number of missing values is of more profound influence on the performance of imputation methods than the relative number of missing values. From the analysis, we draw some guidelines for data analysts who intend to impute missing values. Our work is also of particular relevance for statisticians, as most statistical analyses require complete data.**

***Index Terms*—multiple imputation, interval score, R package mice.**

I. INTRODUCTION

A. Background on Imputation

Missing data are common in real-world applications, such as in large-scale clinical trials [1] and in temporal climate time series [2]. It is considered good practice to investigate the mechanism causing missing data before any analysis on the data set is performed. That mechanism may depend neither on the observed data nor on the missing data, in which case the data are said to be Missing Completely at Random (MCAR) [3]. The incomplete data sample is then likely still representative of the population, meaning that there are no systematic differences between the missing and the observed data values [4]. If the missing mechanism only depends on the observed data, then the missing data are Missing At Random (MAR), which allows prediction of the missing values based on the complete subset [3]. If the mechanism depends on the missing data, and this dependency remains even given the observed data, then data are classified as Missing Not At Random (MNAR) [5].

The importance of identifying the missing data mechanism lies in its relevance for appropriately handling missing data. If the data are MCAR, then one can employ a missing data ignoring technique [6], given the observation that the complete subset is representative of the population. In contrast, when data are missing systematically, improper handling can introduce bias. For example, if women who earn a high salary are more likely to skip a survey question about income than are men who earn a high salary, then ignoring the missing data will artificially inflate male salaries relative to female salaries [7]. The widespread solution in such cases is missing data imputation.

B. Use of Multiple Imputation

Multiple Imputation (MI) is an imputation methodology that proceeds with replicating the incomplete data set multiple times and replacing the missing data in each replicate with plausible values drawn from an imputation model [8]. The statistical analysis of interest is then performed on each completed data set separately. MI is often preferred over single imputation, as it properly accounts for the uncertainty in the imputed values [7]. In particular, MI allows to construct confidence intervals around the imputed values. These confidence intervals may then be exploited in a subsequent analysis of interest to reflect uncertainty in the outcomes of the analysis. Given this feature of MI, it is no surprise that this technique has gained popularity as a powerful statistical tool for handling missing data [9], and that its use is frequently recommended by journal reviewers whenever missingness is present [10].

C. Outline of the Paper

This paper compares some MI methods from the R package `mice`. The philosophy behind the `mice` methodology is that multiple imputation is best done as a sequence of small steps, each of which may require diagnostic checking [11]. The R package `mice` is very convenient, in particular because it implements a lot of MI methods, and changing between methods essentially requires only to adjust the parameter 'method'. The results that are described below may equally well apply to MI methods from other software packages. The imputation methods are applied on five real-world time series from economics that are highly complex, each containing a very large number of missing values, and on one publicly available benchmark data set (cf. Section II). The selected imputation methods are outlined in Section III. It is, obviously, of vital importance to employ an imputation method that is accurate, since the accuracy of the imputed values may have a severe effect on any downstream task. Yet, practitioners frequently overlook that it is of almost equal importance to consider the appropriateness of the resulting confidence intervals for the imputed values. Very wide confidence intervals are evidently undesired, but the same applies to very small confidence intervals if the correct value is mostly outside of the interval. Therefore, the selected imputation methods are not only compared in terms of accuracy, but also in terms of the resulting confidence intervals, which goes beyond most existing experimental work (cf. Section IV-A). Experimental results are described in Section IV.

II. Data sets

A. Financial ratios

In the first experiment, we consider five financial ratios over time, which will be used in a later stage to predict bankruptcy in a recently granted project. The ratios were collected from the Bel-First Finance database, which contains extensive and highly detailed financial information on companies based in Belgium and Luxembourg [12]. The data set has previously been used by colleagues from Ghent University to predict bankruptcy using a Markov model, where imputation was performed by a simple mean method [13].

After consultation with domain experts from economics, it was internally agreed to restrict attention to five financial ratios that are considered most predictive for bankruptcy. An overview of these five ratios is provided in Table I (for the definition of the selected ratios, we refer to the aforementioned paper). Each financial ratio is a time series from 2010 until 2019, and data were collected for about 1 million companies. The table shows the percentage of missing values per ratio. It is observed that the five data sets are highly complex in terms of missingness, with over half of the values missing. Ratio 5 is an extreme case, with 97% of the values missing. Yet, given the very large number of companies and the fact that there are ten time points, even 3% non-missingness (as applies to ratio 5) still corresponds to about 300 000 non-missing values. This paper thus considers the very interesting research question whether multiple imputation methods can handle data sets where missingness in relative terms is very large, but where the amount of non-missing values in absolute terms is still very high. As an illustration of the distribution of missing values, Fig. 1 shows which time points are missing for ratio 3 for the first 5000 companies.

TABLE I
European financial ratios from the BelFirst database used in the case study

Ratio index	Description	% missing values
Ratio 1	Return on total assets	59%
Ratio 2	Interest cover	63%
Ratio 3	Solvency ratio	59%
Ratio 4	Liquidity ratio	61%
Ratio 5	Operating revenue per employee	97%

To gain some further insight into the characteristics of the financial ratios, we computed the correlation between consecutive time points, which turned out to be rather constant

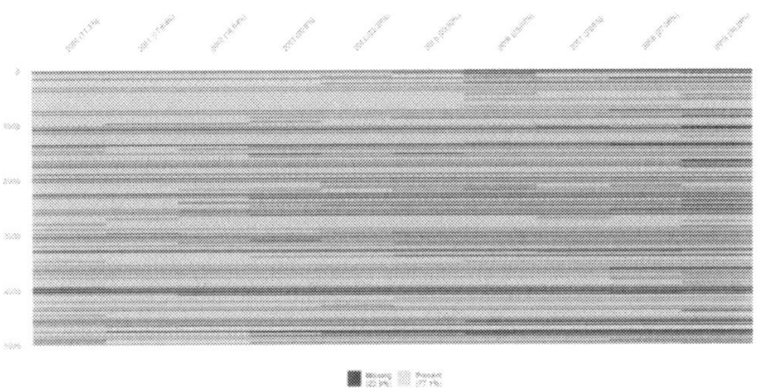

Fig. 1. Missing values for ratio 3 for the first 5000 companies

over time per ratio. Table II contains the average correlation between consecutive time points for all financial ratios. For the first three ratios this correlation is low, while the other ratios display a very high correlation. Since the relative number of missing values for the first four ratios is similar, as shown in Table I, we expect imputation values more accurate for the fourth ratio, given the very high correlation between consecutive time points. For the last ratio, there is also a very high correlation between consecutive time points, but the relative number of missing values is also extremely large. It will be part of the experimental analysis to identify which of both counteracting features has the greatest influence.

TABLE II
Average correlation between consecutive time points

	Correlation
Ratio 1	0.35
Ratio 2	0.5
Ratio 3	0.6
Ratio 4	0.86
Ratio 5	0.87

The correlation between the ratios is shown in Table III. The table clearly shows that the correlation between the ratios is low to very low.

TABLE III
Correlation between the ratios

	Ratio 2	Ratio3	Ratio 4	Ratio 5
Ratio 1	0.23	0.04	0.19	0.01
Ratio 2		0.12	0.20	0.01
Ratio 3			0.40	0
Ratio 4				-0.02

The R method `mcar_test` was applied to verify if the data set is MCAR. The results show that none of the ratios is MCAR, with extremely small p-values. Testing for MAR was performed by applying logistic regression, where for a given time point all missing values are set to 1 and all non-missing values to 0, and predicting these values with the other time points as input. The coefficients of the logistic regression model turned out to be statistically very significant, implying that the data set is at least MAR. Testing for MNAR is, however, not feasible, since this would require to know the missing values.

B. HTRU2 data set

As a second experiment, we also applied the selected imputation methods on the High Time Resolution Universe (HTRU2) data set from the University of California Irvine (UCI) Machine Learning Repository [14], which describes a sample of pulsar candidates collected during the High Time Resolution Universe Survey [15]. It contains 17 898 instances and 9 attributes. The fact that there are no missing values implies that this data set may be used as some sort of control data set. For example, if the considered imputation methods turn out to perform poorly on the financial ratios, while accuracy is high on the HTRU2 data set, it may be hypothesized that the relative number of missing values has a severe influence on the general performance of imputation methods. Table IV shows the pairwise correlations between the variables of the HTRU2 data set. It is seen that the correlations vary significantly, from very small correlations (e.g., between the second and the seventh variable) to very large correlations (in particular, between the third and the fourth variable).

TABLE IV
CORRELATION BETWEEN THE VARIABLES OF THE HTRU2 DATA SET

	2	3	4	5	6	7	8	9
1	0.55	-0.87	-0.74	-0.30	-0.31	0.23	0.14	-0.67
2		-0.52	-0.54	0.01	-0.05	0.03	0.03	-0.36
3			0.95	0.41	0.43	-0.34	-0.21	0.79
4				0.41	0.41	-0.33	-0.20	0.71
5					0.80	-0.62	-0.35	0.40
6						-0.81	-0.58	0.49
7							0.92	-0.39
8								-0.26

C. Introducing missing values

Obviously, evaluating imputation methods requires a ground truth. Therefore, a predefined percentage of non-missing values was randomly set to missing. For the first experiment, concerning the five financial ratios, this percentage was chosen as 2%. In the second experiment, involving the HTRU2 data set, a varying number of percentages was applied, ranging from 0.5% to 20%, in order to evaluate the impact of increasing missingness on the performance of the MI methods.

Each of the considered MI methods was applied 10 times, thus resulting in 10 imputed data sets for each chosen percentage of introduced missing values. To reduce the effect of random influences, in particular to avoid that the performance of the imputation methods is severely affected by an unfortunate random selection of non-missing values that are set to missing, the aforementioned procedure is repeated three times. We refer to these repetitions as "sub-experiments", reserving the term "experiment" to refer to either the financial ratios data set or the HTRU2 data set.

Imputation was performed on all missing values, but evaluation was restricted to the fictitious missing values.

III. IMPUTATION METHODS

We selected five MI methods from the R package `mice`:

- `mean`: Imputes the arithmetic mean of the observed data. This is a very simple and fast method, but imputing the mean of a variable is almost never appropriate [11].
- `norm`: Calculates imputations for missing data by Bayesian linear regression [16].
- `lasso.norm`: Imputes missing normal data using lasso linear regression with bootstrap [17] [18].
- `lasso.select.norm`: Imputes missing data using Bayesian linear regression following a preprocessing lasso variable selection step [17] [18].
- `rf`: Imputes missing data using random forests [19].

The selection includes simple methods, such as `mean`, as well as much more advanced methods, such as `rf`. The methods were selected in terms of applicability and popularity. Linear regression methods, such as `norm.predict`, turned out to fail on the given data sets, due to high correlation between certain variables. Furthermore, we restricted attention to the best known methods, which is why methods such as `2lonly.mean` and `polr` were not considered.

The statement that the `mean` method is very simple lies, in particular, in the fact that it does not take the correlation between the variables into account, while the other methods do. Methods relying on random forests are especially recommended when the variables have high inter-correlations [20].

IV. RESULTS

A. Evaluation measures

The five MI methods were evaluated using two evaluation measures that have also been used in our previous work [21]. Denote the values that were set to missing by ν_i and the corresponding imputed values for the jth imputed data set by $\hat{\nu}_{ij}, j = 1, \ldots, 10$. Furthermore, let $\hat{\nu}_i$ represent the average of the values $\hat{\nu}_{ij}$ over the 10 imputed data sets.

For each imputed data set we compute the Average Relative Difference (ARD):

$$ARD = \frac{1}{N}\sum_{i=1}^{N}\left|\frac{\hat{\nu}_{ij} - \nu_i}{\nu_i}\right| \tag{1}$$

where N refers to the number of non-missing values that were set to missing (cf. Section II). These values are then averaged over the 10 imputed data sets. The range of the ARD is $[0, +\infty)$.

The ARD measure evaluates the quality of the imputed values. It is, however, frequently overlooked in the literature to also evaluate the confidence intervals that result from applying multiple imputation. Given imputed values $\hat{\nu}_{ij}, j = 1, \ldots, 10$, we first compute the average value and the sample variance:

$$m(\hat{\nu}_i) = \frac{1}{10}\sum_{j=1}^{10}\hat{\nu}_{ij} \tag{2}$$

$$v(\hat{\nu}_i) = \frac{1}{9}\sum_{j=1}^{10}\left(\hat{\nu}_i - \hat{\nu}_{ij}\right)^2 \tag{3}$$

A 95% confidence interval for the considered data point can then be constructed as

$$[m(\hat{\nu}_i) - 2\sqrt{v(\hat{\nu}_i)}, m(\hat{\nu}_i) + 2\sqrt{v(\hat{\nu}_i)}]$$

Very wide confidence intervals are undesired, given that they represent large uncertainty about the true value. But very small confidence intervals are also undesired if the true value is frequently found outside this interval. A useful evaluation measure for confidence intervals is the interval score, which rewards narrow intervals, while penalizing lack of coverage [22]. For a $(1-\alpha)\%$ confidence interval $[l, u]$, with $\alpha = 0.05$ chosen in this paper, it is computed as:

$$IS = (u-l) + \frac{2}{\alpha}(l-\nu)\mathbf{1}_{\{\nu<l\}} + \frac{2}{\alpha}(\nu-u)\mathbf{1}_{\{\nu>u\}}$$

where $\mathbf{1}_{\{expr\}}$ refers to the indicator function, being 1 if expression $expr$ holds and 0 otherwise, and where ν refers to the true value. We then define the Average Interval Score, denoted AIS, as the average interval score over all data points that were set to missing, and this for each sub-experiment. The lower the value of AIS, the higher the quality of the confidence interval.

B. Description of the results

1) Experiment 1: Results are shown in Tables V to VII, which present the average ARD for the three sub-experiments of the first experiment, i.e. for the imputed data sets for the financial ratios, where each sub-experiment corresponds to a different random selection of 2% non-missing values that are deliberately set to missing. The value of the best performing MI method is displayed in bold for each financial ratio. The relative performance of the MI methods is consistent over the financial ratios, with `rf` being the best method for the last four ratios. Surprisingly, the very simple `mean` method outperforms the other methods for the first ratio, its average ARD value being even several times smaller than the corresponding value for the other methods.

Another observation is that all average ARD values in the first sub-experiment are much worse than in the other two sub-experiments, at least for the first four ratios. This is also illustrated by Fig. 2, which provides a comparison of the average ARD values for the `rf` method between the sub-experiments. Given that the percentage of missing values is the same for all sub-experiments, this shows that there might be a severe influence of the specific variables that have missing values and/or that the values at the non-missing locations affect performance (since, obviously, the non-missing values also vary over the sub-experiments). Table VIII provides, for completeness, the average ARD values over the three sub-experiments. The ARD values, which represent a percentage error, for the first sub-experiment are so large that they are clearly of no use. For ratio 2, the `rf` MI method even generates imputed values that deviate 1 300% from the real values. In such a case, imputation may even adversely affect any downstream analysis, as in such a case the imputed values are outliers that may distort statistical analyses and violate their assumptions. Results are better for the other sub-experiments, except for ratio 5, for which the errors in imputation are prohibitively large. It is reminded that this ratio comes with an extremely high relative number of missing values (cf. Section II-A), which might be a plausible explanation for the fact that none of the imputation methods is able to produce accurate values.

It is also noticed that results for the fourth ratio are much better than for the other ratios, confirming the hypothesis that the very high serial correlation for this ratio translates into more accurate imputed values (cf. Section II-A).

Tables IX to XI show the AIS for the three sub-experiments of the first experiment. The method `rf` clearly outperforms all other methods, and this for all financial ratios. The discrepancy in performance of the MI methods between the first sub-experiment and the other sub-experiments that was observed for the ARD, is also apparent for the AIS. Compared to the values in the second and the third sub-experiment, the values in the first sub-experiment are extremely large, making it highly unlikely that the 95% confidence intervals have any relevance in the first sub-experiment. The extreme AIS values in this case suggest that the true data values either lie far outside the corresponding confidence interval and/or that the confidence interval is so wide that it is of no practical use. The AIS values for ratio 5 confirm that imputation for this ratio is a meaningless task.

2) Experiment 2: Results are shown in Tables XIII to XV, which present the average ARD for the three sub-experiments of the second experiment, i.e. for the imputed values for the HTRU2 data set, where an increasing number of non-missing values has been set to missing. The leftmost column of each table contains the percentage of missing values.

The `rf` imputation method clearly outperforms the other methods, and this for all ratios and independent of the percentage of missing values. Remarkably, results do not necessarily improve as fewer values are missing. This would be an intuitive hypothesis, as a larger amount of non-missing values represents more information that may be used to estimate plausible imputed values. That this hypothesis does not hold is obvious from, e.g., the second sub-experiment, where the average ARD is 1.10 for 5% missing values and 0.96 for 20% missing values when `rf` was applied. This reinforces the above hypothesis that there might be a severe influence of the specific variables that have missing values and/or that the values at the non-missing locations affect performance. Yet, it is striking that this effect outweighs the fact that there are four times more missing values in the 20% case. The result is also apparent by comparison between experiment 1 and experiment 2. Although the average ARD over the three sub-experiments is much worse in experiment 1 compared to experiment 2 for `rf` (cf. Tables VIII and XVI), this is mainly due to the very poor results in the first sub-experiment of experiment 1. Ignoring this particularly unfortunate sub-experiment provides a more nuanced perspective. For example, compare the second sub-experiment of experiment 1 (cf. Table VI) to the second sub-experiment of experiment 2 (cf. Table XIV). For this sub-experiment it is observed that `rf` performs better on the first four ratios in experiment 1 than on any of the data sets in experiment 2. This is a remarkable observation, since it means, in particular, that imputed values are more accurate for the financial ratios with more than 50% of the data values missing than for the HTRU2 data set with 0.5% missing values. This indicates that the performance of `rf` is not critically dependent on the relative number of missing values.

Another conclusion is that the ARD values are surprisingly high. The lowest ARD is obtained in the third sub-experiment with an ARD value of 0.56 for `rf` for the 0.5% case. So, even though there are very few missing values, the average percentage error is 56%. This result emphasizes the importance of using multiple imputation, since it would be unwise to use the imputed values without taking into account the uncertainty in accuracy. Of course, this only works if the confidence intervals themselves are an accurate representation of this uncertainty, which is why the interval score is an essential validation measure in imputation tasks.

Tables XVII to XIX show that `rf` also performs best in terms of the AIS. Furthermore, the AIS does generally worsen with the increase in the number of missing values for this method. Such a trend was much less obvious for the ARD. Thus although the accuracy of the imputed values might show a rather stable or fluctuating pattern as the number of missing values is increased, the uncertainty related to the accuracy of imputed values increases. As a summary, Table XX shows the average AIS over the three sub-experiments.

TABLE V
MEAN OF AVERAGE RELATIVE DIFFERENCE (ARD): EXPERIMENT 1, SUB-EXPERIMENT 1

	mean	norm	rf	l.norm	l.s.norm
Ratio 1	**2.06**	38.86	8.87	39.01	38.96
Ratio 2	32.58	74.32	**13.00**	73.58	74.21
Ratio 3	13.49	20.85	**3.02**	20.87	20.83
Ratio 4	4.79	2.23	**1.80**	2.19	2.26
Ratio 5	11.73	48.11	**4.78**	44.21	48.17

TABLE VI
MEAN OF AVERAGE RELATIVE DIFFERENCE (ARD): EXPERIMENT 1, SUB-EXPERIMENT 2

	mean	norm	rf	l.norm	l.s.norm
Ratio 1	**0.09**	1.73	0.44	1.71	1.70
Ratio 2	1.70	3.90	**0.54**	3.86	3.83
Ratio 3	0.69	1.08	**0.17**	1.08	1.07
Ratio 4	0.27	0.12	**0.08**	0.11	0.12
Ratio 5	7.78	31.47	**3.57**	28.43	31.22

V. CONCLUSION

This paper describes experimental results related to the application of several multiple imputation methods from the R package `mice` on two data sets with different features. The first data set consists of five financial ratios over time, with

TABLE VII
MEAN OF AVERAGE RELATIVE DIFFERENCE (ARD): EXPERIMENT 1, SUB-EXPERIMENT 3

	mean	norm	rf	l.norm	l.s.norm
Ratio 1	**0.11**	1.98	0.41	1.96	1.95
Ratio 2	1.67	3.90	**0.60**	3.82	3.89
Ratio 3	0.64	1.04	**0.19**	1.02	1.03
Ratio 4	0.24	0.13	**0.12**	0.13	0.13
Ratio 5	7.86	40.55	**4.33**	35.64	40.64

TABLE VIII
MEAN OF AVERAGE RELATIVE DIFFERENCE (ARD): EXPERIMENT 1, AVERAGE OVER SUB-EXPERIMENTS

	mean	norm	rf	l.norm	l.s.norm
Ratio 1	**0.75**	14.19	3.24	14.23	14.20
Ratio 2	11.98	27.37	**4.71**	27.09	27.31
Ratio 3	4.94	7.66	**1.13**	7.66	7.64
Ratio 4	1.77	0.83	**0.67**	0.81	0.83
Ratio 5	9.12	40.04	**4.23**	36.09	40.01

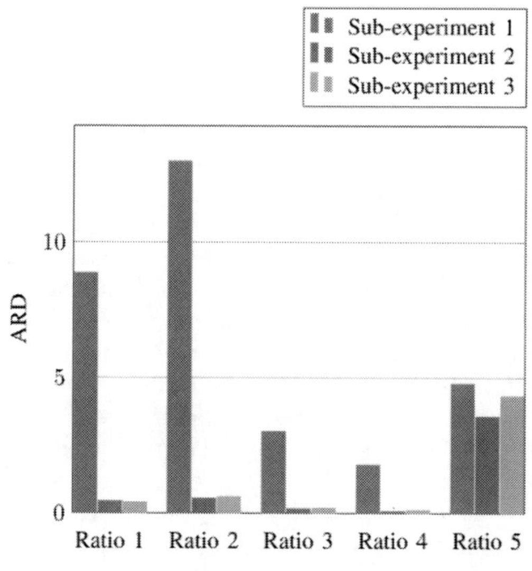

Fig. 2. Comparison of ARD for rf between the sub-experiments of the first experiment

TABLE IX
AVERAGE INTERVAL SCORE (AIS): EXPERIMENT 1, SUB-EXPERIMENT 1

	mean	norm	rf	l.norm	l.s.norm
Ratio 1	794.83	342.44	**239.08**	342.45	342.28
Ratio 2	1977.51	646.24	**458.91**	646.89	648.45
Ratio 3	158.03	47.85	**28.38**	47.82	47.82
Ratio 4	1206.81	116.77	**98.35**	117.24	117.05
Ratio 5	51076.13	25009.93	**11109.64**	23059.73	24990.42

TABLE X
AVERAGE INTERVAL SCORE (AIS): EXPERIMENT 1, SUB-EXPERIMENT 2

	mean	norm	rf	l.norm	l.s.norm
Ratio 1	39.25	16.86	**11.45**	16.69	16.85
Ratio 2	106.75	34.33	**23.72**	33.40	34.06
Ratio 3	7.71	2.34	**1.42**	2.34	2.33
Ratio 4	61.72	5.68	**4.82**	5.77	5.70
Ratio 5	34108	17001	**7948**	15547	17012

TABLE XI
AVERAGE INTERVAL SCORE (AIS): EXPERIMENT 1, SUB-EXPERIMENT 3

	mean	norm	rf	l.norm	l.s.norm
Ratio 1	40.42	17.83	**12.43**	17.61	17.66
Ratio 2	104.88	33.72	**23.40**	33.95	34.05
Ratio 3	7.50	2.28	**1.33**	2.29	2.27
Ratio 4	60.78	5.90	**5.09**	5.86	5.84
Ratio 5	34198.34	19901.34	**7937.03**	17767.43	19868.10

TABLE XII
AVERAGE INTERVAL SCORE (AIS): EXPERIMENT 1, AVERAGE OVER SUB-EXPERIMENTS

	mean	norm	rf	l.norm	l.s.norm
Ratio 1	291.50	125.71	**87.65**	125.58	125.59
Ratio 2	729.71	238.10	**168.68**	238.08	238.85
Ratio 3	57.75	17.49	**10.38**	17.48	17.47
Ratio 4	443.10	42.78	**36.09**	42.95	42.86
Ratio 5	39794.32	20637.30	**8998.09**	18791.31	20623.46

TABLE XIII
MEAN OF AVERAGE RELATIVE DIFFERENCE (ARD): EXPERIMENT 1

	mean	norm	rf	l.norm	l.s.norm
0.5%	6.10	3.25	**0.65**	3.24	3.31
1%	6.40	3.49	**0.45**	3.26	3.34
5%	6.96	4.39	**0.81**	4.17	4.17
10%	14.95	5.73	**0.86**	5.61	5.59
15%	10.48	5.40	**0.97**	5.44	5.21
20%	8.64	5.43	**0.85**	5.30	5.36

TABLE XIV
MEAN OF AVERAGE RELATIVE DIFFERENCE (ARD): EXPERIMENT 2

	mean	norm	rf	l.norm	l.s.norm
0.5%	8.02	4.02	**1.10**	3.81	3.77
1%	8.00	4.19	**0.62**	3.72	3.71
5%	22.90	14.12	**2.32**	14.78	17.19
10%	8.06	4.51	**0.76**	4.42	4.32
15%	15.28	11.03	**1.69**	10.37	9.49
20%	11.59	5.59	**0.96**	5.62	5.62

TABLE XV
MEAN OF AVERAGE RELATIVE DIFFERENCE (ARD): EXPERIMENT 3

	mean	norm	rf	l.norm	l.s.norm
0.5%	4.94	2.60	**0.56**	2.67	2.77
1%	7.90	3.78	**0.68**	3.72	3.77
5%	9.13	4.82	**0.84**	4.95	4.57
10%	9.36	5.22	**0.88**	5.67	6.29
15%	19.82	29.81	**1.95**	19.83	20.81
20%	14.15	10.30	**1.35**	10.66	11.12

TABLE XVI
MEAN OF AVERAGE RELATIVE DIFFERENCE (ARD): AVERAGE OVER EXPERIMENTS

	mean	norm	rf	l.norm	l.s.norm
0.5%	6.35	3.29	**0.77**	3.24	3.28
1%	7.43	3.82	**0.59**	3.56	3.61
5%	13.00	7.78	**1.32**	7.97	8.64
10%	10.79	5.15	**0.83**	5.23	5.40
15%	15.19	15.41	**1.54**	11.88	11.84
20%	11.46	7.10	**1.05**	7.19	7.37

TABLE XVII
AVERAGE INTERVAL SCORE (AIS): EXPERIMENT 1

	mean	norm	rf	l.norm	l.s.norm
0.5%	602.37	43.20	**12.29**	39.77	40.12
1%	539.44	42.33	**12.45**	41.10	42.55
5%	578.09	44.64	**14.00**	43.29	44.87
10%	587.01	49.05	**14.43**	49.22	49.08
15%	599.02	55.21	**16.81**	54.46	55.32
20%	593.21	60.14	**17.89**	61.69	60.29

TABLE XVIII
AVERAGE INTERVAL SCORE (AIS): EXPERIMENT 2

	mean	norm	rf	l.norm	l.s.norm
0.5%	603.13	42.88	**12.02**	42.37	48.59
1%	568.52	47.42	**12.65**	48.32	45.50
5%	601.17	46.52	**13.93**	45.87	46.71
10%	601.11	50.32	**15.53**	51.22	51.36
15%	576.74	53.31	**15.65**	53.75	53.46
20%	598.30	60.48	**18.04**	60.86	60.61

TABLE XIX
AVERAGE INTERVAL SCORE (AIS): EXPERIMENT 3

	mean	norm	rf	l.norm	l.s.norm
0.5%	640.41	55.07	**13.51**	53.56	52.20
1%	550.80	39.32	**12.44**	38.39	37.48
5%	564.94	43.22	**13.22**	43.91	43.39
10%	592.26	51.37	**14.66**	50.90	51.42
15%	602.88	56.76	**16.49**	57.01	57.48
20%	582.27	56.58	**17.47**	56.40	57.27

TABLE XX
AVERAGE INTERVAL SCORE (AIS): AVERAGE OVER EXPERIMENTS

	mean	norm	rf	l.norm	l.s.norm
0.5%	615.30	47.05	**12.60**	45.23	46.97
1%	552.92	43.03	**12.51**	42.60	41.84
5%	581.40	44.79	**13.72**	44.36	44.99
10%	593.46	50.25	**14.87**	50.45	50.62
15%	592.88	55.09	**16.32**	55.07	55.42
20%	591.26	59.07	**17.80**	59.65	59.39

a very high number of missing values in relative terms. The second data set is HTRU2, a publicly available benchmark data set where all data values are non-missing. For the first data set, a certain percentage of the number of non-missing values is deliberately set to missing in order to evaluate five selected multiple imputation methods. For the HTRU2 data set, an increasing number of non-missing values is set to zero to allow an analysis of the influence of the relative number of missing values on the performance of the imputation methods.

A number of interesting results can be deduced from the experimental analysis:

- The `rf` method, which relies on random forests, is superior to the other imputation methods, both in terms of average relative difference as well as with respect to the average interval score.
- For a fixed number of missing and non-missing values for a given data set, the performance of imputation methods may vary significantly according to the specific data points that are missing.
- The relative number of missing values might not be a determining factor for the performance of imputation methods, except if that relative number is extremely high. Performance of all imputation methods with respect to financial ratio 5, with 97% of its values missing, was observed to be disastrous. In general, however, the absolute number of non-missing values is probably of more significance for the accuracy of the imputed values.
- It is of crucial importance to perform a preliminary imputation analysis, where non-missing values are deliberately set to missing, to check the acceptability of the imputed values. The reason is that the scenario where imputation introduces outliers cannot be excluded a priori.
- If the preliminary analysis indicates that a chosen multiple imputation method is feasible for the data set at hand, meaning that ARD and AIS values are below predefined thresholds, the confidence interval should always be computed and taken into account. Only in this way the multiple imputation methodology is fully exploited, by providing a measure of uncertainty about the accuracy of the imputed values.

These results may act as guidelines for practitioners, although future experimental work is needed to verify the generality of the above working hypotheses.

Acknowledgment

This work was supported by the Research Foundation - Flanders (Grant number G006421N).

References

[1] P. Austin, I. White, D. Lee, and S. van Buuren, "Missing data in clinical research: A tutorial on multiple imputation," Canadian Journal of Cardiology, vol. 37, pp. 1322–1331, September 2021.

[2] E. Afrifa-Yamoah, U. A. Mueller, S. M. Taylor, and A. J. Fisher, "Missing data imputation of high-resolution temporal climate time series data," Meteorological Applications, vol. 27, e1873, January 2020.

[3] J.D. Dziura, L.A. Post, Q. Zhao, Z. Fu, and P. Peduzzi, "Strategies for dealing with missing data in clinical trials: from design to analysis," Yale J Biol Med., vol. 86, pp. 343–358, September 2020.

[4] K. Bhaskaran and L. Smeeth, "What is the difference between missing completely at random and missing at random?," Int J Epidemiol, vol. 43, pp. 1336–1339, August 2014.

[5] J.C. Jakobsen, C. Gluud, J. Wetterslev, and P. Winkel, "When and how should multiple imputation be used for handling missing data in randomised clinical trials – a practical guide with flowcharts," BMC Med Res Methodol, vol. 17, 162, December 2017.

[6] P. Roth, "Missing data: a conceptual review for applied psychologists," Personnel Psychology, vol. 47, pp. 537—560, September 1994.

[7] K. Sainani, "Dealing with missing data," PM R., vol. 7, pp. 990–994, September 2015.

[8] P. Hayati Rezvan, K.J. Lee, and J.A. Simpson, "The rise of multiple imputation: a review of the reporting and implementation of the method in medical research," BMC Med Res Methodol, vol. 15, 30, April 2015.

[9] A. Mackinnon, "The use and reporting of multiple imputation in medical research - a review," J Intern Med, vol. 268, pp. 586–593, December 2010.

[10] J.H. Ware, D. Harrington, D.J. Hunter, and R.B. D'Agostino, "Missing data," N Engl J Med, vol. 367, pp. 1353–1354, October 2012.

[11] S. van Buuren and K. Groothuis-Oudshoorn, "mice: Multivariate imputation by chained equations in R," Journal of Statistical Software, vol. 45, pp. 1–67, December 2011.

[12] Bel-First Finance database, https://www.bvdinfo.com/en-us/our-products/data/national/bel-first (Accessed: 21 July 2022).

[13] A. Volkov, D. Benoit, and D. Van den Poel, "Incorporating sequential information in bankruptcy prediction with predictors based on Markov for discrimination," Decision Support Systems, vol. 98, pp. 59–68, June 2017.

[14] HTRU2 data set from the UCI Machine Learning Repository, https://archive.ics.uci.edu/ml/datasets/HTRU2 (Accessed: 21 July 2022).

[15] M. J. Keith et al., "The high time resolution universe pulsar survey – I. System configuration and initial discoveries," Monthly Notices of the Royal Astronomical Society, vol. 409, pp. 619–627, December 2010.

[16] D.B. Rubin, Multiple imputation for nonresponse in surveys. New York: Wiley 1987.

[17] Y. Deng, C. Chang, M.S. Ido, and Q. Long, "Multiple imputation for general missing data patterns in the presence of high-dimensional data," Scientific reports, vol. 6, pp. 1–10, February 2016.

[18] Y. Zhao and Q. Long, "Multiple imputation in the presence of high-dimensional data," Statistical Methods in Medical Research, vol. 25, pp. 2021–2035, October 2016.

[19] L.L. Doove, S. van Buuren, and E. Dusseldorp, "Recursive partitioning for missing data imputation in the presence of interaction effects," Computational Statistics & Data Analysis, vol. 72, pp. 92–104, April 2014.

[20] F. Tang and H. Ishwaran, "Random forest missing data algorithms," Statistical Analysis and Data Mining, vol. 10, pp. 363–377, June 2017.

[21] W. De Mulder, B. Rengs, G. Molenberghs, T. Fent, and G. Verbeke, "Statistical emulation applied to a very large data set generated by an agent-based model," SIMUL 2015 : The Seventh International Conference on Advances in System Simulation, pp. 43–48, 2015.

[22] T. Gneiting and A. Raftery, "Strictly proper scoring rules, prediction, and estimation," Journal of the American Statistical Association, vol. 102, pp. 359–378, March 2007.

Heatmap Weighted A* Algorithm for NPC Pathfinding

Paul Williamson
School of Computing and Mathematics
University of South Wales
CF37 1DL, Pontypridd
e-mail: paul.williamson@southwales.ac.uk

Christopher Tubb
School of Computing and Mathematics
University of South Wales
CF37 1DL, Pontypridd
e-mail: christopher.tubb@southwales.ac.uk

Abstract— **Non-Player Characters (NPCs) are characters within a video game, which are not controlled by a human participant. While they are mainly used to fulfil a role not designated for a human player, there are occasions when an NPC needs to play in a human role, and therefore needs to imitate appropriate gameplay behaviours, in such a way that it is not easily distinguished from a human player. Navigation is a fundamental gameplay behaviour, focused on how a player traverses the environment when undertaking objectives. This paper explores the possibility of modelling human navigation by modifying A* algorithm with a heatmap derived from human-based data. This is achieved by having participants complete a search and collect experiment. The data is saved for analysis and to develop a navigation model. NPCs using the model undertake the same experiment, but with a heatmap weighted A* graph. The experiment explores adjusting the weight of the heatmap so its influence on the pathfinding varies and a comparison can be made to see which weight better reflects the human results.**

Keywords—NPC; Player Modelling; Pathfinding; Gameplay; A* Algorithm.

I. INTRODUCTION

In the context of an NPC, pathfinding is the mechanism used to find a suitable route between two points on a map. The type of game genre and size of the map can influence which technique is more practical because some solutions are only viable under predefined constraints. In First Person Shooter (FPS) games, a common technique used is A* algorithm, or some variant of this method, where a 2D grid is superimposed over the map, then using cost and heuristic the algorithm calculates a shortest cost path.

This paper expands on the A* algorithm. It focuses on adjusting the weight cost of nodes in accordance with a heatmap. For the purposes of this experiment, the heatmap is generated from data captured from human players roaming the environment, undertaking an experiment in which they need to find and collect eight coins. This data enabled a model to be developed, which captures not only the general areas of navigation, but also intricate behaviours associated with the act of roaming, and the influence they have on pathfinding.

Secondly, this research uses a tagged environment to help determine pathing based decisions. This limits the distance of the routing decisions to only what is within view from the perspective of the NPC. This technique drastically reduces performance cost because, despite the size of the A* graph, the distance between the NPC and destination node is always relatively short.

In Section II, this paper discusses the motivation behind a player driven A* algorithm solution. It states why it is important for NPCs to use the same navigational behaviours as human players and why heatmaps generate a useful tool for this purpose. Section III examines research in the field of improving the usefulness of A* algorithm for pathfinding solutions, and some implications of the limitation of these methods. In Section IV, the method for the data capture experiment is explained, which involves human subjects roaming the map to collect several coins. Section V uses the same experiment as Section IV, except in this experiment, NPCs with the roaming model are used and a thorough evaluation of the results is conducted to determine the applicability of the model and how it compares to the human subject results. Finally, Section VI concludes the paper.

II. MOTIVATION

While roaming may appear a random action, it is often a more strategic behaviour where a player tries to maximise scanning efficiency by positioning their character to visually cover as much of the map as possible. This increases the likelihood they will spot their objective and reduce the chance of checking already checked areas of the map [1].

The motivation for this paper is to address how NPCs can roam the environment and increase the likelihood it will interact with a human player. This is important in both single and multiplayer games. In single player games, the game should revolve around the player, so ensuring regular engagement from NPCs is crucial. Regarding multiplayer games or roles generally reserved for a human player, it is important that NPCs can imitate the general behaviours seen in a human player, which include using roaming in a way which is consistent with the routes a player might take. For example, during a death match scenario, players roam the map in search for opponents to eliminate. When NPCs pathfinding is not modelled to reflect the same generalised routes as a human player, it can cause them to patrol areas rarely visited by players.

Heat maps offer a good overview of which parts of the map contain the most interactions. Utilising this information can help develop NPCs that are not hard coded to patrol a certain route, a technique which is commonly used, which is predictable and often recognised by a player. Instead, providing the NPC with human player acquired data so they can undertake roaming with a more human-like characteristic. This should enable naturally occurring interactions, rather than forced encounters where the NPC can appear omniscient.

The perception of omniscience is a common issue with NPCs, which is often caused by making decisions and/or performing actions with information that it should not have. For instance, in some cases an NPC will shoot at a wall with a player on the other side. They should not know the player is there. However, they are provided with an extra layer of information, which can influence actions. An important part of making NPCs appear more human-like is therefore removing this perception. The development of a new model of navigation, as discussed here, is intended to do this. To achieve this goal NPCs can only make decisions based on what they can 'see' and internal parameters such as health or ammunition count.

III. BACKGROUND AND RELATED RESEARCH

Pathfinding is a crucial aspect of an NPCs core mechanics. Some form of navigation is essential in games where the NPC is required to move. The complexity of the pathfinding has increased as games have become more intricate. A* algorithm has remained an important technique in modern games [2].

In FPS games, A* is popular because of its graph-based nature. It can find an optimal route between two points. However, this can lead to predictable routes, which can be exploited. Furthermore, an exponential performance cost can occur when increasing the size of the map, as it increases the size of the graph [3], thus, adding more nodes that could be checked when forming a route.

Comparison analysis was conducted by Permana et al. [4], in which they looked at A*, Dijkstra and Breadth First Search (BFS) in a maze runner genre. They focused primarily on the performance impact of each technique, as well as the efficiency in context of functionality. The results suggest that all methods are capable of pathfinding, however, A* was more efficient computationally.

There has been substantial research to modify A* so it can excel at certain tasks. Sazaki et al. [5] showed that some of the limitations of A* can be overcome by developing a model, which was used in a car racing scenario. This model focused on assisting A* with a Dynamic Pathing Algorithm (DPA). The results demonstrated that it could avoid moving obstacles. This addresses one of the problems with A*; the need to continually update the graph if the map is not static. This suggests that combining pathfinding models and techniques can yield positive results and shows that the effectiveness of A* can be enhanced when aided with other techniques.

Makarov et al. [6] used Voronoi-based pathfinding that has been developed with obstacle avoidance and tactical elements to reduce the probability NPCs will traverse the dangerous areas of the map. They showed that including what NPCs can visually 'see', it was able to make tactical and logistical decisions. When incorporating internal information, such as previous enemy encounters, the NPC uses all the data to make decisions, including navigation. This indicates that when making navigation decisions, providing the NPC with more specific data about itself can lead to an adaptable NPC, which could appear more human-like.

Like the forementioned work, the research in this paper uses NPCs vision to make decisions on navigation. NPCs can only move to a location it can visually 'see'. This significantly reduces the size of the pathing and low computational overhead. When using a non-static map, the A* graph needs to be updated on a regular basis, so NPCs do not attempt to traverse non-walkable areas. This can have a negative impact on performance. While significant research has been undertaken to address this issue, it is still a problem that needs to be considered when using A*. The approach proposed in this research could be useful as the NPC could update the graph based on what is in its view.

Research undertaken by Sturtevant et al. [7] has shown that dynamically adjusting the cost of A* nodes based on the terrain they occupy can yield useful results. They used this technique by creating an abstraction layer which deals with terrain cost and dynamic terrain. They determined that from a performance perspective, when used with several different terrain types, the solution can be up to ten times faster in finding a suitable path, while remaining 2-6% optimal. This is important to this research because it shows that weighted environments can be used with other techniques to positively impact the overall pathfinding. This is supported by Pan [8] who proposes a multi-technique approach. They used a bootstrap Jump Point Space (JPS) technique when there are no threats present, then switch to a waypoint-based solution when the NPC detects a threat. This is an interesting approach to a dynamic pathfinding system which responds to the current circumstance of the NPC. When combined with a weighted A* graph, this could help develop a more realistic navigation system because the pathfinding technique will change to reflect the behaviour expected to be displayed.

IV. HUMAN ROAMING MODELLING

The modelling phase involved having human subjects undertake a roaming experiment. So, generalised behaviours can be identified and incorporated into a model, which will aim to imitate an average human player roaming characteristics.

A. *Data Capture Experiment*

The data capture experiment was conducted by having subjects roam the map in search of eight coins. A heatmap was generated by adding a standard A* graph, each node was given a collider detection and when a subject intersected with the collider, a counter specific to that node was incremented by one. Constraints were added to prolong the overall length of the experiment, so a more accurate model of roaming could be achieved. Only one coin is present on the map at any given time. This was to prevent chaining where the subject spots a coin as they are moving to collect another coin. When a new coin spawns, it can spawn anywhere on the map, but not in view of the subject current position and cannot collide with terrain. This was to prevent the chance of coins repeatedly spawning close to subjects.

The purpose of this method was due to the separation of the navigation model and A* graph. Wherein, the NPCs uses the graph to plot a route, but it is not part of the overall navigation model.

Non-model related data was captured so a comparison can be made as to the efficiency of model in relation to the overall performance of the roaming behaviour. This was to conclude if the act of roaming is random, or if there was a more significant strategy as to why subjects used certain doorways and routes. Therefore, the position and rotation of the subject was logged every 0.5 seconds, which can be input back into the experiment for behaviour observation by a researcher.

B. Results and Analysis

A total of 30 subjects took part in the experiment. Figure 1 shows the combined heatmap of all subjects (left image) and the breakdown of the map with numbered rooms (right image). The result shows an interesting trend where subjects were more likely to traverse the outer edge of the map, which influenced which doorways were likely to be used.

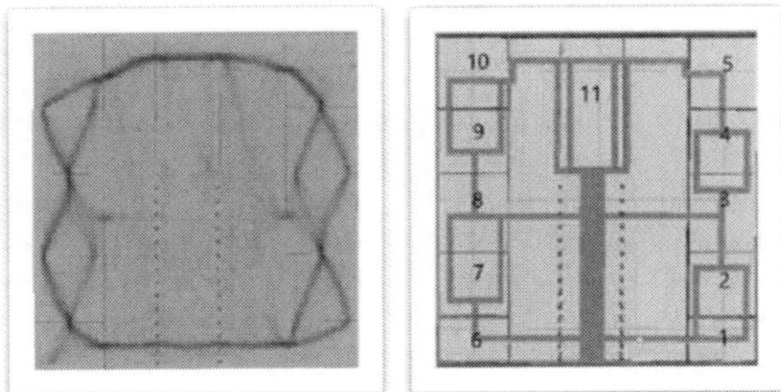

Figure 1. Heatmap and Room Numbers.

This demonstrates that roaming is very strategic, and subjects increase their likelihood of finding a coin by increasing their viewing coverage. It also highlights that roaming routes are funnelled via doorways, and it is likely that subjects' navigation decision-making was primarily limited to the space between doorways. The experiment confirmed initial results, which showed that human players had preferred routes through the map [1]. While this is not surprising as subjects need to use the doorways to traverse the environment, as the map resembles a typical office, it indicates the importance of map design and the strategic value of funnel points. Even in open world maps, generally there are points of interest, with routes, such as roads, leading directly to these areas.

As roaming is strategic, map coverage is therefore an important objective. Figure 2 shows an example of the amount of map uncovered by a randomly selected subject. It shows that at the end of the experiment >95% of the map has been revealed, with a small area in the corner of room 4, which was not uncovered.

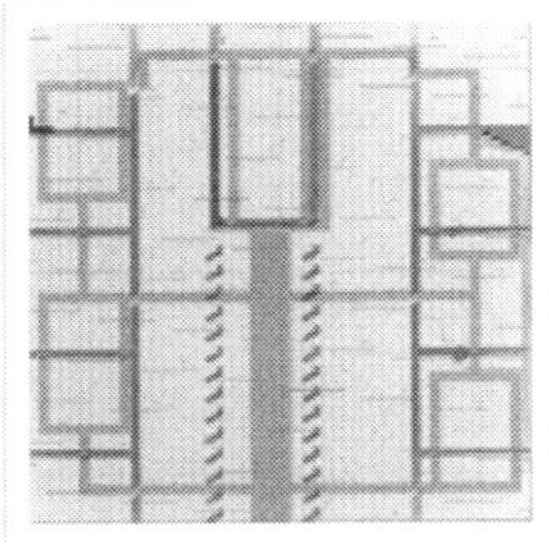

Figure 2. Map Coverage.

There were three key generalised characteristics:

- Player Positioning: Subjects were more likely to traverse the outer edge of the map, thus, increasing viewing angle to cover more map.
- Peeking: Subjects occasionally 'peeked' into the foyer area, this involved moving to the doorway connecting to the foyer for a quick look, before continuing their intended route.
- Rapid Room Scanning: Upon entering a room, subjects were likely to quickly scan the room as they continued to move towards the next doorway.

These behaviours were consistent across most subjects and emphasise that there is a clear logic behind roaming that is not a random undertaking. It is an organised activity where the objective is maximising the efficiency of map coverage.

A critical behaviour that emerged was the speed in which subjects' navigation behaviours changed when new information was presented. While the roaming was methodical, when subjects identify a coin, the behaviour shifts immediately to acquiring the coin. The behaviour changes from looking around the map, to a focused behaviour where the subject remained fixated on the coin and moved directly to retrieve it. Figure 3 shows the results from one subject. The circles show where the subject spotted a coin and immediately breaks away from the roaming route, then after collection they resume on the same roaming route. In one instance, the subject can be seen to traverse the width of the map in a near straight line when spotting a coin.

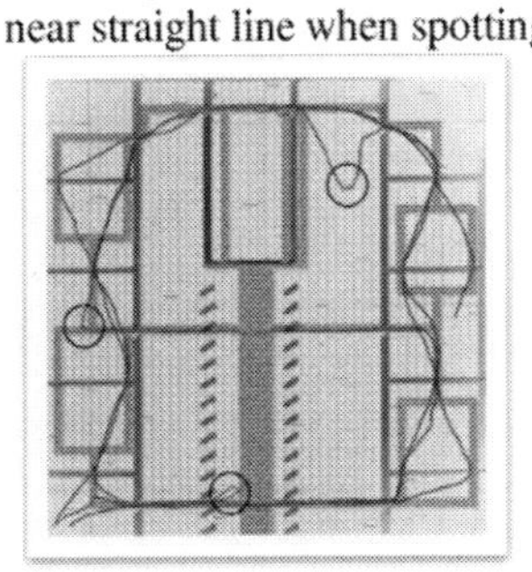

Figure 3. Beeline Behaviour.

This suggests that the navigation model could require a subset of models for the various behaviours associated with moving throughout the map. This could lead to establishing that navigation is more than point to point pathing, but an expression of behaviours related to fulfilling specific objectives. This could explain why subjects were scanning the surroundings when roaming and why they were fixated on their target when collecting coins.

V. Roaming Model Analysis

A roaming model analysis experiment was conducted to determine if the roaming model developed represented the characteristics of an average human subject. The objective was to compare the human data and NPCs directly, to establish the accuracy of the model and determine if there were any negative consequences from using a heatmap.

A. Pathfinding and Roaming Model

There is a distinction between pathfinding and roaming. Pathfinding uses the heatmap weighted A* algorithm to plot a route between two points on the map. Whereas the roaming model controls the navigation decision-making and behaviour of the NPC as it moves between these two points.

The technique uses the heatmap to adjust individual node cost in the A* graph. This was achieved by adding all the specific node counters from the data capture experiment, then subtracting this weight from individual nodes when creating the A* graph. Figure 4 is a pseudo code example of the method used to create the A* graph with heatmap.

```
Loop X grid size
  Loop Y grid size
    create node world position
    check if node is walkable
      int movement penalty = 100
      walkable = True
      movement penalty -= heat weight value
    Else
      walkable = False
    Add node to array
```

Figure 4. Pseudo Code for Heatmap A* Graph.

As the distribution of cost between neighbouring nodes can vary significantly. It was decided that a smoothing technique was required to blur the differences. This was also required to help prevent NPCs occasionally traversing very close to walls as nodes neighbouring non-walkable nodes, such as walls, had their cost increased.

The smoothing technique used a box blur algorithm to normalise the cost of a node. A compromise was made where the box blur was set to 3x3, because when testing 2x2 the blur was not enough and when using 4x4 and 5x5, the smoothing was so significant that the heatmap had no effect. Figure 5 displays the box blur equation. Each number represents the weight cost of a node, the centre number is the node being blurred by adding all weights then dividing by the number of neighbouring nodes.

$$\frac{1}{9}\begin{bmatrix}1,1,1\\1,1,1\\1,1,1\end{bmatrix}$$

Figure 5. Box Blur Equation

Subjects showed that doorways provided pivotal and strategic points on the map, as they are funnel points and are the only means of traversing between rooms. Therefore, as NPCs were restricted to information only in view, doorways became a central point to the model. Each NPC stored personal data about doorways and assigned a dynamic weight cost to each doorway, which reflected the heat observed from the subject experiment. The NPC will attempt to prioritise the doorway in view with the highest weight value. When successfully using the door, it will temporarily decrease the weight to prevent room cycling.

Unpredictability is an element of human players gameplay in an FPS game. There is a probability of performing a certain action in a scenario, but it is never certain. This was reflected in the roaming model, which aims to reduce predictability, but remain logical and consistent with human behaviour. This was achieved by implementing a random number generator of between one and ten, which represented the probabilistic outcome.

When entering a room, NPCs had an 80% chance to scan the room as they moved to the next location, as well as apply special attention to looking at other doorways. Peeking had a special importance when roaming because subjects used this technique to tactically scan open spaces without entering the area.

Lastly, when traversing open spaces, human subjects showed an awareness of their surrounds and took advantage by occasionally looking towards the open spaces, while still moving towards their intended location. This gave the appearance of the subject strafing as they were not moving in a forward-facing direction. This was modelled by enabling the NPC to have awareness of the distance between itself and open spaces to their left and right. Using this distance and a probabilistic algorithm, the model decided whether the NPC should scan the left or right side. After the NPC has successfully scanned the environment, a timer is started to ensure that the NPC does not keep repeating this action in a short space of time, a behaviour not seen in human subjects.

B. Experimental Protocol

The purpose of this experiment was to directly compare human subjects and NPCs. It was decided that having NPCs undertake the same experiment as the data capture experiment would provide a good basis to compare the results.

To remain consistent, NPCs run the experiment several times, varying the weight impact of the heatmap, so it could be determined which weight better represented the characteristics of the average subject. There were four different weight profiles. The heavier the weight profile, the higher the base node cost on the graph, which is represented by the darker the colour (Figure 6).

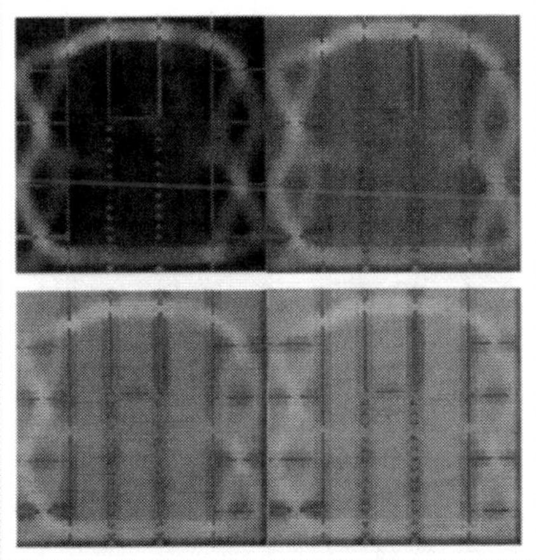

Figure 6. Heatmaps Comparison.

It shows the significant difference between weight costs of the different profiles. The top left profile aims to aggressively influence the NPC to adhere to the heatmap. While the bottom right profile was aimed at being more of a light influence on the pathfinding. This is a promising sign because it means the heatmap is working as intended and the degree of change between the profiles demonstrates that the model should be flexible in its application. This presents a novel approach to pathfinding as the heatmap is not strictly limited to player data. It could be used to prevent NPCs roaming the same areas by increasing the weight cost of nodes based on its own heatmap which is calculated over a set length of time.

Figure 7 shows an example of the A* graph without the heatmap. While this profile was only used once in this experiment, it is a good comparison to show the influence the heatmap has on the A* graph.

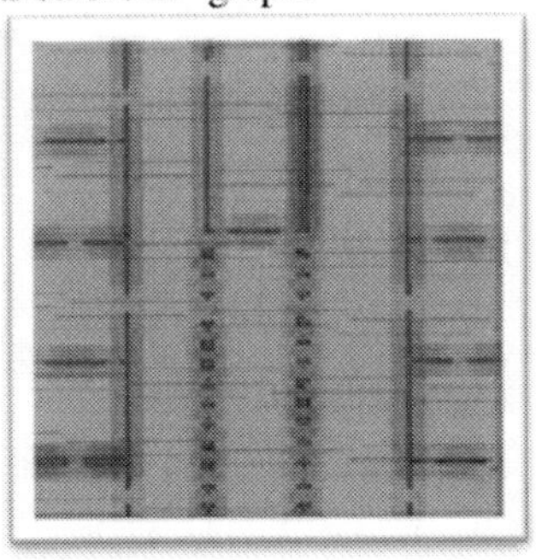

Figure 7. No Heatmap Example.

The node cost smoothing technique was added to all the graphs. This ensured that neighbouring nodes did not have wildly different movement costs. This was essential because in a heatmap, some neighbouring nodes could have significant variation in cost, which would result in the NPC having a jerking motion as they moved.

While some NPCs were required to collect eight coins for a direct comparison with individual human subjects, other NPCs were required to collect forty coins per run, which was the equivalent of five subjects. This number was decided as the purpose of the experiment was to analyse the generalised roaming route of the NPCs. A line renderer was used to track NPCs routing. Therefore, a compromise was required where it would provide enough data to make conclusions, but not too many where the lines become saturated and confusing.

As with the the human subject experiment, the whole map is covered with a black fog, which is instantly removed when entering the view of the NPC. The fog provided a measure of the areas of the map the NPC has scanned and allowed comparison with observations of the human subjects.

C. Results and Analysis

When directly comparing the four weight profiles. The results show that amplifying the significance of the heatmap on the cost of the A* nodes, NPCs pathfinding was noticeably affected. Generally, the model has a positive effect on the navigation and each of the heatmaps accurately reflects the roaming patterns observed in the human subject experiment (Figure 8). However, it also had an adverse effect when not roaming. NPCs were taking very inefficient routes to reach a specified location, such as moving to a coin location. On some occasions, NPCs were not making a beeline behaviour after identifying a coin. They would lose sight of the coin and move through multiple rooms, before finally acquiring the coin. Although this behaviour is clearly at odds with that exhibited by the human subjects it does comply with the lowest cost path calculated by the modified A* Algorithm.

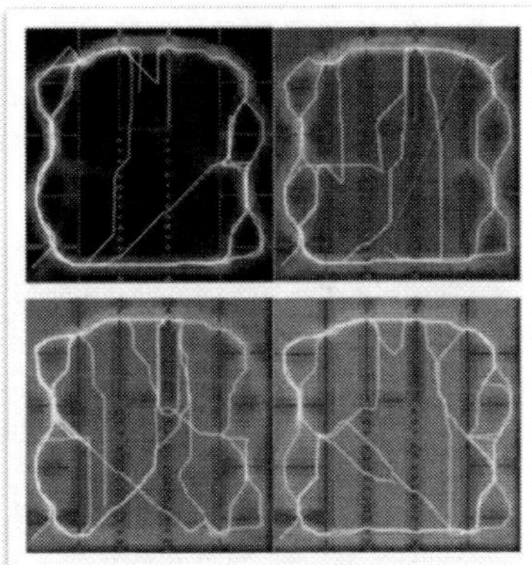

Figure 8. Heatmaps Analysis.

An important observation is in the centre of the map because there is a correlation between the base node cost and likelihood of cutting across the map to reach a destination when roaming. This opens the pathfinding to a degree of flexibility because multiple graphs could be created and the model decides which to use, or if the graph is regularly updated, it can decide how aggressive the roaming should be in relation to the heatmap. This could be useful in a scenario where NPCs are tasked with tracking players and the developer does not want to use scripting to force interactions. Similar research has been undertaken where NPCs are influenced by pheromones, which are generated by other game agents with positive results [9]-[11]. While these examples are generally focused on real-time strategy games, and are intended to explore swarm intelligence, commonality can be derived with the technique presented in this paper. Subject to further investigation, research could be undertaken where the players emit pheromones that temporarily decreases the cost of nodes within the vicinity.

Analysing the model when the coin count was set to forty. The results remain consistent with what was observed with eight coins (Figure 9). In this example, a moderately aggressive base node cost was chosen to help prevent NPCs using the middle of the map to roam, but not too costly that NPCs would take inefficient and irregular route when moving to a coin. The results show the heatmap has a very strong influence on roaming, and when moving to a coin, the NPC would use the middle of the map.

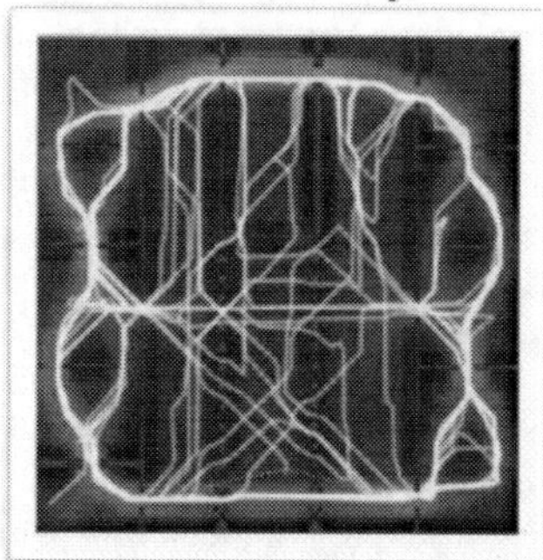

Figure 9. Forty Coin Heatmap Analysis.

When comparing the heatmap against a normal A* graph. The results appear somewhat similar, however, when scrutinising the straightness of the paths, it shows a degree of difference. Figure 10 shows the heatmap A* (left image) and the standard A* (right image). The heatmap lines show they are not straight, but instead having a meandering characteristic.

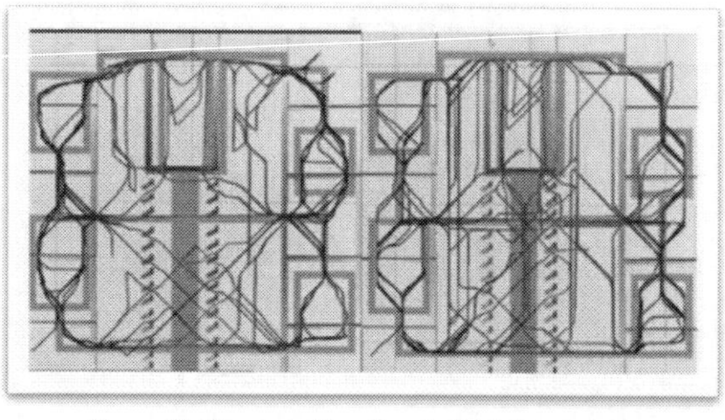

Figure 10. Heatmap A* vs Standard A* Comparison.

Zooming in to specific areas further highlights intricate differences between the heatmap and non-heatmap A*. Figure 11 focuses on a single room. The right image shows a uniform pattern, whereas the left image is less structured that is more reminiscent of human subjects.

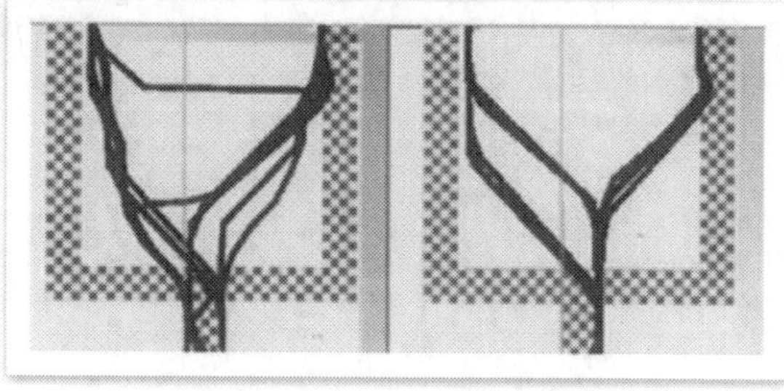

Figure 11. Room Comparison.

When compared to a human subject in a similar room (Figure 12). It shows NPCs using the heatmap is more akin to the subject than the NPC using the standard A* graph.

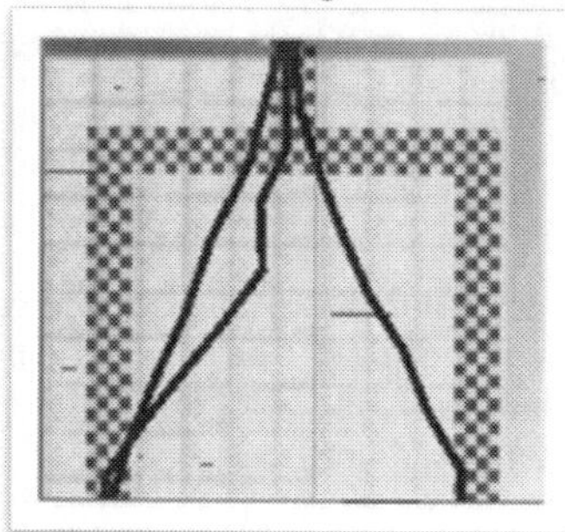

Figure 12. Human Subject Room Analysis.

A key feature of the roaming model was imitating how human subjects entered a room and the time it takes to start moving to a new location. Figure 13 shows the doorway exit and entrance trajectory. The results indicate that the model is working as intended. There are no identical paths, but adheres to a logical tactic, and there was little pathing efficiency cost.

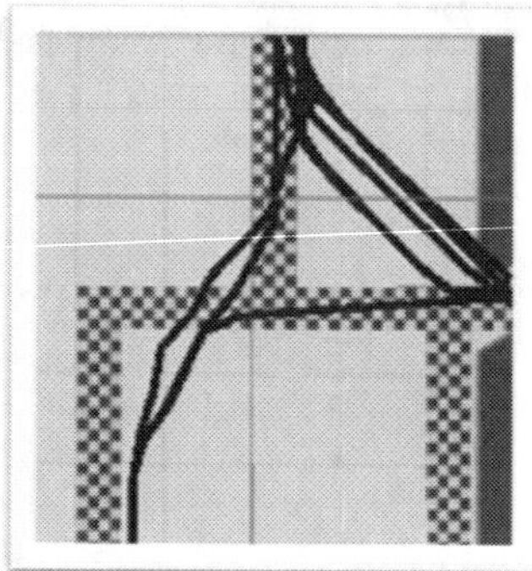

Figure 13. Door Trajectory Analysis.

A key strategy used by human subjects was peeking into large areas. The effect of peeking can be seen most clearly when looking at the fog, the red line indicates the path the NPC followed (Figure 14). It moved into the room, peeked into the foyer area before resuming initial route. Such characteristics are integral to having an accurate imitating roaming model because it projects a degree of intelligence when observed by a player.

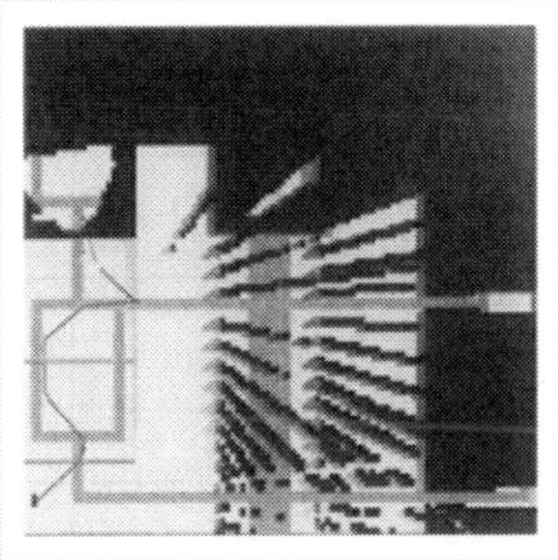

Figure 14. NPC Peeking Identification.

Finally, when discussing the map view coverage, with the objective set to collect eight coins. NPCs showed approximately the same level of map coverage as human subjects was achieved (Figure 15). This shows that the roaming model can comfortably seek out and acquire anything within the realms of the A* graph.

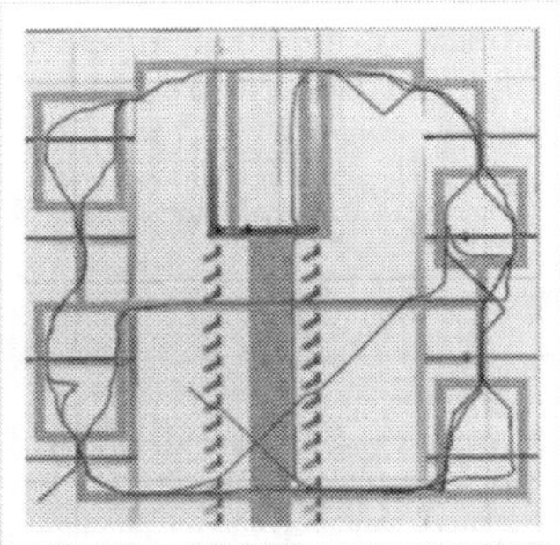

Figure 15. Roaming Model Map Coverage.

Being able to fully scan the environment is a crucial aspect of navigation. When the goal location is not predetermined, if the NPC cannot scan and analyse the entire map, some goals might become impossible to complete.

VI. CONCLUSION

The objective of this paper was to explore if human player navigation data can be used to create a heatmap, for the purpose of adjusting the weight cost in an A* graph to influence the pathfinding.

The roaming model demonstrates that using a method, which restricts pathing decisions based on what it can see, and using a heatmap weighted A* algorithm, a good imitation of the general roaming behaviours of a human player can be achieved. This hybrid model was able to take advantage of tags in the environment so the NPC could make decisions based on what was in view. Thus, removing omniscient characteristics often associated with NPCs and which can be clearly identified by players. The heatmap weighted A* offers a unique approach to influencing pathfinding so that NPCs use frequently travelled areas, making the NPC interactions more natural, than scripted interactions that can appear forced.

However, it was clear that using a designated A* roaming graph had negative implications when used for other navigation tasks. Therefore, the practical application of the model would need to incorporate a multiple graph solution, in which the A* would be applied to an appropriate graph, based on the task the NPC is undertaking. This is currently being researched, in which NPCs can instantly switch graphs suited for the current task being undertaken.

REFERENCES

[1] P. Williamson, "Modelling Human Behaviour in a Virtual Environment." [Unpublished Masters Thesis]. University of South Wales, 2019.

[2] D. Foead, A. Ghifari, M. B. Kusuma, N. Hanafiah, and E. Gunawan, "A systematic literature review of A* pathfinding," Procedia Computer Science, pp. 507-514, 2021.

[3] W. Ziqiang, H. Xiaoguang, and L. Xiaoxiao, "Overview of Global Path Planning Algorithms for Mobile Robots," Comput. Sci., vol. 48, pp. 1-16, 2021.

[4] S. Permana, K. Bintoro, B. Arifitama and A. Syahputra. "Comparative analysis of pathfinding algorithms a*, dijkstra, and bfs on maze runner game," IJISTECH International J. Inf. Syst. Technol., vol. 1, no. 2, pp. 1, 2018.

[5] Y. Sazaki, H. Satria, and M. Syahroyni. "Comparison of A* and dynamic pathfinding algorithm with dynamic pathfinding algorithm for NPC on car racing game," 11th International Conference on Telecommunication Systems Services and Applications, pp. 1-6, 2017.

[6] I. Makarov, P. Polyakov, and R. Karpichev, "Voronoi-based Path Planning based on Visibility and Kill/Death Ratio Tactical Component," In AIST, pp. 129-140, 2018.

[7] N. R. Sturtevant, D. Sigurdson, B. Taylor, and T. Gibson, "Pathfinding and abstraction with dynamic terrain costs," In Proceedings of the AAAI Conference on Artificial Intelligence and Interactive Digital Entertainment, vol. 15, no. 1, pp. 80-86, 2019.

[8] H. Pan, "Pathfinding and Map Feature Learning in RTS Games with Partial Observability," In AIIDE Workshops 2021.

[9] D. Daylamani-Zad, L. B. Graham, and I. T. Paraskevopoulos, "September. Swarm intelligence for autonomous cooperative agents in battles for real-time strategy games," 9th International Conference on Virtual Worlds and Games for Serious Applications, pp. 39-46, 2017.

[10] X. Chen, et al., "Towards believable resource gathering behaviours in real-time strategy games with a memetic ant colony system," Procedia Computer Science, vol. 24, pp. 143-151, 2013.

[11] A. Rafiq, T. Kadir, and S. N. Ihsan, "Pathfinding algorithms in game development," In IOP Conference Series: Materials Science and Engineering. vol. 769, no. 1, pp. 1-12, 2020.

Modelling Player Combat Behaviour for Dynamic Difficulty Scaling in First Person Shooter Games

Paul Williamson
School of Computing and Mathematics
University of South Wales
CF37 1DL, Pontypridd
e-mail: paul.williamson@southwales.ac.uk

Christopher Tubb
School of Computing and Mathematics
University of South Wales
CF37 1DL, Pontypridd
e-mail: christopher.tubb@southwales.ac.uk

Abstract—**Non-Player Characters (NPC) are a core aspect of a modern video game. They fulfil a wide range of roles and features in most genres. How they are perceived can have an impact on the overall enjoyment of the game, and when the NPCs are poorly modelled, the experience can be negative. This paper explores modelling human player behaviour to develop a combat model for NPCs, which will provide a dynamic solution for skill scaling. Game difficulty is a subjective notion and when games have a predefined classification, being able to satisfy all players is not realistic. This paper investigates if the combat model can therefore be used to scale the difficulty of the NPC in real-time, by dynamically adjusting a skill attribute, which is used by several key combat behaviours.**

Keywords—NPC; Player Modelling; Difficulty; Combat Behaviour; Gameplay; FPS.

I. Introduction

This paper explores a player driven approach for dynamically adjusting the difficulty of Non-Player Characters (NPCs) in real-time. This is achieved by modelling player combat gameplay. The model is then applied directly to NPCs. The combat efficiency is controlled by dynamically adjusting the variable parameters in real-time for the purpose of difficulty scaling. The reasoning behind modelling human-player gameplay is to help define the generalised upper and lower skill level of average players. These bounds are then, in determining how skilfully an NPC should behave, based on data rather than developer interpretation.

This paper conducts two experiments. The first experiment uses predetermined combat scenarios that records the data of human subjects, which is used to model generalised combat behaviours. The second experiment applies the combat model to NPCs, then evaluates the perception of the model when human subjects conduct a deathmatch scenario with the skill of the NPC increasing with each round.

The results show that generalising human combat data provides a suitable base for controlling the combat effectiveness of NPCs. It demonstrates that by using a variable to denote the skill level of the NPC, the difficulty can be dynamically adjusted to reflect a desired outcome.

In Section II, this paper provides a background for NPCs in FPS games and the role of difficulty. Section III discusses the motivation behind this paper and what impact this research could have on the gaming industry. In Section IV, a literature review is undertaken to discuss relative research, which is consistent with the NPCs in the FPS genre. Section V details the two experiments. The first is used to capture and model human subject combat behaviour, while the second experiment evaluates the model by having human subjects compete against NPCs with the combat model in a deathmatch scenario. In Section VI, the results of the experiments are analysed and displayed. Firstly, a numerical comparison between the human subject data and NPCs is discussed along with an evaluation of the feedback from human subjects, regarding the perception of the combat model. Lastly, an assessment of the combat model as a suitable solution for dynamic skill scaling. Section VII concludes the paper and discusses the impact of the combat model. Finally, Section VIII discusses potential future work that can be undertaken to build upon the work presented in this paper.

II. Background

A. Non-Player Characters in FPS Games

An NPC is a character that exists within a video game that is not being controlled by a human player. NPCs can occupy any range of characters and can exhibit a variety of levels of perceived intelligence.

There are multiple roles an NPC can fulfil, and their stance towards a player can be friendly, neutral, or enemy [1]. This paper is only focused on NPCs in the role of an enemy and therefore a threat.

The purpose of an NPC is dependent upon the specific role it was designed to fulfil. However, NPCs should strive to appear as authentic as possible to maintain immersion. This is especially important when the NPC operates as a member of a team with human players, because if the NPC is identified, it can become the focus of the opposition if the NPC performs at a low level.

Poorly designed NPCs can have a significant effect on a game, because when the immersion is broken it can ripple through other parts of the game [2]. Therefore, careful consideration should be undertaken when designing the role and function of an NPC because it can negatively impact the game.

B. Difficulty in Games

Difficulty is one of the areas where poorly developed NPCs can damage the overall enjoyment of a game. When NPCs are too easy, they do not represent a challenge and when they are too difficult, they can be frustrating and appear as unfair opposition.

This signifies a problem when discussing difficulty settings in video games. The term is subjective and so what is 'easy' to one player may not necessarily be 'easy' to other players. The issue exists when hardcoding arbitrary characteristics to perform at a defined level. The focus is not player-centric, but rather a generalised interpretation of what is considered 'easy' by the developers.

In First Person Shooter games (FPS), NPCs 'difficulty' is often expressed in their combat efficiency, and so difficulty settings reflect adeptness regarding individual combat behaviours, such as accuracy and reaction time. Part of this paper is to explore whether the skill of the NPC can be changed in real-time, and if the combat behaviours correspond precisely to the skill level. This would enable a player-centric based difficulty. The players skill is calculated in real-time, and then the NPCs are modified accordingly depending on the difficulty classification selected.

III. MOTIVATION

The motivation of the paper is to address the purpose of varying difficulty and ultimately the distinction between the different difficulty classifications. While this is a subjective discussion, the difficulty of a game can impact how it is perceived by an individual. When a particular difficulty is selected, it is important that it is perceived accordingly otherwise there is a risk of a negative experience.

A combat game in the form of an FPS was chosen as the case study because it represents a well-founded genre and have heavily featured in the gaming industry since the early 1990s. As game genres can differ in gameplay and technicality, it was important to isolate one genre so that the scope of the research remains narrow so a conclusion can be derived from the data. Furthermore, in FPS games, the metric of difficulty is commonly associated with combat 'skill', such as reaction speed, precision, and decision-making. Therefore, it is a standard practice in the video game industry to statically increase reaction time, damage dealt and precision when increasing difficulty levels.

The motivation for exploring real-time skill scaling centres around the notion that one size does not fit all. When a game has static pre-determined difficulty settings, they cannot accurately cater to all potential players. By having NPCs skill based on the performance of the player, it could usher in a new player-centric style of difficulty, and ultimately provide more control to the player.

Williamson and Tubb [3] showed that player gameplay can be broken down into key behaviours and the patterns that emerged can be modelled. They also indicated that when an NPCs were poorly modelled, and the combat efficiency was too high, the resulting NPC was perceived as a player using cheats.

IV. RELATED RESEARCH

A. Non-Player Characters in Combat Roles

When discussing NPCs in a combat role, the focus will be primarily on the FPS genre. While NPCs have been present since the inception of the FPS genre, there has been some progress in the scope of their capabilities. Orkin [4] showed that NPCs could display seemingly complex characteristics, such as tactics, by using Goal Orientated Action Planner (GOAP), which enabled individual actions to be undertaken based on current circumstance. This technique sparked a host of research based around maximising the effectiveness of using action planners. Influenced by GOAP, Pezzato et al. [5] researched a technique that uses active interference and Behavioural Trees (BT) to develop decision-based plans, which are adaptable and created in real-time for robotics.

However, Agis et al. [6] suggest that because GOAP are individual by design, NPCs are not actively cooperating with allies and just giving the illusion of working as a team. They proposed using a new form of Event Driven Behavioural Tree (EDBT), where three extra nodes are added for communication purposes between same team NPCs. These nodes facilitate actions in a sub-tree, so the sender can request the receiver/s to perform certain actions.

Neufeld et al. [7] propose that behavioural trees are a good approach to NPC decision-making, when combined with a Hierarchical Task Network (HTN). The HTN was able to instruct multiple NPCs what to do but leave the low-level execution of tasks to the BTs. When comparing this hybrid approach against a pure HTN solution. The results showed the hybrid approach to be more flexible and fail less often.

B. Human Imitation

The idea to measure and quantify the skill of human players is not a new idea and in essence this research is akin to work undertaken to develop NPCs to appear more believable. While believability can have many interpretations depending on the context of the topic, this paper is focused on NPCs with a generalised skill level. Camilleri et al. [8] identify believability as:

> *Player believability is a highly subjective notion commonly viewed as the ability of a game playing character to convince observers that it is being controlled by a human player*

This suggests that for an NPC to be deemed as a believable character, it needs to exhibit human-like behaviours. So, observers are convinced the character is human controlled. In the context of the FPS genre, these behaviours will range from combat efficiency to pathfinding characteristics and decisions.

Polceanu et al. [9] presented two solutions for imitating human player behaviour. The first is a human behaviour mirror technique, while the second uses interactive genetic algorithms. This is supported by Mora et al. [10], they combined the techniques to create a hybridisation model. When experimented in a Turin Test scenario, the results showed that a high level of "humanness" was achieved.

The importance of imitating human players extends beyond difficulty scaling. Wehbe et al. [11] argue that the difference between playing with other human participants and NPC is profound because it intersects the artificial world of the game with real life. They also imply that quasi-feudalistic tendencies of human players should be encouraged in NPCs where possible.

C. Difficulty Control in FPS Games

When discussing difficulty control, it is important to define the terminology in the context of a video game. Smeddinck et al. [12] states:

> *Game difficulty choices that are presented in menus with typical labels such as "easy, medium, hard" can be found even in very early and simple games. The "classic way to*

present difficulty choices" has arguably evolved largely as a matter of technical circumstance

This suggests that difficulty has been part of video games for a long time and has needed to evolve out of necessity.

Hendrix et al. [13] showed a positive result when developing a six-point system, which gathers data and applies an algorithm to determine the capabilities of the player through engagement.

Blom et al. [14] have taken a different approach to identifying the currently perceived difficulty experienced by the player. They developed a system that monitors facial expressions to determine the difficulty the subject is experiencing, achieving 72% accuracy. The model was able to adapt to the individual's performance level via their facial expression and establish which tasks or challenges presented the most difficulty.

The research shows that while difficulty may be an easily defined concept, problems occur when putting the theory into practice. For the remainder of this paper, difficulty will be defined as:

The degree of challenge presented to an individual when undertaking game related tasks or mechanics

These tasks can range from game objectives, such as solving puzzles or combat interactions that relies on eliminating opponents.

The idea of a personalised approach to NPC development is not a novel idea. Research by Bakkes [15] discusses the notion of using player models to generate an individualistic experience. Their research shows that a few viable techniques have been examined [16]-[18]. These techniques mainly use NPC training methods or manipulate external constraints, such as environmental, to achieve the desired outcome. However, the purpose of this paper is to use generalised player data to control the combat efficiency of NPCs, which can be adapted in real-time.

V. EXPERIMENTS

A series of experiments were conducted to analyse the combat efficiency of human subjects so they can be directly modelled. This also enabled the same experiment to be undertaken by the NPCs, so a direct comparison could be performed and ensure combat efficiency was changing in accordance with the skill level set. Evaluating the perception of difficulty, an experiment was undertaken where human subjects played a series of deathmatch rounds against two NPCs. As the rounds progressed, the base skill level of the NPCs also increased.

The objective of these experiments is to identify the generalised combat efficiency of human players, use this data to develop a combat model that adjusts combat efficiency based on current skill level, and then evaluate the model by having human subjects compete against NPCs.

A. Experimantal Environment

The experiments in this paper were developed using Unity3D, the files were upload to an online server. Each subject download and ran the experiment on their local machine. The first experiment took approximately fifteen minutes to complete. After each stage data was saved and uploaded to an online database. The second experiment took ten minutes, with the data also being saved online after each stage. There was also an accompanying questionnaire at the end of this experiment, which was completed via a web browser.

All subjects in both experiments were anonymous, no details were requested, and no experience was required. The data that was uploaded from their experiment session did not record any information which could be tracked to an individual.

B. Combat Behaviour Experimental Protocol

The modelling experiment focused on five scenarios, which analysed and recorded the decisions and behaviours of the subjects as they undertook each scenario. Each scenario has three settings where targets spawns near, medium distance or far from the subject. During the experiment the subject cannot move except to rotate and targets randomly spawn in view. The scenarios in this experiment were used because they reflect commonly occurring combat situation in FPS games. While it is understood that in some modern games more complicated scenarios could appear, it was decided to model the fundamental scenarios only and gauge the effectiveness of the skill scaling.

The experiment runs four times. Each time the weapon or weapon aim stance will change, in the order as follows:

- Pistol: Off hip
- Pistol: Aiming down sights
- Assault Rifle: Off hip
- Assault Rifle: Aiming down sights

The purpose of these experiments is to identify if individual weapons have an impact on combat behaviours and the degree of change in combat efficiency when the weapon aim stance changes. This will help determine the specific and generalised weapon behaviours that will need to be modelled and what impact they may have on difficulty.

All targets use the same model and texture, they each have the equivalence of fifty health points and are immediately destroyed when its health is reduced to zero.

a) Normal Scenario

The normal scenario is a typical encounter in a video game. A single target appears, and the subject has a limited amount of time to dispatch it. Subjects have 2 seconds to eliminate the target before it disappears. As the three stages represent near, medium, and far distances. This experiment analyses what effect this has on accuracy, reaction time and helps determine a baseline for average reaction time.

b) Increased Spawn Rate

The increasing spawn rate analyses the effect of targets appearing in view when subjects are in the process of eliminating another target, and if the new targets have a negative effect on reaction time. The purpose of this experiment was to determine if external influence can have a negative effect on combat efficiency, and if so to what degree.

c) Grouped Targets

It is frequent in a modern game that multiple opponents can be present at a given time. This scenario analyses the pattern exhibited when numerous opponents suddenly appear.

Continuing with the three-stage approach, this scenario also increases the number of targets that simultaneously spawn as the stages advance. The near stage has three targets, medium stage has five targets, and the far stage has seven targets. All targets remain for five seconds before disappearing.

d) Varying Size

This scenario is a repeat of the normal scenario stage. However, the target size is decreased to determine the degree of correlation between target size and combat efficiency.

e) Moving Target

In this scenario, targets spawn every 2.5s and self-destruct at 5s. They move from left to right at a constant speed, changing direction when reaching the edge of a predefined boundary. This enables some overlap of targets on screen if they are not eliminated fast enough. This scenario explores if a moving target has an influence on combat efficiency of an individual.

C. Dynamic Difficulty Experimental Protocol

Evaluating the effect of dynamic difficulty, the experiment is a deathmatch. The objective is to achieve a set number of eliminations before the opposition. In this experiment, the requirement is set to 5 eliminations. There are three stages, as the stages progress the base skill level of the NPCs is increased. The stages are as follows:

- Stage One: NPC Base Skill is 3
- Stage Two: NPC Base Skill is 6
- Stage Three: NPC Base Skill is 9

There are two NPCs opponents, which operate in an all verses all scenario. One of the NPCs will use a pistol and the other will use the assault rifle. Each weapon has a sub model that influences attack distance and has its own attributes such as clip size and bullet damage.

The subject will have access to three weapons. Each weapon has its own ammunition stash and can be equipped by pressing 1, 2 or 3 on the keyboard. The weapon characteristics are as follows:

- Pistol: The pistol has high recoil and kickback, slow fire-rate, but deals high damage
- Assault Rifle: This weapon has high fire-rate, medium damage, and moderate recoil
- Shotgun: The shotgun fires 12 pellets per shot, each of which deal low damage, high recoil, and high pellet spread over range

There are three medic-packs and three ammunition-pack throughout the map. The medic-pack provide 50% health and the ammunition provides one clip for the equipped weapon. When a medic-pack or ammunition has been collected, it will respawn in the same location after five seconds.

The purpose of this experiment is to evaluate the combat model and to determine if increasing the base skill level has an effect on combat efficiency. The skill scaling is important because in a real-world setting, there is a spectrum of player skill levels, this flexibility needs to be reflected in the model. If NPCs are able to increase or decrease their combat efficiency in real-time, it would provide a suitable solution to improving challenging NPCs. As NPCs could be changed during a game to match the skill of the current player.

a) Combat Model

The combat model being used in this paper was derived from subject data captured in the 'Combat Behaviour Experiment'. The purpose of this model is to have NPCs imitate human-like combat behaviours, with key behaviours directly linked to a skill variable, so the combat efficiency accurately reflects the NPC skill at a given time. For this paper, the skill of the NPC will be between 1 and 10, with 10 representing very high combat efficiency and 1 very poor efficiency. Therefore, an NPC with a skill of 5 will represent the generalised combat efficiency resulting from the combat behaviour experiment. The definition of skill will therefore be based around improving or worsening the generalised data.

As the combat model was used to influence key combat behaviours by modifying how the NPC operates in combat situations. This means the purpose of the combat model was to represent a generalised combat behaviour exhibited by human subjects during combat encounters. As the data used for this model was directly sourced from human subjects, it was generalised to provide a base level for how an average skilled NPC should play.

As the development techniques being deployed are standard in the gaming industry, it was important that a range of these techniques were compatible with the data acquired. Therefore, when developing the model, it was decided that the best approach would be to use object orientated programming to encapsulate the functionality of the model. After an object of the class is generated, the other components of the NPC can directly access the combat model. This is vital because during run time, several scripts and coroutines are running at the same time and potentially require access to the same data.

Ensuring NPCs did not appear generic, it was decided that the skill attribute should be influenced by modifiers but have an upper and lower restriction. This would stop NPCs snowballing and becoming too good or regressing and becoming too bad. It was important that the influence applied by the skill attribute is a direct reflection of the previous passage of play, accumulating from the past few combat interaction outcomes. The modifiers are:

- Death: Being eliminated has a negative effect and decreases skill modifier
- Eliminations: Eliminating an opponent is positive and increases the skill modifier

The modifier change is +0.5 for an elimination and -0.5 for a death. This amount is added to an accumulative counter but is capped at +2.5 and -2.5. This limitation was added to stop NPCs diverging too far from their base skill. For instance, a run of eliminations without being eliminated will take an NPC to peak performance of base skill level + 2.5.

Players generally have a preferred weapon of choice. Therefore, NPCs generate a preferred weapon order when initially spawned. The top three weapons have a positive influence on active skill, the amount is determined by the weapons position in the weapons order. For this experiment however, NPCs were not given the option to change weapon and were equipped with a predefined weapon. The weapon skill modifier was always set to +1.

When calculating the active skill, the base skill, weapon modifier and a hot-streak/cold-streak modifier are all added together. This approach means the active skill will always be close to the base skill but has some arbitrary variation because there is potential for the NPC be having a "good" or "bad" round.

Equation (1) shows how the initial reaction time was calculated using an active skill calculation.

$$\text{Reaction Time} = \frac{Ts + ((S * M) * Dx)}{Dz} \qquad (1)$$

Where, *Ts* is the target size, *S* the active skill attribute, *M* is a generic modifier, *Dx* the 2D distance from the centre of the screen to the target and *Dz* the Euclidean distance from the NPC to the target. This represents a comprehensive approach to targeting because it considers not only the size of the target (*Ts*), but also the distance (*Dz*). This was required because the further away the target was in game, the smaller it would appear on the screen. This underscores the importance of precision when determining the initial reaction targeting speed.

Equations (2) and (3) are for accuracy. It was decided to separate the two shooting stances as looking down sights should provide better control than shooting off the hip.

$$\text{Aiming} = \text{Vp} + \text{Vf} * (\text{Mx} + (\text{My} * \text{S})) \qquad (2)$$

Vp is the vector position and *Vf* the vector forward direction of the NPC, *Mx* and *My* are generic modifiers and *S* the active skill of the NPC.

$$\text{Off Hip} = \frac{\text{Vp} + \text{Vf} * (\text{Mx} * \text{S})}{Sx * Ws} \qquad (3)$$

Like the aiming equation, *Vp* is the vector position and *Vf* the vector forward direction of the NPC, *Mx* a generic modifier and *S* the active skill of the NPC. However, *Sx* is the locale scale of the crosshair and *Ws* is the equipped weapon bullet spread. When shooting off the hip, the crosshair momentarily increases in size, this effect is accumulative, so the longer the weapon is being continuously fired, the more inaccurate it becomes.

The shooting stances therefore have unique characteristics that display different combat behaviours based on the weapon being used and active skill of the NPC.

VI. Results

The results indicate that modelling human behaviour is a suitable method for having dynamically skilled NPCs and it is possible to generalise combat efficiency. While the skill scaling proved to be a very effective solution for modifying the NPC combat efficiency in real-time.

a) Combat Model Analysis Comparison

The results suggest that while the performance of the model was well received, there were some areas of combat that require more attention. Figure 1 details the average accuracy for both NPCs at each stage and subjects at stage 1. It shows that while the scaling worked, they were in general over-tuned.

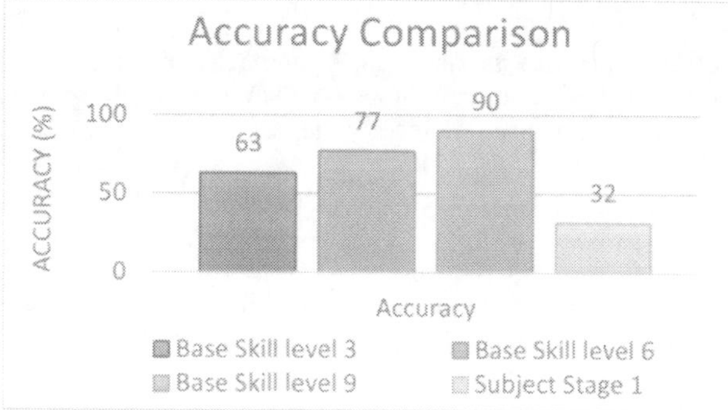

Figure 1. Accuracy Comparison.

When specifying where combat believability was the weakest, it follows a similar trend. Figure 2 shows that when asked about specific behaviours of combat, 85.7% of the responses thought accuracy was not realistic.

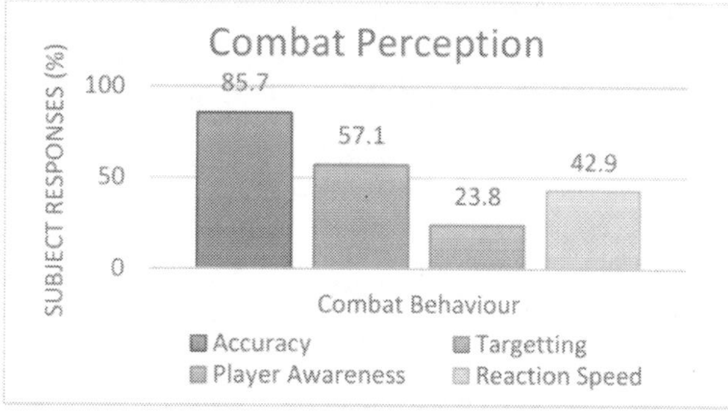

Figure 2. Combat Perception Analysis.

Reaction time was also elevated. This suggests that subjects had a difficult time competing with the NPCs. However, this problem can be solved by reducing the weight of the modifier system in the combat model, which suggests more experimentation is required to tweak the model.

Figure 3 shows the overall combat perception of the NPCs. While 50% thought the NPCs were somewhat human-like, the rest thought they did not display a good representation of a human player.

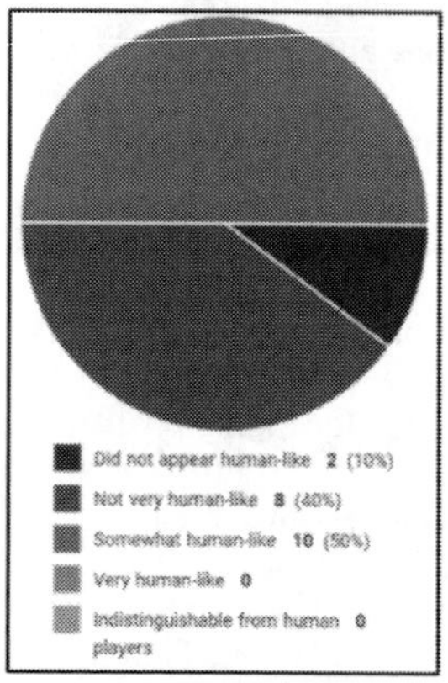

Figure 3. Combat Feedback.

While these results may not suggest the NPCs accurately imitated human players, it shows that this method does hold some promise and by fine tuning the model it could yield better results.

b) Gameplay Influence

When analysing the feedback, it became apparent that the other gameplay behaviours were having a direct influence on the perception of the combat believability. This meant that the perception of the pathfinding was negatively affecting the opinions of the subjects regarding the combat of the NPCs. As subjects were requested to fill out a questionnaire at the end of the deathmatch experiment, a question was specifically asked about the combat behaviours exhibited by NPCs. Figure 4 singles out a reply from one of the subjects. It underlines that other gameplay behaviours, such as navigation, can have an impact on the perception of combat.

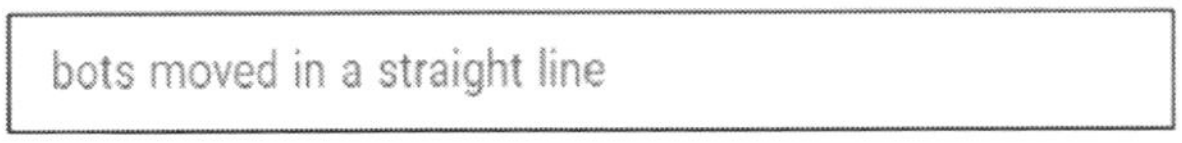

Figure 4. Specific Combat Subject Feedback.

When one behaviour is modelled poorly, it can affect the perception of other behaviours and have undesirable effects. When modelling certain behaviours, it is important to be aware of how it may affect the other behaviours in certain scenarios.

c) Skill Scaling

The skill scaling showed a high degree of effectiveness when asking the subject if they noticed a change in difficulty as they progressed through the stages (Figure 5). While 57.1% noticed a change in difficulty, none of the subjects thought the difficulty did not change.

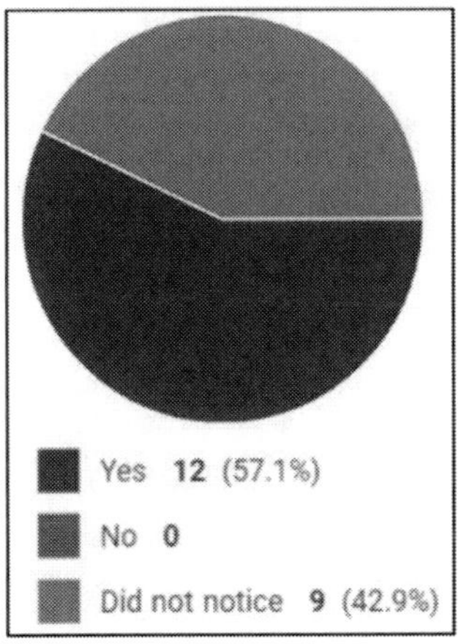

Figure 5. Difficulty Identification Feedback.

This shows the combat model could be a suitable solution for enabling real-time adaptive NPC difficulty. This further confirms that players, to a degree, have awareness about the combat efficiency of opponents. This emphasises that generalisation of difficulties cannot satisfy all players.

When analysing the pistol combat performance between the three difficulties (Figure 6). A positive trend is evident where the amount of damage done by the NPC increased as the base skill is increased.

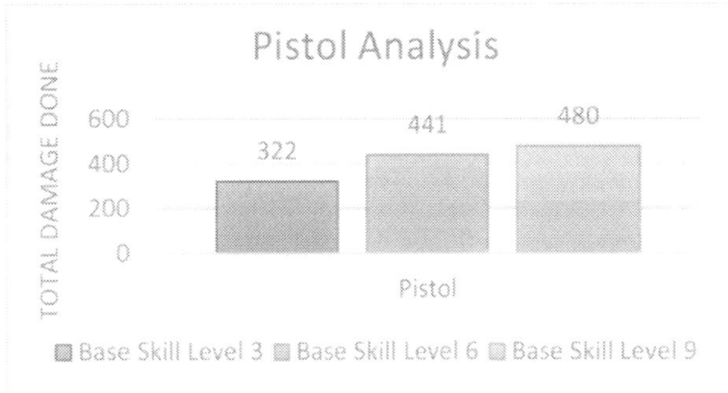

Figure 6. Pistol Damage Done Skill Comparison.

Combat efficiency increased with base skill level. This is supported when analysing the average initial reaction time for the assault rifle across all three stages (Figure 7). The results show a slight correlation between reaction time and active skill level. While there is some deviation, this could be due to the fluctuation in active skill level, due to hot and cold streak being triggered.

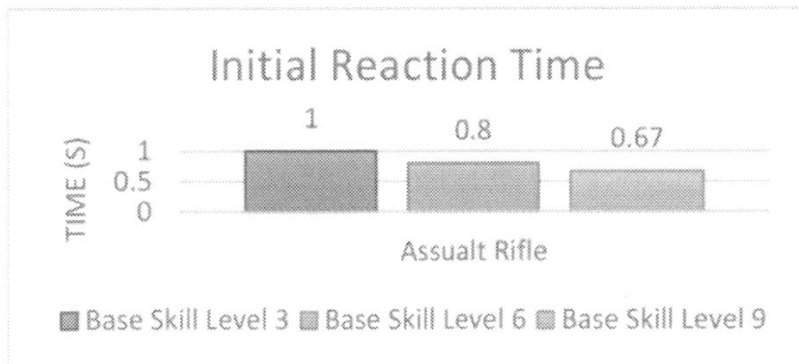

Figure 7. NPC Skill Reaction Time Initial Comparison.

When analysing the 1st and 3rd stages (Figure 8) the average number of eliminations achieved for each character was considered. On average, subjects did not perform very well and the NPC with the assault rifle was overly efficient especially on stage 1.

Figure 8. Eliminations Comparison.

This data supports the suggestion that the performance of the NPCs was over tuned. However, when analysing the NPC with the pistol, the data shows that it did get better as its skill was increased. This had a significant effect because both the subject and assault rifle NPC elimination count dropped. While more experimentation and fine tuning of the model is needed, this represents a positive result.

The novelty of this model and algorithms is that the skill variable directly influences the behaviour and efficiency of the

NPC in combat. Further research is required to capture real-time skill of the player, so the NPC can tweak its skill to match the desired difficulty outcome. This would represent a personalised difficulty structure, where the player skill is taken into consideration.

VII. Conclusion

The objective of this research was to develop a dynamic skill scaling combat model based on data acquired from human subjects. This paper has shown that the combat model provided a good solution for modelling human combat behaviours, however, more data is required to improve the modifier weights in relation to the active skill of the NPC. There is evidence to suggest that modelling combat alone would not be enough to create dynamic NPCs, several subjects, when asked to comment on combat behaviours, mentioned pathfinding and navigation issues. Gameplay behaviours are intertwined and when one gameplay behaviour is poorly modelled, it can influence perception of other behaviours.

The skill scaling showed a positive result, the data highlighted that there is a somewhat linear change in reaction time and accuracy, as the skill of the NPC was increased. This was noted by 57.1% of the subjects, with zero subjects stating that they thought the NPCs did not increase in difficulty. However, the combat efficiency of the NPC was deemed to be too high, even on the easiest difficulty stage, this was supported when analysing the number of eliminations achieved and the NPC with the assault rifle significantly outperformed the subjects.

VIII. Future Work

As the results indicated the combat behaviour was negatively impacted by the other gameplay behaviours, research is required to determine the extent of this influence. Navigation and decision-making models will need to be included in the NPC, the experiment repeated, and results compared.

Identifying real-time player skill level could further enhance the effectiveness of dynamic skill scaling. Research in this area could help determine if dynamically adjusting NPC skill based on the current player perform provides a more engaging experience.

References

[1] H. Warpefelt, "The Non-Player Character: Exploring the believability of NPC presentation and behavior," Doctoral dissertation, Department of Computer and Systems Sciences, Stockholm University, 2016.

[2] P. Lankoski and S. Björk, "Gameplay Design Patterns for Believable Non-Player Characters," DiGRA Conference, pp. 416-423, 2007.

[3] P. Williamson and C. Tubb, "Modelling Player Combat Behaviour For NPC Imitation And Combat Awareness Analysis," ECMS, pp. 205-212, 2021.

[4] J. Orkin, "Three states and a plan: the AI of FEAR," Game developers conference, pp. 4, 2006.

[5] C. Pezzato, C. Hernandez, S. Bonhof, and M. Wisse, "Active Inference and Behavior Trees for Reactive Action Planning and Execution in Robotics," arXiv preprint arXiv:2011.09756, 2020.

[6] R. A. Agis, S. Gottifredi, and A. J. García, "An event-driven behavior trees extension to facilitate non-player multi-agent coordination in video games," Expert Systems with Applications, pp. 155, 2020.

[7] X. Neufeld, S. Mostaghim, and S. Brand, "A hybrid approach to planning and execution in dynamic environments through hierarchical task networks and behavior trees," In Proceedings of the Fourteenth AAAI Conference on Artificial Intelligence and Interactive Digital Entertainment, pp. 201-207, 2018.

[8] E. Camilleri, G. N. Yannakakis, and A. Dingli, "Platformer level design for player believability," Conference on Computational Intelligence and Games, pp. 1-8, 2016.

[9] M. Polceanu, A. M. Mora, J. L. Jimenez, C. Buche, and A.J. Fernandez-Leiva, "The believability gene in virtual bots," The Twenty-Ninth International Flairs Conference, pp. 346-349, 2016.

[10] A. M. Mora, A. Gutiérrez-Rodrıguez, and A. J. Fernández-Leiva, "Optimising Humanness: Designing the Best Human-Like Bot for Unreal Tournament 2004," In International Work-Conference on Artificial Neural Networks, pp. 681-693, 2017.

[11] R. R. Wehbe, E. Lank, and L. E. Nacke, "Left the 4 dead: Perception of humans versus non-player character teammates in cooperative gameplay," In Proceedings of the 2017 Conference on Designing Interactive Systems, pp. 403-415, 2017.

[12] J. D. Smeddinck et al. "How to present game difficulty choices? Exploring the impact on player experience," CHI Conference on Human Factors in Computing Systems, pp. 5595-5607, 2016.

[13] M. Hendrix, T. Bellamy-Wood, S. McKay, V. Bloom, and I. Dunwell, "Implementing adaptive game difficulty balancing in serious games," IEEE Transactions on Games, pp. 320-327, 2018.

[14] P. M. Blom, S. Bakkes, and P. Spronck, "Modeling and adjusting in-game difficulty based on facial expression analysis," Entertainment Computing 31, 2019.

[15] S. Bakkes, C. T. Tan, and Y. Pisan, "Personalised gaming: a motivation and overview of literature," In Proceedings of the 8th Australasian Conference on Interactive Entertainment: Playing the System, pp. 1-10, 2012.

[16] P. H. M. Spronck, I. G. Sprinkhuizen-Kuyper, and E. O. Postma, "Difficulty scaling of game AI," In Proceedings of the 5th International Conference on Intelligent Games and Simulation, pp. 33-37, 2004.

[17] P. Demasi and A. J. de. O. Cruz, "Online coevolution for action games," International Journal of Intelligent Games and Simulation, vol. 2, pp. 80-88, 2002.

[18] G. N. Yannakakis and J. Hallam, "Towards optimizing entertainment in computer games," Applied Artificial Intelligence, vol. 21, pp. 933-971, 2007.

Augmented Reality Simulation for Testing Advanced Driver Assistance Systems in Future Automotive Vehicles

Michael Weber
Institute of Energy Efficient Mobility
Hochschule Karlsruhe -
University of Applied Sciences, HKA
Karlsruhe, Germany
email: michael.weber@h-ka.de

Tobias Weiss
Institute of Energy Efficient Mobility
Hochschule Karlsruhe -
University of Applied Sciences, HKA
Karlsruhe, Germany
email: tobias.weiss@h-ka.de

Franck Gechter
CIAD (UMR 7533)
Univ. Bourgogne Franche-Comte, UTBM
Belfort, France

LORIA-MOSEL (UMR 7503)
Université de Lorraine
Nancy, France
email: franck.gechter@utbm.fr

Reiner Kriesten
Institute of Energy Efficient Mobility
Hochschule Karlsruhe -
University of Applied Sciences, HKA
Karlsruhe, Germany
email: reiner.kriesten@h-ka.de

***Abstract*—To take advantage of Advanced Driver Assistance Systems (ADAS) testing in simulation and reality, this paper presents a new approach to using Augmented Reality (AR) in future automotive vehicles to test ADAS. Our procedure creates a connection between simulation and reality and should enable a faster development process for ADAS tests and future mobility solutions, which will become increasingly complex in the future. Complex automotive environmental conditions, such as high vehicle speed and fewer possible orientation points on an urban test track compared to using AR applications inside a building, require high computing power for our approach. Using Image Segmentation (IS), Artificial Intelligence (AI) for object recognition and visual Simultaneous Localization and Mapping (vSLAM), a three-dimensional model with accurate information about the urban test site is generated. The use of AI and IS aims to significantly improve performance, such as calculation speed and accuracy for AR applications in complex automobiles.**

***Index Terms*—Artificial Intelligence, Augmented Reality, Advanced Driver Assistance Systems, Visual Simultaneous Localization and Mapping.**

I. Introduction

Advanced Driver Assistance Systems (ADAS) are more and more spread in current and future cars because they are increasing vehicle safety by recognizing road signs, keeping the car in its lane, or regulating the speed adaptively. These complex systems go through an extensive test phase, resulting in the potential for optimization in terms of quality, reproducibility, and costs. Due to the increasing complexity of vehicle communication and the rising demands on these systems in terms of reliability to function safely even in a complex environment and to support the driver, test scenarios for ADAS are constantly being further developed to meet higher requirements. The European New Car Assessment Program (Euro NCAP) has included a series of new safety tests for ADAS in its program and has drawn up a roadmap up to the year 2025 [1] [2].

Current testing methods of ADAS can be divided into simulation and reality. The core idea of using simulation is to transfer the behavior of the vehicle to the virtual test drives as realistically as possible. The approach of using simulation aims to use the advantages like reproducibility, flexibility, and cost reduction. In this way, the specifications and solutions derived from this should be able to be tested and evaluated at an early stage of the development process. Using suitable simulation methods enables the efficient design, development, and application of vehicles and vehicle components. However, simulation cannot yet replace real test drives in all respects. Due to the complex physical conditions under which a vehicle is handed over during ADAS tests, real test drives are still required for the current status. For example, weather, road surface conditions, and other influencing parameters play a crucial role in the evaluation of ADAS road tests [3] [4].

However, the test and evaluation effort correlate with the complexity of an ADAS. The more complex the system, the greater the testing effort. The robustness, functional safety, and reliability of the ADAS must be proven in increasingly dynamic, complex, and chaotic traffic situations. This also includes the interaction with different road users, each with their natural movements, such as, e.g., the interaction of road users with each other. Therefore, new and efficient test methods are required to pave the way for future ADAS [5]. This paper describes the usage of Augmented Reality (AR) for testing camera-based Advanced Driver Assistance Systems. In Section II a description of ADAS basics is presented. Section III describes the current methods used for testing ADASs. Section IV, shows a possible usage of Augmented Reality and its challenges. The paper is concluded by Section V, where the research, results, and lessons learned are discussed.

II. Advanced Driver Assistance Systems

ADAS supports the driver when operating a vehicle. Depending on the type, they ensure more driving comfort, increase safety, reduce energy consumption or enable more efficient traffic flow. The systems record the driving situation via sensors, process the collected information with powerful computers, and give the driver optical, acoustic, or haptic feedback. In some cases, they intervene automatically, semi-autonomously, or autonomously in the control and operation of the vehicle, for instance by accelerating, braking, signaling, or steering. These can extend to fully autonomous driving. The main requirements for ADAS are fast data processing in almost real-time and high system reliability [6] [7]. A growing number of environment sensors, such as radar, camera, ultrasonic, and lidar sensors enable the use of ADAS in modern vehicles and related functions for autonomous driving. At the same time, each sensor is severely limited in its scope and cannot provide all of the information about the vehicle's surroundings that is required for safety functions. Only the combination of data from different sensors (sensorfusion) results in a complete environment model, a basic requirement for the reliability and safety of driver assistance systems and autonomous driving [8].

III. Testing of Advanced Driver Assistance Systems

Simulated test procedures during the development process, as well as real test procedures, are used to evaluate the functionality of individual ADAS sensors and their joint interaction in ADAS-relevant scenarios. While all test drive components remain virtual in the first concept phase, virtual components are successively exchanged for associated real test elements over the various integration stages in the course of development. Up to entirely real test drives with real drivers and road users, the simulation components have entirely given way to reality [9].

A. Testing Advanced Driver Assistance Systems in Simulation

The guiding principle of the virtual test drive is to transfer the real test drive to the virtual world as realistically as possible. The aim is to use the characteristic strengths of simulation in terms of reproducibility, flexibility, and cost reduction and to establish a test and evaluation option for the specifications and solutions derived from this early on in the vehicle development process. Using suitable simulation methods enables vehicles and vehicle components to be designed, developed, and used more efficiently. They serve as a bridge and shorten the time until real vehicle prototypes are available. With real test drives and the reliability of real test results as a template, Using simulation techniques is an optimization task in which the modeling, parameterization, and simulation effort must be matched to the efficiency achieved. The methods used for this approach mainly come from the repertoire of integrated mechatronic system development. Here, the methods: Model in the Loop (MiL), Software in the Loop (SiL), Hardware in the Loop (HiL), and Vehicle in the Loop (ViL) come into question [3].

B. Testing Advanced Driver Assistance Systems in Reality

While vehicle dynamics control systems can still be validated in real driving tests with great effort, despite all their complexity and variety, this is no longer economically viable for ADAS today due to the complex system, the complexity of the test cases, and the necessary scope of the tests. Even if the tests are supposed to be performed in the same way, in practice it is impossible to perform the tests under the same conditions due to the many potential and sometimes unknown or ignored influences. The reproducibility of the results is therefore not given because on the one hand the functionally relevant features can contain the necessary interaction of several road users and on the other hand a complex interaction of a general nature can be subject to conditions, such as low glare, simultaneous sun, and reflection on a wet road surface at a specific angle. Current ADAS functions access information about the environment, sometimes collected from multiple sensors with different functions and processed into a representation of the environment [4] [10].

We use the Euro NCAP as the standard. That is a Europe-wide standardized test procedure for ADAS with real driving tests. The focus is on the behavior and reaction of the vehicle in safety-critical situations. In simulated dangerous circumstances, dummies in the form of vehicles driving ahead, pedestrians, and cyclists are used to test the functionality of ADAS systems. In a further step, the reaction time of the hazard message for the driver is evaluated. Due to the constantly increasing traffic safety, the test procedures of Euro NCAP will also contain more complex test scenarios in the future. Therefore, the roadmap up to 2025 also includes other road users, such as scooters, motorcycles, and wild animals to increase road user safety [11]. An Autonomous Emergency Braking (AEB) test scenario in which a pedestrian (child or adult as a dummy) crosses the street in which a car is turning is shown in Figure 1. The test vehicle must detect the pedestrian and avoid personal injury or property damage by braking [12].

C. Combining Virtual and Real Testing

To enable the testing of camera-based assistance systems in real environments earlier in the development phase and thus increase the quality of the systems, the use of AR as a link

Fig. 1. Pedestrian is crossing a road in which a car is turning [12]

Fig. 2. Pokémon Go-App on the left side of the figure [17] and a self-created Augmented Reality application showing a possible scenery on the right side of the figure

between virtual and real testing lends itself to this. Using AR to test camera-based systems combines the advantages of a virtual environment and these of the real world: Reproducible, complex scenes with realistic environmental conditions. AR thus makes it possible to dispense with test dummies or second vehicles including drivers even in the initial phases of testing. This reduces the costs of the tests and increases the safety of the test engineers. The combination of different test situations is also possible: The display of several vehicles, lane markings, and road signs allow the simultaneous testing of all camera-based driver assistance systems. The unlimited variety of test scenarios allows a significant increase in the depth of testing at an early stage of development. That increases the quality of the testing and thus of the overall system. In 2010, a Swedish team led by Jonas Nilsson presented a software framework at a conference that used AR to evaluate a pedestrian detection system. The framework was able to augment the images from the vehicle camera to include a walking pedestrian. The resulting detection system results were comparable to test results obtained with real obstacles. As summarized in this paper, deeper investigations are needed to further advance an AR test system [20]. In the following, an AR-approach will be discussed.

IV. Augmented Reality Simulation in Advanced Driver Assistance Systems

Different criteria are required for the use of AR in testing automotive ADAS than for conventional AR applications, such as on a smartphone. This section describes the test criteria for this approach.

A. *Augmented Reality for regular Applications*

According to Azuma's proposal, AR can be defined as a combination of three fundamental characteristics: the combination of real and virtual worlds and the precise three-dimensional registration of real and virtual objects, both in a real-time interactive environment [13]. The basic principle of AR is mainly known from the mobile game Pokémon Go [17]. Within this game, users can interact with digital creatures through their smartphones. These creatures are placed virtually in the user's environment. One such AR application is shown in Figure 2. Figure 2 shows also a self-created AR-App for demonstrating a possible scenery with traffic signs and a pedestrian. The three parts of the algorithms behind AR are image analysis, 3D modeling, and augmentation.

Image analysis serves to identify points or areas of interest within the given image. Feature detection, such as corner detection is often used for this step [14]. A three-dimensional model of the environment is created using the results of the image analysis. The types of algorithms used for this step vary depending on the type of AR application. Simultaneous Localization and Mapping (SLAM) or Structure-of-Motion (SfM) algorithms are often used for AR in unknown locations [14]. The augmentation is based on the results of 3D modelling. The scene model is typically provided as a positional description of a plane or coordinate system that represents the real world [14]. With this information, a virtual object can be placed on the plane or in the coordinate system with appropriate characteristics, such as size and orientation. After object placement, the virtual content is combined with the real image [14].

There are different versions of applications for AR. These applications are very diverse in their fields, from the use of AR in psychology [13] to use in hospital operating rooms [14] to mobile games [14] to military applications [14]. What all these apps have in common is that human reality is expanded. With humans as users of AR, there are implications for the application. One is that, in most cases, the human user is forgiving of not accurately placed virtual objects, if the error lies within a small margin. In addition, the speed of human movement, and therefore the distance covered in a given time, is limited. Because of these limitations, localization, mapping, object placement, and runtime requirements are not as strict and demanding as in the automotive environment given in this paper.

B. Approach for Using Augmented Reality in Advanced Driver Assistance Systems

With a focus on the camera-based ADAS sensors, the area around the test field is recorded, as shown in Figure 3. The path between the sensor fusion module and the Electronic Control Unit for Advanced Driver Assistance Systems (ADAS-ECU), which causes the vehicle to intervene, for example by braking, has to be disrupted and a new path has to be found through the Augmented Reality Electronic Control Unit (AR-ECU). Within the AR-ECU, the captured environmental data is augmented with virtual objects, such as traffic signs or lane markings. The aim here, is a realistic and consistent behavior of the ADAS-ECU as in real object detection. For the final

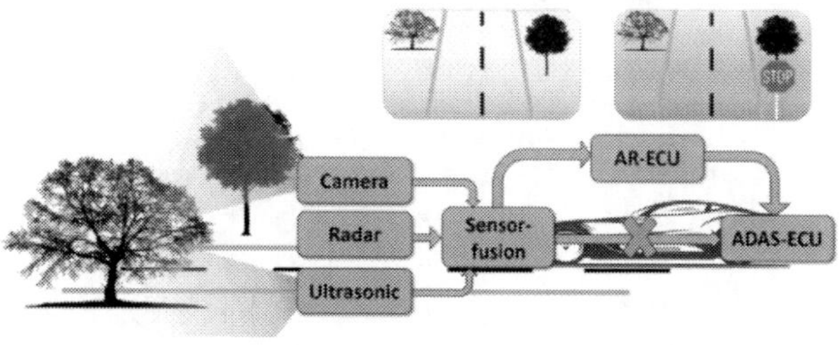

Fig. 3. Our approach for using Augmented Reality in Advanced Driver Assistance Systems

augmentation of the virtual objects on the real image of the sensor, a detailed 3D environment of the test environment must first be created. For this purpose, a visual Simultaneous Localization and Mapping (vSLAM) approach is chosen. The vSLAM method uses only visual inputs to perform localization and mapping. That means no vehicle sensors other than the vehicle's camera system are needed to create a 3D model of the environment, making this approach more flexible than lidar, radar, and ultrasonic. The vSLAM algorithm framework mainly consists of three basic modules: initialization, tracking, and mapping, and two additional modules: relocation and global map optimization (including loop closure) [15]. Several approaches with the vSLAM algorithm are available for using vSLAM in automotive vehicles and the associated properties, such as fast scene changes and low environmental textures, which can be found in [16]. Based on [16], various vSLAM approaches are compared in terms of accuracy and robustness, among other things.

C. Oriented FAST and Rotated BRIEF (ORB) as approach for visual Simultaneous Localization and Mapping

The approach "Oriented Features from accelerated Segment Test (FAST) and Rotated Binary Robust Independent Elementary Features (BRIEF) (ORB)-SLAM" was first introduced in 2015 and seems to be state-of-the-art because it has higher accuracy than comparable SLAM algorithms [16]. Here, ORB-SLAM represents a complete SLAM system for monocular, stereo, and red-green-blue-depth (RGBD) cameras. The system works in real-time and achieves remarkable results in terms of accuracy and robustness in a variety of different environments. ORB-SLAM is used for indoor sequences, drones, and cars driving through a city. The ORB-SLAM consists of three parallel main threads: Tracking, Local Mapping, and Loop Closure. A fourth thread can be created to run the Bundle Adjustment (BA) after a closed loop. This algorithm is a feature-based approach that represents the detected feature points in a three-dimensional MapPoint [16]. Figure 4 shows a MapPoint on the left side created from internally acquired image sequences. Detected Feature Points that are used creating the MapPoint are displayed on the right side of the figure. The increase in accuracy of the MapPoint created by ORB-

Fig. 4. Selfcreated MapPoint on the left side of the figure and the detected feature points (green rectangles) on the right side of the figure

Fig. 5. Original image on the left side of the figure and the recognized objects using Image Segmentation (Pole, Ego Vehicle (Hood), Terrain, Vegetation, Road and Sky) on the right side of the figure

SLAM with correspondingly recognized objects and surfaces is made possible by using IS and AI. Figure 5 shows the object detection. On the left is the original picture of the front view of the car. Since the Euro NCAP tests are conducted in dedicated test areas with low texture and therefore less information about the environment (see Figure 1), the recognized classes for our approach are pylons, own vehicle (hood), terrain, vegetation, road, and sky. More classes should be added in the further project progress. This means deriving plans from MapPoint, recognizing the road surface, and realistically enlarging objects on the virtual map. Another focus of this work is the realism of magnification, such as occlusion, reflection, and shadows. The vSLAM location mode is used to augment individual camera pixels to present the vehicle with a real-life hazard situation.

D. Advantages of our Approach

Our approach will combine the specific advantages of testing in simulation (reproducibility, flexibility and cost reduction) and reality (vehicle and environment complexity) and thus represent a link between these test methods. It should make it possible to test more complex scenarios and thus increase the safety of road users. The lane crossing enables, for example, a lane departure warning system to be tested independently of the test site. Scenarios, such as the appearance of temporary lane markings or missing sections, can be tested in the same test area. Narrowing and widening of lanes can be displayed, as well as international differences between lane markings. Vehicles driving ahead can be superimposed on the camera image to test traffic jam assistants. In the first test phase, there is no need for a second vehicle including driver, which reduces test costs and increases safety for test engineers. In addition, test cases with traffic signs, pedestrians and cyclists can be added quickly and situationally. It is also possible to combine different test situations. The unlimited variety of test scenarios enables a significant increase in test depth at an early stage of development. This increases the quality of the tests and thus of the system in general. Due to the increasing number of ADAS and the constant development towards autonomous driving, the application area of the software program can be expanded as desired.

E. Challenges for our Approach

Various advances and improvements in terms of accuracy, robustness, etc. can be found in later developments based on this ORB-SLAM approach [16]. While ORB-SLAM's performance is impressive on well-structured sequences, error conditions can occur on poorly-structured sequences, such as Euro NCAP test scenarios or when feature points temporarily disappear, for example due to motion blur [16]. In addition to accuracy, the execution time of the global algorithm is also of great importance. Camera systems in automotive vehicles today work with a frame rate of 30 to 60 frames per second [fps] [7]. For a successful evaluation of ADAS test scenarios, the AR system must be able to orientate itself very precisely in the environment [16]. One cause is the missing feedback about the impact intensity of test dummies when crashing them. Because of this, it is necessary to know the exact position of the car on the test track in order to calculate the intensity of the impact based on the braking distance. Using Euro NCAP test scenarios, speeds up to 130 km/h, which is equal to 36.111 m/s, are proven [11]. The algorithm must have a faster execution time compared to the speed of the camera system. The distance d that the vehicle covers within one frame at a given speed and frame rate can be calculated. At a speed of 130 km/h and using a camera framerate of 30 fps, the vehicle travels

$$d = \frac{36.111\,[\frac{m}{s}]}{30\,[\frac{frames}{s}]} = 1.204\,\frac{m}{frame}. \quad (1)$$

So at a frame rate of 60 fps at the same speed, a distance of

$$d = \frac{36.111\,[\frac{m}{s}]}{60\,[\frac{frames}{s}]} = 0.602\,\frac{m}{frame} \quad (2)$$

is covered. A slowdown of one frame means that the test results deviate from 0.602 to 1,204 meters. Due to the high speed of the car and camera, as well as the need for high precision in object placement, it is clear that the requirements for this AR application are much stricter than the usual human user application.

F. Visualisation for the Testdriver

The main task of the Human-Machine-Interface (HMI) is to make the AR perceptible to the test driver in real time that the ADAS functions of the test vehicle, as well as the human interaction, can be evaluated. The acceptance of the HMI as an interface for the experience plays an important role. This depends for the most part on the quality of the display, interaction and haptics [18]. For our approach, the selection of a suitable HMI concept focuses on visualization and interaction. To display AR visibly, the use of a suitable HMI or a corresponding display is necessary. Possible screen approaches are classified into feature classes based on their properties. Displays that use a medium-direct view through to the real environment in 3D belong to the class of see-through (ST) displays. Monitor-based (MB) displays only allow an indirect view of the real environment. Live or stored videos (2D) are used for this technology. Indirect displays (3D objects: video ST), which visualise AR in 3D using video, also belong to the group of ST displays. The 3D concept is crucial here. The processing of the 2D camera data of the real environment used, through 3D scene modelling, makes it possible in the first place to integrate the virtual objects in the correct perspective (2D). Video-based ST displays (video ST) are used if the recording and playback of this same AR on an indirect display take place almost simultaneously. Optical ST displays (3D-Objects:optical ST) are used when the reproduction of the virtual objects in combination with the direct view of the real environment is correctly integrated. The visualisation of AR according to Azuma limits the AR-capable displays to those that can display virtual 3-dimensional objects correctly oriented in perspective [13]. For the identification of suitable HMI approaches for testing camera-based ADAS, only these ST displays fulfil the necessary criteria.

HMI approaches in which stationary displays are mechanically fixed to the vehicle for the duration of the test belong to the Head-Up-Display (HUD) group. Head-Up-Displays used in automotive vehicles to show the driver the actual speed or using the display of a smartphone or tablet belongs to this category. Those in which the display is attached to the head like when using Virtual Reality (VR)-glasses or AR-glasses belong to the Head-Mounted-Display (HMD) group [19]. In both HMD and HUD, HMI approaches of optical and video-based ST displays are identified. In the further progress of the approach to use AR as a visualization for the driver, different evaluations must be carried out.

G. Further Thoughts about Using Augmented Reality Simulation for Testing Advanced Driver Assistance Systems in Future Automotive Vehicles

In the first step, the focus of our approach will shift to camera-based sensors. Only a few ADAS functions, such as traffic sign recognition or Lane Departure Warning (LDW), access the camera's sensors. To evaluate further tests and to achieve the identical behavior of the ADAS-ECU (see Figure 3) in reality as when using AR, the integration of more sensors, such as radar or lidar, is required. It should also be mentioned that the Euro NCAP test scenarios are only carried out under ideal conditions according to the current status of the position of the sun at midday with little or no shadows and reflections, no other road users, no rain, etc. [16]. Our approach aims to further increase the complexity and realism of Euro NCAP test scenarios.

V. Conclusion

In this article, we proposed an approach to using AR in automobiles. Using AR in ADAS aims to combine the advantages of simulated test procedures, such as reproducibility and cost savings, with the benefits of real test procedures (complexity of the entire vehicle and the environment). We model the problem of creating an urban environment to use AR for testing in high-speed ADAS. Our approach is based on a combination of vSLAM algorithms with AI and IS for object detection. That should help get better overall performance in terms of computational speed and accuracy. The creation of a virtual 3D environment with a better understanding of individual objects should make it possible in a later step to enrich other sensors, such as car radar and lidar, with objects in addition to camera data. That should further increase the overall performance of the entire system. The lessons learned so far are mainly regarding the SLAM-Algorithms. In automotive test fields, the current state-of-the-art SLAM algorithms are not well suited for environmental conditions such as low textured environment and high camera velocity. Further problems are the software runtime since the test system must work in real-time and the reproducibility. We hope to overcome at least some of these challenges, as mentioned beforehand, by combining neural networks with modern SLAM algorithms. This approach is intended not only to create a link between real and virtual test procedures but also to increase the complexity of potential test procedures, accelerate the development speed of ADAS functions and improve safety for future mobility solutions.

References

[1] K. Bengler et al., "Three decades of driver assistance systems: Review and future perspectives." In: IEEE Intelligent Transportation Systems Magazine vol. 6, no.4 , pp. 6–22, Winter 2014.

[2] F. Schuldt, F. Saust, B. Lichte, M. Maurer, and S. Scholz, "Efficient systematic test generation for driver assistance systems in virtual environments - Effiziente systematische Testgenerierung für Fahrerassistenzsysteme in virtuellen Umgebungen." 2013. [Online]. Available from: https://publikationsserver.tu-braunschweig.de/servlets/MCRFileNodeServlet/dbbs-derivate-00031187/AAET-Schuldt-Saust-Lichte-Maurer-Scholz.pdf Accessed 2022.07.29

[3] B.-J. Kim and S.-B. Lee, "A study on the evaluation method of autonomous emergency vehicle braking for pedestrians test using monocular cameras." Applied Sciences 10, no. 13: 4683, July 2020, doi: 10.3390/sapp10134683

[4] C. Miquet et al., "New test method for reproducible real-time tests of ADAS ECUs: "Vehicle-in-the-loop" connects real-world vehicles with the virtual world." In: 5th International Munich Chassis Symposium 2014, pp. 575-589, July 2014.

[5] J.E. Stellet et al., "Testing of Advanced Driver Assistance Towards Automated Driving: A Survey and Taxonomy on Existing Approaches and Open Questions." In: 2015 IEEE 18th International Conference on Intelligent Transportation Systems, pp. 1455–1462, September 2015.

[6] M. Nagai, "Research into ADAS with autonomous driving intelligence for future innovation." In: 5th International Munich Chassis Symposium 2014, pp. 779–793, January 2014

[7] H. Winner, S. Hakuli, F. Lotz, and C. Singer, "Manual Driver Assistance Systems - Basics, Components and Systems for Active Safety and Comfort - Handbuch Fahrerassistenzsysteme - Grundlagen, Komponenten und Systeme fuer Aktive Sicherheit und Komfort." Springer Vieweg, Wiesbaden, March 2015. [Online]. Available from: https://link.springer.com/content/pdf/10.1007/978-3-658-05734-3.pdf Accessed 2022.07.29

[8] M. Darms, "A Basic System Architecture for Sensor Data Fusion of Environmental Sensors for Driver Assistance Systems - Eine basis-systemarchitektur zur Sensordatenfusion von Umfeldsensoren fuer Fahrerassistenzsysteme." PhD thesis, Technische Universität Darmstadt, 2007. [Online]. Available from: https://tuprints.ulb.tu-darmstadt.de/914/ Accessed 2022.07.29

[9] T.M. Gasser, A. Seeck, and B.W. Smith, "Virtual Integration" In: "Framework Conditions for Driver Assistance Development - Rahmenbedingungen fuer die Fahrerassistenzentwicklung", pp. 27–54. Springer Vieweg, March 2015.

[10] P. Seiniger and A. Weitzel, "Testing Procedures for Consumer Protection and Legislation - Testverfahren fuer Verbraucherschutz und Gesetzgebung." In: Manual Driver Assistance Systems - Basics, Components and Systems for Active Safety and Comfort - Handbuch Fahrerassistenzsysteme - Grundlagen, Komponenten und Systeme fuer Aktive Sicherheit und Komfort, pp. 167–182. Springer Vieweg, Wiesbaden, March 2015. [Online]. Available from: https://link.springer.com/content/pdf/10.1007/978-3-658-05734-3.pdf Accessed 2022.07.29

[11] R. Fredriksson, M.G. Lenné, S. van Montfort, and C. Grover, "European NCAP Program Developments to Address Driver Distraction, Drowsiness and Sudden Sickness" November 2021. [Online]. Available from: https://www.frontiersin.org/articles/10.3389/fnrgo.2021.786674/full Accessed 2022.07.29

[12] Euro NCAP "AEB Pedestrian". [Online]. Available from: https://www.euroncap.com/en/vehicle-safety/the-ratings-explained/vulnerable-road-user-vru-protection/aeb-pedestrian/ Accessed 2022.07.30

[13] R.T. Azuma, "A Survey of Augmented Reality." In: Teleoperators and Virtual Environments, pp. 355–385, August 1997.

[14] A. State, G. Hirota, D. Chen, W. Garrett, and M. Livingston, "Superior Augmented Reality Registration by Integrating Landmark Tracking and Magnetic Tracking." In: SIGGRAPH '96: Proceedings of the 23rd annual conference on Computer graphics and interactive techniques, pp. 429-438, August 1996.

[15] T. Taketomi, H. Uchiyama, and S. Ikeda, "Visual Slam Algorithms: a Survey from 2010 to 2016." In: IPSJ Transactions on Computer Vision and Applications, Article number: 16, 2017.

[16] C. Campos, R. Elvira, J.J.G. Rodrıguez, M. Montie, and D. Tardos, "Orb-slam3: An Accurate Open-Source Library for Visual, Visual–Inertial and Multimap Slam." In: IEEE Transactions on Robotics, pp. 1–17, July 2020, doi: 10.1109/TRO.2021.2075644

[17] Pokémon GO, "Developer Niantic is working on a game for tourists - Pokémon GO: Entwickler Niantic arbeitet an einem Spiel für Touristen." [Online] Available from: https://mein-mmo.de/pokemon-go-entwickler-app-touristen/ Accessed 2022.07.29

[18] J. Brade and A. Koegel, "Presence in Virtual Reality - Key to Acceptance and Transferability?!" In: 5. Fachkonferenz zu VR/AR-Technologien in Anwendung und Forschung, VAR² 2019, pp. 59-71, December 2019.

[19] R. Doerner, "Fundamentals and Methods of Virtual and Augmented Reality - Grundlagen und Methoden der Virtuellen und Augmentierten Realitaet." In: Virtual and Augmented Reality (VR/AR), Springer Viweg, pp. 1-143, 2019.

[20] J. Nilsson et al., "Performance Evaluation Method for Mobile Computer Vision Systems Using Augmented Reality". In: 2010 IEEE Virtual Reality Conference (VR), pp. 19–22, March 2010.

Optimal Usage of Marketing and Sales to Push Residential Refurbishment

An emperically grounded Agent-Based Simulation on How to Push Refurbishment Decisions

Mart Verhoog
Marketing and Communication Department
IU International University of Applied Sciences
Bad Honnef, Germany
e-mail: mart.verhoog@iu.org

Abstract—**Agent-based models can be used to assess the impact of different mixes of marketing and sales measures on home-owner's energetic refurbishment decision-making. During the last two decades, governments have been using especially marketing-like measures (e.g., mass media campaigns) to push residential refurbishment – for a large part, unsuccessfully. Only recently, more sales-like activities (e.g., visits of energy consultants) have been offered for that purpose. The question now rises, whether this will be a more successful approach. This idea contribution addresses the research question asking what mix of marketing and sales measures is optimal to support homeowners during their refurbishment decision-making.**

Keywords— Agent-Based Modeling (ABM); refurbishment Decision-Making (DM); marketing and sales; empirically grounded.

I. INTRODUCTION

Much research has been published about the importance of residential refurbishment for sustainability. Germany's building stock has been erected for the largest part before the existence of any energetic building standards. Furthermore, German homeowners tend to energetically refurbish their property slowly and doubtingly. Consequently, heating residential buildings consumes too much energy and is accompanied by a huge ecological footprint [1].

More recently, the dependence of many European countries on Russian gas for heating buildings and the war Russia has been fighting against Ukraine has recharged the debate that energy efficiency in housing should be improved and refurbishment should be speeded up to lessen the dependency on Russian gas.

This idea contribution deals with the question asking how governments can optimally push homeowners in the direction of a positive refurbishing decision with the help of marketing and sales measures. In the past, governments used mass media campaigns to do this. More recently, local governments have been offering visits of energy consultants at a reduced (or even at no) charge to convince homeowners to refurbish. The question is whether there are optimal (e.g., cost efficient) mixes of marketing and sales measures that help homeowners make this decision positively. An empirically grounded Agent-Based Model (ABM) for refurbishment could be developed and the impact of different mixes of marketing and sales on refurbishment Decision-Making (DM) could be simulated.

Science has applied ABM in the context of the current energy transition numerous times before. Du et al. [2] conclude in their review that ABM have been developed to model socio-demographic factors, housing factors, social influences, and environmental attitudes as drivers of DM in a context of energy transition. Most ABM, however, have focused on solar energy diffusion and less research was done to study refurbishment. Furthermore, Du et al. [2] conclude "Future studies can also evaluate the effectiveness of market-based policies […]" (p. 8).

Jager already stated in 2007 that the effectiveness of marketing could benefit from social simulations like ABM [3]. He proposes different formalizations of the 4 P's commonly used in marketing to be implemented in ABM (Product, Price, Place and Promotion). Delre et al. [4] focus especially on promotional activities, which is the category where mass and personal communication can be classified. Until today, however, ABM applied in consumer behavior DM studies do not differentiate between marketing and sales.

For both the literature concerning DM in an energy transition context, and ABM literature in the field of marketing, modeling an optimal usage of marketing and sales to push residential refurbishment is an interesting contribution.

This short description of the idea contribution is structured as follows. In Section II, this work briefly explains the key concepts used for this idea. Here, the Hierarchy Of Effects (HOE) model is explained, as this concept uses it to assess the impact of communication on DM. Furthermore, this section discusses the ABM modeling approach that is very suitable to answer the research question. The last concept explained is the Sinus lifestyle segmentation approach. The Sinus lifestyle typology differentiates the German society in ten groups. This typology can be used to simulate the refurbishment DM of 17 mi. homeowners in Germany, empirically grounded, in a differentiated way. Section III documents some thoughts concerning the development of such an ABM for refurbishment. It describes how the DM process concerning refurbishment for different agents and touchpoints can be modeled. Finally, Section IV summarizes this idea contribution and briefly gives an outlook concerning future work and the implementation of the ABM for refurbishment.

II. KEY CONCEPTS USED IN THIS IDEA

The objective of commercial communication (or "touchpoints") is to have an impact on consumers and to support consumers in buying DM. A large body of research exists to assess this impact. HOE models represent a family of models that examine this impact of touchpoints on different steps in the buying behavior. In this logic, HOE models assume forthcoming steps in the DM process can only be reached when previous ones have been effectively completed. Consequently, the number of people who reach a next step in the process is usually reduced, compared to the previous step. This transfer from a previous step onto the next is called conversion. HOE models enable the calculation of transfer rates under the influence of communication – and as well under the influence of different kinds of communication: mass and personal communication.

As mentioned in Section I, ABM have not distinguished between marketing and sales until today. HOE models can do exactly this: The first stages in the model are primarily impacted by marketing (mass communication touchpoints), and the last stages primarily by sales (personal communication touchpoints). This is the main rationale behind applying the HOE logic within the ABM for refurbishment.

In previous research, the author developed a HOE model for energetic refurbishment of residential buildings [5]. The resulting model is based on Lewis [6], Lavidge and Steiner [7] and is shown in Figure 1. This model assesses the impact of touchpoints on DM for energetic refurbishment.

This idea contribution proposes to develop an ABM. This modeling approach simulates decisions and/or behavior of different individual agents. These agents can interact with their environment, as well as with each other. Within an ABM, usually different agents behave according to their individual preferences, their characteristics, their interactions, as well as their environment. Software for ABM allows for the setup and description of different agents, their preferences, interactions, as well as their environment. In this way, the aggregated system with its dynamics (that emerges from many different individual behaviors) can be simulated.

Agent-based models are especially interesting when problems of emergence are studied [8]. The idea is to use this approach to study refurbishment intention (after interactions with marketing and sales) at a lifestyle and system level.

The last concept described is the Sinus Lifestyle typology. The typology is used in marketing & sales, both in practice and in academics. The Sinus Institute has been monitoring sociocultural developments and trends in the German society since the 1980ies and small adaptations to the lifestyle typology are carried out regularly. The lifestyles are positioned in a two-dimensional space. The x-axis describes their orientation: Traditional towards progressive lifestyles. The y-axis describes social status: Lower class towards upper class.

Figure 1. HOE model for energetic refurbishment [5]

Ten lifestyles are located within this two-dimensional space. Previous research by the author [5] showed that depending on the Sinus lifestyle, German homeowners have very diverse attitudes and behaviors concerning energetic refurbishment of residential housing. This idea contribution uses the Sinus lifestyle approach as it forms an efficient segmentation approach to create differentiated, empirically grounded, agents within the ABM.

After this description of the key concepts of the idea, Section III will document some thoughts about the ABM that could be developed to simulate the impact of marketing and sales on homeowners' refurbishment DM.

III. ABM FOR REFURBISHMENT

The ABM for refurbishment can be based on empirical data, taken from [5], as displayed in Table I. The representative sample (n = 4471) describes the status quo of the decision concerning energetic refurbishment of 17 mi. homeowners in Germany. The ABM will focus on the interaction of agents with various (mass and personal communication) touchpoints. This idea contribution does not take other drivers of DM (e.g., social influences) into account.

It comprises Sinus lifestyle data and their status quo concerning the DM process in the format of the developed HOE model, as described in Section II.

With the help of this data, conversion rates can be calculated, e.g., 65% of the social ecological lifestyle is converted from knowledge (80.0%) to attitude (52.3%). Within the ABM for refurbishment, 17 mi. agents (homeowners) can be set up according to the distribution of the status quo in their refurbishment DM (as displayed in Table I).

The ABM can simulate the impact of touchpoints on each individual agent with the support of a threshold variable. As a result of the interaction with a touchpoint during a period, the value of the threshold variable is increased. It is assumed that an agent needs to reach a threshold variable with a value of 4 prior to being transferred to the next step in the HOE model. Hence, as soon as an agent's threshold variable reaches the value of 4, the agent is transferred towards the next step. Once an agent has been transferred, the threshold variable is set to 0. During the initialization of the model, the threshold variable can be set randomly between 0 and 3 to incorporate variability into the model.

TABLE I. EMPIRICAL DATA FROM [5]

German's Sinus lifestyle	Status quo in DM				
	Aware -ness [%]	Know-ledge [%]	Atti-tude [%]	Con-viction [%]	Inten-tion [%]
1. Established conservat.	99.0	80.1	51.0	33.7	14.9
2. Liberal-intellectual	99.7	82.9	57.9	40.6	13.3
3. High achiever	98.9	79.5	48.4	32.9	18.4
4. Movers and shakers	98.4	76.9	52.3	34.6	16.6
5. Adaptive pragmatics	99.5	69.0	53.9	42.4	22.4
6. Social-ecological	99.7	80,0	52.3	36.2	17.0
7. New middle class	98.5	76.9	44.1	32.6	11.8
8. Traditional	99.0	78.8	44.5	30.8	10.6
9. Precarious	99.6	64.4	36.1	20.6	9.3
10. Escapists	92.8	59.3	33.7	21.9	12.2

However, touchpoints come in different forms and should not be generalized. Not every touchpoint generates the same impact. It is generally acknowledged in marketing and sales, that mass communication touchpoints (e.g., advertising campaigns and information brochures) are best suitable to transfer consumers through the first stages of DM, especially awareness, but knowledge as well and, to a lesser extent, interest. Furthermore, personal communication touchpoints (e.g., sales talks) are best suitable to transfer consumers through the last stages of DM, especially intention, but conviction as well and, to a lesser extent, interest [9]. Hence, we detect an increased impact in the beginning and a decreased impact towards the end of DM, due to mass communication. Furthermore, we detect a decreased impact in the beginning and an increased impact towards the end of DM, due to personal communication. This phenomena of different impacts of touchpoints can be reflected in the ABM by incorporating a correction factor in the additions to the threshold variable. The correction factor is decreasing for mass communication and increasing for personal communication with every following step in the DM process.

Within the model, different amounts of mass and personal communication that an agent is exposed to in a period, can be set. The model can calculate the costs of these different mixes (of mass and personal communication), as these two types of communication vary greatly in price.

By varying the mixes of mass and personal communication, the model can explore:

1. How many homeowners reach a refurbishment intention under the impact of a set mix of mass and personal communication, and,
2. the costs for that specific mass and personal communication mix.

As described in Section I, time and especially acceleration of refurbishment behavior is important. For this reason, a budget can be set. The simulation can explore the impact of different mass and personal communication mixes in time, as long as the total costs are below the budget. In this way, the factor time (acceleration) can be considered as well.

IV. CONCLUSION AND FUTURE WORK

Heating Germany's residential buildings consumes too much energy and is accompanied by a huge ecological footprint. Governments have been using especially marketing-like measures (e.g., mass media campaigns) to push residential refurbishment among homeowners. Only recently, more sales-like activities (e.g., visits of energy consultants) have been offered for that purpose. This idea contribution deals with the question asking, how governments can optimally push homeowners in the direction of a positive refurbishing decision with the help of marketing and sales measures.

Future work consists of implementing (developing and coding) an ABM for refurbishment within an ABM modeling environment, according to the logic described in Section III. During the initialization (or set up) of the model, different agent groups should be created according to the size and distribution of Sinus lifestyles in Germany to take representativeness into account. This counts as well, for the status quo of the agents' refurbishment DM, as displayed in Table I. Furthermore, attention will be paid to the following tasks:

A. *Costs of mass and personal communication touchpoints*

As discussed in Section III, many different touchpoints exist. Modeling results will be driven directly and strongly by the average costs assumed for mass and personal communication, which is why they should be researched carefully.

B. *Mixes of mass and personal communication*

Different mixes of mass and personal communication can be seen as scenarios for system refurbishment behavior. So, it is important to develop mixes of mass and personal communication that help the evaluation of policy effectiveness.

C. *Budgetting approach*

Speed is an important aspect of refurbishment, which can be simulated by a budgeting approach (see Section III). A budget must be developed to simulate time factors.

After successful implementation of these tasks, the ABM will enable the assessment of the impact of different mixes of mass and personal communication to push refurbishment. In this way, it can lead to recommendations on cost and time efficient approaches to push energetic refurbishment among German homeowners.

REFERENCES

[1] M. Verhoog, "Steuerung von Akteuren und Entscheidungen in Baunetzwerken [in English: Controlling Actors and Decisions in Construction Networks]", Springer Gabler, Wiesbaden, 2018, ISBN 978-3658205867.

[2] H. Du, Q. Han, and B. de Vries, Modelling energy-efficient renovation adoption and diffusion process for households: a review and a way forward, in: Sustainable Cities and Society, Vol. 77, pp. 1-10, 2022, https://doi.org/10.1016/j.scs.2021.103560.

[3] W. Jager, "The four P's in social simulation, a perspective on how marketing could benefit from the use of social simulation", in: Journal of Business Research, Vol. 60, Issue 8, pp. 868–875, 2007, https://doi.org/10.1016/j.jbusres.2007.02.003.

[4] S.A. Delre, W. Jager, T.H.A. Bijmolt and M.A. Janssen, "Targeting and timing promotional activities: An agent-based model for the takeoff of new products" in: Journal of Business Research, Vol. 60, Issue 8, pp. 826–835, 2007, https://doi.org/10.1016/j.jbusres.2007.02.002.

[5] M. Verhoog, "A target group-specific communication approach to push refurbishment", Energy for Sustainability International Conference, Funchal, pp. 1-9, 2017.

[6] T. Barry, "The Development of the Hierarchy of Effects: An Historical Perspective", in: Current Issues & Research in Advertising, Vol. 10, Issue 2, pp. 251-295, 1987, DOI: 10.1080/01633392.1987.10504921.

[7] R. Lavidge and G. Steiner, "A Model For Predictive Measurements of Advertising Effectiveness.", in: Journal of Marketing 25, pp. 59-62, 1961, https://doi.org/10.1177/002224296102500611.

[8] S. Railsback and V. Grimm, "Agent-Based and Individual-Based Modeling", University Press, Princeton, 2012, ISBN 978-0691136745.

[9] P. de Pelsmacker, M. Geuens and J. Van den Bergh, "Marketing communications", 6th edition, Pearson Education, Harlow, 2017, ISBN 978-1292135762.

Informal Ways to Educate about Formal Modeling and Simulation with Petri Nets

Lara Zakfeld, Stefan Haag and Carlo Simon

Hochschule Worms
Erenburgerstr. 19, 67549 Worms, Germany
Email: {zakfeld, haag, simon}@hs-worms.de

Abstract—**Linking current research and advanced teaching is one pillar of higher education. Students need to be prepared for finding novel solutions for challenges that arise from the digitalization of products, services, and production. To address these challenges, planing and forecasting play essential roles. These tasks can be handled by modeling to understand a real-world system, and simulating these models to gain insight into possible consequences of change. Formal modeling and simulation are highly complex activities that require experience and fitting tools. When lecturers integrate such exciting and cutting-edge topics, classical head-on teaching is not enough. Instead, they need inspirational approaches and reliable tools to provide learners with an easy-to-grasp, direct, and engaging introduction into modeling and simulation. This paper presents different approaches to engage students in this task. Case studies illustrate theoretical and practical business knowledge. The firing rule of Petri nets can be explained with mazes. Learners experience the implications of digitalization in production with real models of assembly lines controlled by Petri nets. Students are enabled to act as consultants who develop simulation models that incorporate planing and forecasting. Such extensive user interaction requires elaborated tool support but offers the possibility to intertwine teaching, theoretical learning, practical application, and current research.**

Keywords—**Modeling; Simulation; Interactive Education; Digital Twins; Petri Nets.**

I. Introduction

In recent years, there has been a shift away from fact-based teaching to more involving methods such as problem-based and research-oriented learning. As a result, new concepts like inverted classrooms, blended learning or case studies become more commonly used by lecturers. These varied and active learning experiences encourage student engagement and secure a lasting learning success.

This ongoing process alters the roles of lecturers and students alike. While teachers shift more into the role of mentors and trainers, learners become more responsible to actively acquire new knowledge. Thus, the connection of current research, teaching strategies, and student motivation needs to be considered [1].

Experience shows that high engagement leads to more attendance in lectures and a striking correlation between course attendance and exam results of competency tests can be observed. Consequently, the acquisition of professional competencies is significantly promoted [2]. In a survey of 463 teachers on inverted classrooms, 67 % reported that the grade point average had improved and 99 % confirmed that the concept would be maintained [3].

Interactive engagement can induce such positive effects. A contemporary method is gamification. This catchphrase refers to the idea of using game design elements in a non-game context to motivate and increase user activity and retention. Gamification is an approach already used in areas as diverse as finance and education [4]. Yet, it raises the question about how other game-based or interactive techniques can improve students' learning experience.

The *Group of Applied Process Simulation* (*GAPS*) at Worms University of Applied Sciences pursues the goal to integrate active research in modeling and simulation with Petri nets with interactive teaching. The technological backbone is the *Process-Simulation.Center* (*P-S.C*), a Petri net WebApp which is used as a virtual laboratory. It incorporates features of integrated management systems based on Petri nets, organization charts, and process maps and is the hub for gamification, blended and interactive learning, and case studies.

- Semester-long case studies evolve student's competencies regarding business processes and their simulation in an organized and coherent fashion.
- Petri net mazes teach operational rules in a game setting: the faster a maze is solved, the more points are awarded.
- Real world assembly lines in toy size improve the understanding on how production processes can be modeled, predicted, and controlled with Petri nets.
- Consulting projects deliver more insights into the complex challenges that the real world poses.

This approach goes beyond the work of [5] and [6], which explain how to teach basic Petri net modeling techniques. However, they do not include teaching a case study nor enable teachers and learners to cooperate within the tool. Hence, it provides practical experiences and suggestions to lectures in the field of simulation and develop existing approaches further.

The following Section II classifies the approaches presented in this contribution. Section III explains some basics on Petri nets while Section IV provides information about the *P-S.C*. Section V shows how to connect business process management with simulation and modeling by using case studies. Then, Section VI describes how gamification can be used for teaching Petri net fundamentals. Practical modeling aspects in an engaging live setting are outlined in Section VII. Afterwards, Section VIII describes the use of current research as an example application. A conclusion and future work is detailed in Section IX.

II. Learning Pyramid

How can lecturers ensure that the approaches they choose and practice will achieve the desired outcome? How to activate a learning group? These and comparable questions arise for lecturers when they want to improve their teaching, since different approaches enhance competencies at different strengths.

The learning pyramid as depicted in Figure 1 classifies different approaches and their retention rates. The figures on the left show the different learning coefficients (average retention rate) based on the teaching methods (shown directly in the pyramid). The most active and participative methods have the highest learning coefficients [7].

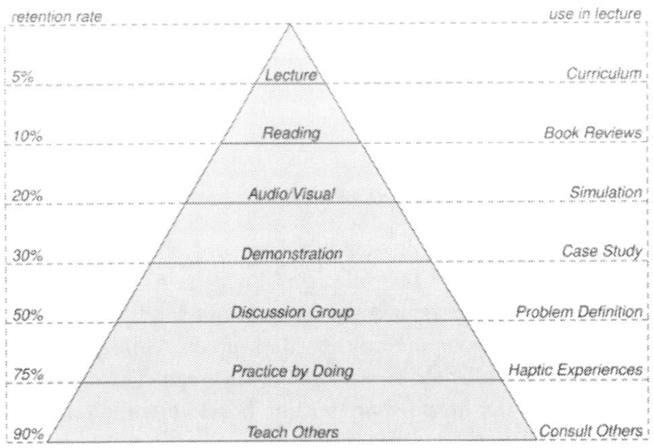

Fig. 1. Learning Pyramid.

The figure's right side shows the methods with which the specific retention is aspired in the presented courses. A head-on lecture or an assignment to write a book review have low retention rates. The use of an integrated case study in combination with a problem-based introduction to the respective unit increases the retention rate considerably. Haptic experiences with suitable tools have exciting effects, as discussed in the next sections. The weekly presentation of results and, thus, teaching by students leads to the highest retention rate.

III. Enabler Petri Nets

As a formal modeling language, Petri nets can be used to model and simulate the behavior of dynamic systems. A Petri net consists of two node-sets: places are marked with information and transitions can operate on this information. The allocation of information on places indicates the systems' state. Information flow is established by alternately linking places and transitions with directed arcs [8].

Originally, in Place/Transition (P/T) nets, information is depicted as anonymous tokens. In high-level nets, like Predicate/Transition (Pr/T) nets, the marking may contain arbitrary data and can be regarded akin to data sets in a database.

The so-called firing rule formalizes state changes: a transition is enabled iff its pre-set places carry sufficient information and its post-set can receive information produced when the transition fires. When an enabled transition fires, the information flow is established [8].

The expressiveness of Petri nets can further be enhanced by time concepts which is relevant for modeling real world processes or real world technical systems [9].

However, the dilemma of explanations like in this section, textbooks, or papers on Petri nets is that they cannot convey the actual dynamics of an operating Petri net. A dedicated tool is needed to experience this and to profit from their capabilities.

IV. The Process-Simulation.Center Our Simulation Lab

The *P-S.C* is an integrated management system that allows for modeling the structural and process organization of corporate entities. It uses P/T and Pr/T nets to establish simulatable models and integrates swimlanes, organizational charts and process maps [10]. Real-world data can be incorporated and used for simulation, planing and forecasting purposes [11]. The development process combines Design Science Research Guidelines and Evolutionary Prototyping [12][13].

Figure 2 depicts the process of academic user registration inside the tool. When a new user registers with the system, they receive the general role of guest. If the corresponding mail address is connected to an education tenant, they may adopt a lecturer or a student role. A lecturer then may define groups and assign tasks to the student groups.

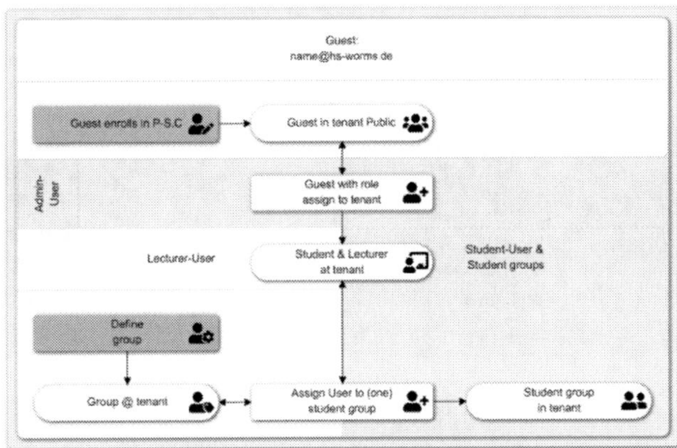

Fig. 2. The Laboratory in Action. (P-S.C export)

As a WebApp, the *P-S.C* can be used on personal computers or mobile devices. The *P-S.C Cloud* is set up to serve different tenants (and clients) simultaneously. Users in multitenancy system can work without getting insight into other tenant's settings, users, or data, just as if the environment was exclusively available to them (as stipulated by [14]).

Additionally, the *P-S.C* and a dedicated interface can be executed on a Raspberry Pi™, a simple but capable single-board computer. External sensors and actuators then can be connected to its input and output pins. Input and output data is put on a Petri net model's places, which allows for computation and further processing. Thus, the *P-S.C* is able to control real-world devices [15].

V. Case Study Based Semester Schedule

University teaching aims to train young adults in the best possible way for the challenges they face after graduation. To put this to practice, a case study was developed in which students are guided by the concept of problem-based or research-oriented learning. Initial approaches have already been presented [15]. Through the continuous development of the *P-S.C* as well as the case study "bureau4us GmbH", new opportunities open up.

The pivotal point here is the *P-S.C* as presented in Section IV. Through a dedicated tenant for the respective course, a learning group of 2-3 students can also exchange and work with each other in the virtual lab. During a semester, students model and simulate processes of the fictitious company "bureau4us GmbH".

Furthermore, to increase the identification between the case study and the learners, the protagonist of the case study, Tina Nett, is also a student in the respective semester. Tina works with some fellow students as an intern in the fictitious company and is assigned to the various departments. The learning group acts as a consulting team to Tina and presents the developed solution to the actual auditorium in the following week. The fictitious student group is pictured in Figure 3.

Fig. 3. A Fictitious Student Working Group.
(photo by Jason Goodman on Unsplash)

This schedules a single lecture and exercise unit as follows:

1) A unit starts with a presentation of the current problem at bureau4us GmbH given by the fictitious protagonists.
2) The lecturer teaches the named topic and delivers the current unit.
3) Then, the problem is transformed into a direct work assignment for the students.
4) Students are provided with workspaces such as free models in the *P-S.C*. Small student learning groups operate in their workspace.
5) Feedback is given within the tool as an integral part of an approval workflow.
6) The students present their results in the auditorium using the *P-S.C*.

This loop takes place iteratively from week to week. Thus, students are further immersed in the real problems of a fictitious company. The case study and the presented workflow have been successfully used for three semesters in Bachelor and Master courses. This setting motivates lecturers and students to continuously develop the case study further, for example concerning the following topics:

- A website of the bureau4us GmbH for deeper immersion.
- An interactive purchase order interface which directly connects bureaus4us and simulations on its data.
- Strategically anchor the individual process goals and, thus, further develop the *P-S.C* as an integrated management system.

Through such active and interactive teaching, both sides, learners and lecturers, can continuously develop in their skills. The knowledge gained is also incorporated into the accompanying industrial projects, one of which serves as an application example and is described in Section VIII.

VI. Petri Net Mazes

A maze game as depicted in Figure 4 allows for an easy introduction to the basic rules of Petri nets. As the *P-S.C* also runs on tablets, users may tap on transitions to make them fire. Enabled transitions are colored dark-green while places with tokens to be collected are colored light-green. The objective is to clear the net in the shortest time possible while leaving no tokens inside. A timer starts running as soon as the transition in the upper left fires. It stops when the last transition in the lower right fires. Remaining tokens lead to penalties.

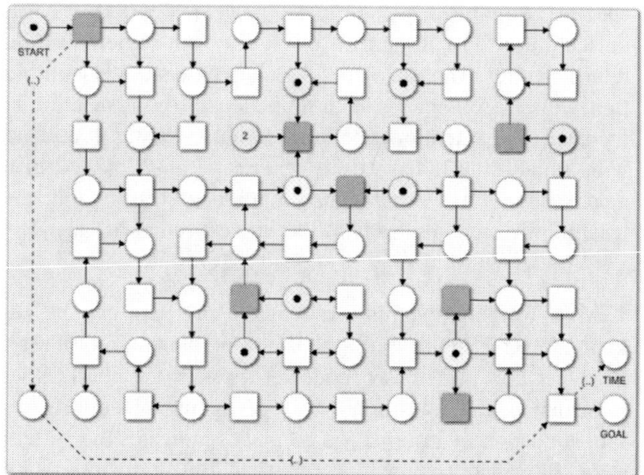

Fig. 4. A medium-sized Maze. (P-S.C export)

Both the mazes' playability on tablets and the race for high scores strongly activate users and, thus, impart knowledge on how Petri nets work. The mazes have been used successfully at several occasions from eight-year-old pupils' STEM courses via lectures for students in their twenties to presentations for seasoned professionals.

VII. Digital Twins in Education

The Industrial Internet of Things (IIoT) and digitalization are prominent topics in public discourse. To ready students for the challenges these and other technological developments pose, the connection of real world applications and business processes has to be conveyed. To this end, cyber-physical systems seem beneficial.

Such systems consist of at least two components: A real-world one, and a digital one. These components are considered twins in the sense that the digital and real twin behave correspondingly. To be more precise, the digital twin, when executed with real data, should calculate the same state that the real twin reaches while providing this data [16].

Figure 5 shows a complete setup suitable for teaching the concepts of digital twins, IIoT, and digitalization. A fischertechnik™ assembly line model features several different sensors and actuators. The sensors are connected to the input pins of a Raspberry Pi™. The output pins in turn are connected to the actuators of the model. This setup corresponds to wiring connections that are used in real-world industrial applications.

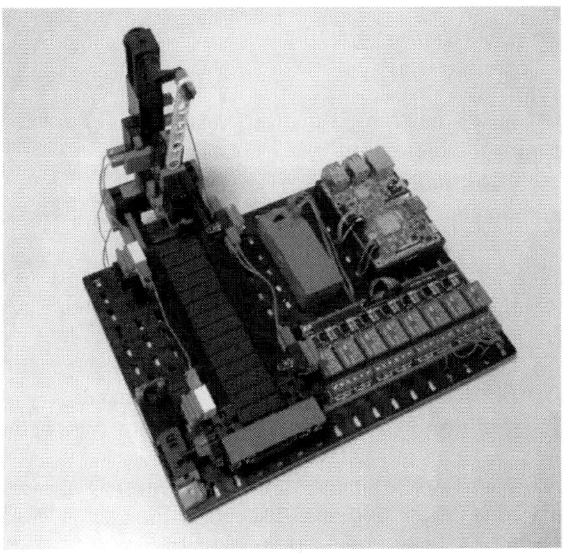

Fig. 5. Raspberry Pi™ (upper right) Connected to a fischertechnik™ Model (left) and a Mutli-Channel Relay (lower right). (photo by Stefan Haag)

The digital twin is implemented as a Petri net model in the *P-S.C*, as shown in Figure 6. The tool is installed on a Raspberry Pi™ and runs in a browser. An interface program that is also installed on the Raspberry Pi™ routes incoming signals to the Petri net model. These signals are used on special input places where they act as tokens and, thus, allow the Petri net to reach the next system state. Correspondingly, special output places are used to control the fischertechnik™ model: When a token is placed, the interface translates the token's data into control commands for the actuators. As is the case in industrial applications, the control signals do not directly influence the actuators, but use relays for load control.

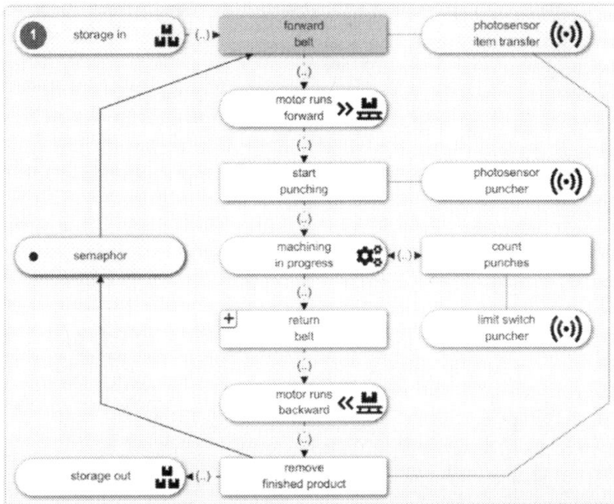

Fig. 6. Control Petri Net of the Digital Twin.

By interweaving imported data, business logic and process models with input and output places, this configuration acts as real and digital twin. The setup lets learners experience the concept of digitalization in an industrial setting first-hand [15].

VIII. Industry

The ways to educate students about formal modeling and simulation presented so far are the first steps. When lecturers include real examples with real challenges, the previously described path as well as the teaching content is rounded off.

The focus of a current knowledge transfer project with an industrial partner is to simulate a new warehouse, which is currently under construction. The warehouse is dedicated for dangerous chemical and pharmaceutical substances and offers space for more than 22,000 palettes. A simulation must be flexible enough to compare different delivery strategies in front and within the warehouse.

GAPS faces the challenge to simulate these processes in a user-friendly way to give the industry partner a feeling for the future operational processes on site. The simulation is part of the resource planning of manpower and investments into forklifts for the warehouse.

Figure 7 shows process description and model of the loading area in the yard. The sub-process involves coordinating trucks booked into the system at the yard, allocating the correct loading ramp, loading the goods provided and measuring the required truck throughput time. The goal of this process is to establish a sound foundation for operations. This is also shown in the process description in the left side area.

An important finding was to evaluate the exported data from the simulation in a visually appealing way as shown in Figure 8. Trucks are depicted on their corresponding locations in the yard. When being loaded, the otherwise white trailer gets filled. A timer on the right side tracks time in the current working shift. Even non-modelers and non-simulationists can directly grasp the added value of the simulation.

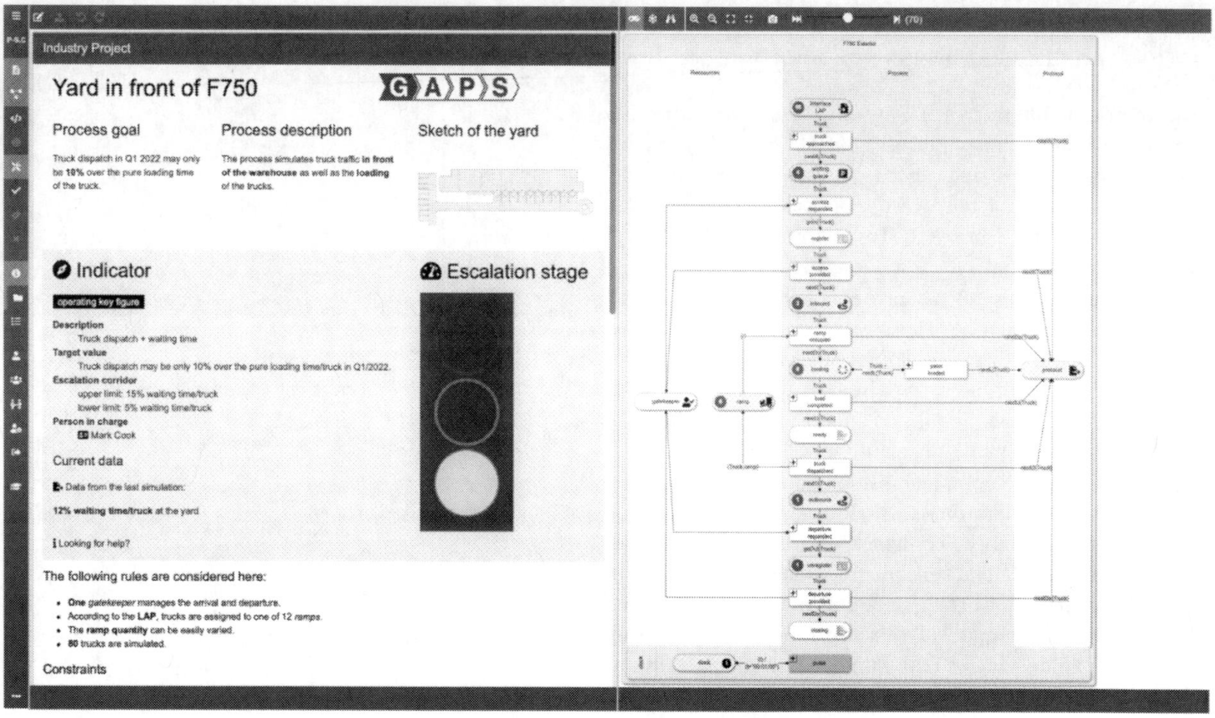

Fig. 7. One Model from an Industry Project. (P-S.C screenshot)

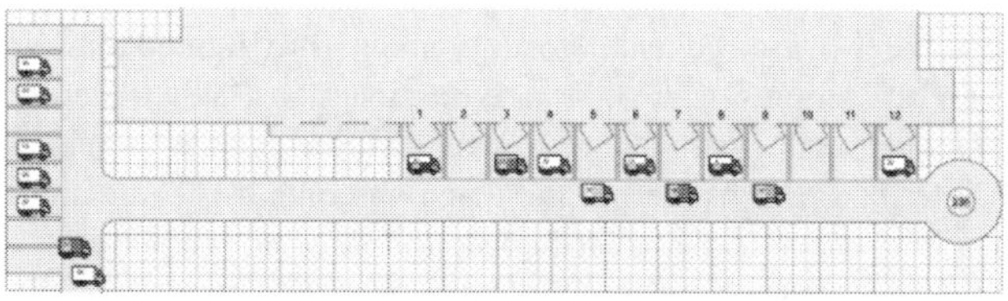

Fig. 8. Visualization of the Yard. (P-S.C screenshot)

This realization is also important for students. Appropriately holistic modeling and simulation tasks in the lecture train and develop these skills. They can transfer their observations from the case study described in Section V to a real world scenario.

The next step is to model the inside of the warehouse and, thus, simulate the goods provided as well. This will further enrich the experiences the students can gather.

IX. Conclusion

Modeling and simulation play crucial parts in practice. They enable a better understanding of complex systems as well as better planning and forecasting. However, as the complexity of the systems increases, so do the requirements for their modeling.

Thus, learners need a thorough and deep understanding of modeling techniques and how to handle simulations. To prepare students for this tasks, and to lower the entry barrier for new modelers, engaging and active learning methods are beneficial. In consequence, this necessitates proper tool support.

By using the *P-S.C*, five different examples for holistic teaching are presented:

1) Case studies let learners experience how modeling and simulation can help to deal with manifold business and technological challenges.
2) Mazes provide an interactive and fun activity to learn the basic Petri net rules and establish an entry point to model with formal methods.
3) Digital twins show the relevance to combine different fields of expertise in an accessible, haptic way. Also, they give first insights into the complex reality students face after graduation.
4) Real world examples further deepen the understanding of complex systems. They also provide guidance to handle these tasks in a structured manner.
5) Feedback is given immediately within the tool in form of an approval process.

The natural extension of this list is one possible research path for the future: Which other interactive methods to teach modeling and simulation can be introduced within the *P-S.C*? What functionality does the *P-S.C* have to provide for these methods?

In addition to methods that rely on the tool, what kinds of engaging, haptic methods can be employed? Further, can such methods be adopted to inspire enthusiasm in STEM courses?

Engaging teaching methods provide for motivated learners. In turn, motivated learners provide feedback on methods, technologies, and content. Thus, they improve education, research and practice alike. A worthwhile endeavor.

REFERENCES

[1] J. Hattie, *Visible Learning for Teachers*. Routledge, 2011.

[2] E. Grosskurth and J. Handke, *Inverted Classroom and Beyond*, 1st ed. Marburg: Tectum Verlag, 2016.

[3] B. Goodwin and K. Miller, "Evidence on flipped classrooms is still coming in," *Educational Leadership*, vol. 70, no. 6, pp. 78–80, 2013.

[4] S. Deterding, D. Dixon, R. Khaled, and L. Nacke, "From Game Design Elements to Gamefulness: Defining "Gamification"," in *MindTrek 11*. New York, NY, USA: ACM, 2011, pp. 9–15.

[5] J. F. i Jové, A. Guasch, P. F. i Casas, and J. Casanovas, "Teaching system modelling and simulation through Petri Nets and Arena," *Proceedings of the Winter Simulation Conference 2014*, pp. 3662–3673, 2014.

[6] D. Gasevic and V. Devedzic, "Teaching petri nets using p3," *Educational Technology and Society*, vol. 7, pp. 153–166, 2004.

[7] J.Artal-Sevil, A. Gargallo, and M. Valero, "Flipped teaching and interactive tools. A multidisciplinary innovation experience in higher education." Sixth International Conference on Higher Education Advances, 2020, pp. 1–8.

[8] W. Reisig, *Understanding Petri Nets*. Berlin, Heidelberg, Germany: Springer, 2013.

[9] C. Simon, S. Haag, and L. Zakfeld, "Simulation of Push- and Pull-Processes in Logistics - Usage, Limitations, and Result Presentation of Clock Pulse and Event Triggered Models," *International Journal On Advances in Software*, vol. 14, no. 1&2, pp. 88–106, 2021.

[10] C. Simon, L. Zakfeld, and S. Haag, "Das Process-Simulation.Center," in *Tagungsband AKWI*, F. Nees, I. Stengel, V. G. Meister, T. Barton, F. Herrmann, C. Müller, and M. Wolf, Eds., 2022.

[11] C. Simon and S. Haag, "Simulatable Reference Models To Transform Enterprises For The Digital Age – A Case Study," in *European Conference on Modeling and Simulation (Wildau, DEU)*. Saarbrücken, Germany: Pirrot, 2020, pp. 294–300.

[12] A. R. Hevner, S. T. March, J. Park, and S. Ram, "Design Science in Information Systems Research," *MIS Q.*, vol. 28, no. 1, pp. 75–105, Mar 2004.

[13] C. Floyd, "A Systematic Look at Prototyping," in *Approaches to Prototyping*. Berlin, Heidelberg: Springer, 1984, pp. 1–18.

[14] H. R. Hansen, J. Mendling, and G. Neumann, *Wirtschaftsinformatik*, 12th ed. Berlin: De Gruyter - Oldenbourg, 2019, German, transl. *Business Information Systems*.

[15] C. Simon and S. Haag, "A Case-Study to Teach Process-Aware Information Systems," *EMISA Forum*, vol. 40, no. 1, pp. 9–10, 2020.

[16] F. Tao, J. Cheng, Q. Qi, M. Zhang, H. Zhang, and F. Sui, "Digital twin-driven product design, manufacturing and service with big data," *The International Journal of Advanced Manufacturing Technology*, vol. 94, no. 9-12, pp. 3563–3576, Februar 2018.

Real-Time Simulation of Hybrid Electric Vehicle Efficiency using Functional Reactive Programming

Volker Schwarzer
Department of Computer Science
University of Applied Science, Worms
Worms, Germany
email: schwarzer@hs-worms.de

Abstract—**An idea is proposed to compute the overall powertrain efficiency of a Hybrid Electric Vehicle (HEV) in real-time using the reactive programming paradigm. Multi-domain vehicle models typically depend on the availability of a multitude of real-time sensor data within a short timeframe (usually one discrete timestep). While using a fully imperative simulation approach is fast and efficient, it is not suitable when required data is not provided within fixed time intervals. Reactive programming would solve this problem by asynchronously responding to real-time data streams instead of actively being triggered by function calls. The advantage of the proposed idea would be a fast and stable simulation process and the ability to partially compute system states as soon as the required corresponding data is available.**

Keywords - Real-Time Vehicle Simulation; HEV Efficiency; Connected Powertrain; Reactive Programming.

I. INTRODUCTION

The efficient hybridization of powertrains presents a complex challenge to car manufacturers. The challenge ranges from early design decisions, such as determining powertrain component sizing, to late-stage decisions, such as the optimization of the energy management. Overall powertrain efficiency of Hybrid Electric Vehicles (HEVs) frequently does not meet expectations due to time constraints in the automotive development cycle and dependencies on shared modular design requirements within the fleet and third-party components.

While suboptimal powertrain efficiency can easily be identified by overall fuel consumption, a precise quantification and determination of drivetrain losses is not straightforward. Multi-domain and multi-physics modeling of electric and hybrid vehicles is a simulation technique to compare powertrain efficiencies for standard drive cycles to test bench results [1][2]. Efficiencies can then be computed by aligning and evaluating the obtained data offline. However, the multi-domain complexity of the underlying stochastic distribution significantly impedes simple correlations and the identification of potential improvements. Furthermore, standard drive cycles do not depict real-life driving conditions with all possible efficiency scenarios.The core idea of the proposed research is that human pattern-recognition could overcome the challenges described above. Instead of comparing significant amounts of offline test bench data with simulation data, it is intended to utilize a real-time, multi-domain HEV model based on live On-Board Diagnostics (OBD) and additional sensor data. Overall powertrain efficiency would be computed and displayed in near real-time. An HEV operator, when noticing below-average powertrain efficiency during certain driving maneuvers and/or vehicle states, could arbitrarily recreate similar states to generate more relevant data and isolate the decisive events.

A well-performing efficiency simulation could certainly be achieved using imperative programming techniques. However, the reactive programming paradigm is a better choice when considering the limited availabilty due to the synchronous nature of most OBD-communication protocols. A deterministic, discrete approach requires all available sensor data to be provided within fixed time intervals. Reactive programming solves this problem by asynchronously responding to real-time data streams instead of actively being triggered by function calls. Fast and stable simulation processes, as well as the ability to partially compute system states can be achieved as soon as the required corresponding data is available.

The rest of this paper is organized as follows. Section II introduces functional reactive programming. Section III describes the proposed reactive simulation methodology. The conclusion closes the article.

II. FUNCTIONAL REACTIVE PROGRAMMING

Functional reactive programming is a declarative paradigm that allows users the benefits of functional programming languages and an easy interface to a reactive environment [3]. It is based on data streams, so called observables, and their propagation of change, which is achieved by observers using various functional operators. While purely functional programming languages are available (e.g., Haskell), the reactive programming paradigm needs further software tools to be fully integrable in a simulation code base. ReactiveX (also known as Reactive Extensions) is a software tool kit for asynchronous programming with observable streams. It is based on the ideas of the observer pattern and the functional programming paradigm. It can be utilized to program various imperative languages (e.g., Java, Scale, C#, C++, Clojure, JavaScript and Python) reactively and is therefore integrable into various simulation frameworks. Observables are rendered as time-series of events. The observation of a stream is called subscribing. Functions are defined as observers and the observables are the subjects being observed.

III. Reactive HEV Efficiency Simulation

Figure 1 visualizes the proposed real-time, reactive simulation methodology. Powertrain sensor data is collected and published to a central Message Queuing Telemetry Transport (MQTT) broker. A client subscribes to all relevant topics and publishes each topic as a separate observable. The multi-domain powertrain model is composed of a collection of observers. Each observer subscribes to the observables needed to compute state variables using a set of operators. Since multiple required observable events will not necessarily occur synchronously, a lifetime parameter must be introduced. Events will last for a predetermined amount of time depending on the physical properties of the variables, which they represent. If all observable events (that an observer is subscribed to) overlap, the observer will react and propagate the data utilizing its operators. The resulting data stream will then be forwarded to a MQTT client, which will publish the data to the main MQTT broker. Eventually, the data stream will be transformed into another observable to which other observers can subscribe to.

To simulate the efficiency of a connected HEV powertrain in real-time, each of the observers would compute a specific state variable [4]. The closed feedback loop enables a nested component structure. Hence, a top-down modelling approach can be chosen, and simulation granularity could be increased over time. The higher the granularity, the more precise the outcome of the simulation.

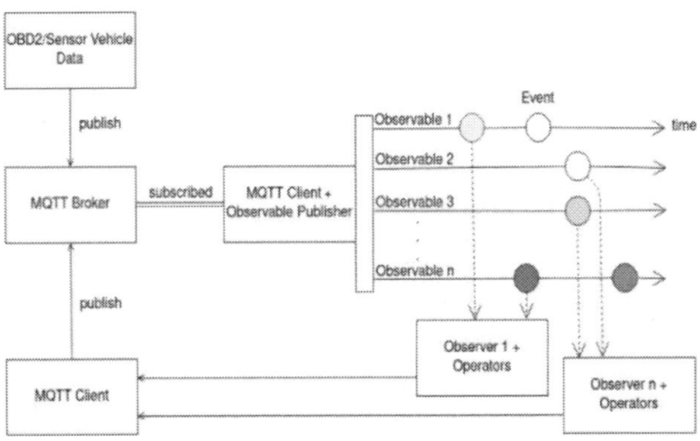

Figure 1. Proposed real-time HEV efficiency simulation engine using MQTT as a transport protocol. Computation of state variables in a closed feedback loop. All system variables are modelled as data streams (observables).

IV. Conclusion

A reactive simulation approach for HEV powertrain efficiency has been proposed. The main advantage of the discussed idea could be a fast and stable simulation process and the ability to partially compute system states as soon as the required corresponding data is available. Even if sensor data is faulty or temporarily not available, the simulation could still be capable of computing and publishing certain state variables and therefore approximate powertrain efficiency.

References

[1] D. W. Gao, C. Mi, and A. Emadi, "Modeling and Simulation of Electric and Hybrid Vehicles," in Proceedings of the IEEE, vol. 95, no. 4, pp. 729–745, April 2007.

[2] V. Rallabandi, D. Lawhorn, D. M. Ionel, and X. Li, "Multi-Physics Modeling for Electric and Hybrid Vehicles with In-Wheel Electric Motors," IEEE Transportation Electrification Conference and Expo (ITEC), pp. 146-151, 2018, doi: 10.1109/ITEC.2018.8450091.

[3] B. Finkbeiner, F. Klein, R. Piskac, and M. Santolucito, "Vehicle Platooning Simulations with Functional Reactive Programming," Proceedings of the 1st International Workshop on Safe Control of Connected and Autonomous Vehicles, SCAV@CPSWeek, pp. 43-47, 2017, doi: 10.1145/3055378.3055385.

[4] F. Boussinot, B. Monasse, and J. Susini, "Reactive Programming of Simulations in Physics", International Journal of Modern Physics C, vol. 26, no. 12, pp. 1-16, 2014, doi: 10.1142/S0129183115501326.

A Method for Accelerated Simulations of Reinforcement Learning Tasks of UAVs in AirSim

Alberto Musa, Luca Zanatta, Francesco Barchi, Andrea Bartolini, Andrea Acquaviva
Università di Bologna
Viale del Risorgimento, 2, Bologna, Italy
alberto.musa@unibo.it, luca.zanatta3@unibo.it, francesco.barchi@unibo.it,
a.bartolini@unibo.it, andrea.acquaviva@unibo.it

***Abstract*—Reinforcement Learning (RL) is widely used for training Unmanned Aerial Vehicles (UAVs) involving complex perception information (e.g., camera, lidar). RL achievable performance is affected by the time needed to learn from the direct interaction of the agent with the environment. AirSim is a widely used simulator for autonomous UAV research, and its photorealism is suitable for algorithms using cameras for making or assisting flying control decisions. This work aims to reduce the RL time by reducing the simulation time step. This impairs simulation accuracy, so the impact on RL training must be quantitatively assessed. We characterise the AirSim acceleration impact on RL training time and accuracy while performing an obstacle avoidance task in a UAV application. We observed that using 5x as the Airsim acceleration factor, the RL task performance degrades by 95%. The observed performance increase is due to the latencies present in the AirSim command chain. We overcome this limitation by proposing a new command approach which allows accelerating without performance degradation until 10x. When pushing the acceleration factor to the extreme (100x), the RL task performance degrades by 38% with a measured speed-up of 15x.**

***Index Terms*—Simulation Engine, Reinforcement Learning, Airsim, Profiling.**

I. INTRODUCTION

Reinforcement Learning (RL) is a branch of Artificial Intelligence (AI) that aims to extract knowledge from the interaction of an agent with the environment. In robotics, specifically Unmanned Aerial Vehicles (UAVs), RL algorithms are used to train and implement control tasks such as navigation, landing, and obstacle avoidance [1]. These tasks require accounting for complex relationships between different sensors and complex dynamics that are difficult to catch with a dataset of use case samples. To bypass this problem, RL enables an agent's training in a task thanks to a reinforcement signal.

RL training requires the agent to directly interact with the environment experiencing the task to be learned and learn the task through a reinforcement signal. Practically, this requires performing the task (called game) repeatedly until the RL algorithm has learned the task. This can easily require thousands or millions of games [2]. According to which RL algorithm is used, stochastic gradient descent and back-propagation step are repeated continuously after profiling a series of actions and collecting the rewards within each game. In practical terms, several weeks to train the drone are required; most of the training time is spent in the simulation steps.

Software simulators facilitate the setting up of the training environment. Simulators are designed to replicate the agent capabilities (e.g., the UAV flight) and real environments through complex mathematical models that simulate agents' real-world physics rules and perception capabilities. Simulators implement all the forces that act in the simulated scenario, such as gravity, rotors actuation, and collisions.

If the task to be performed by the agent leverages camera sensors, accurate and photorealistic rendering of the scene becomes mandatory to obtain a simulation close to the real scenarios. RL combined with a photorealistic simulator reduces time-to-market, increasing the chances that trained models in the simulation can be deployed in the field as it is. According to a recent review [3], the most suitable simulators for UAV applications are: AirSim [4], Flightmare [5], Gazebo [6] and Webots [7]. These are all open-source simulators.

Gazebo and Webots are used by the robotic community but are not photorealistic. Airsim and Flightmare leverage graphical engines for the video game industry to provide photorealism. While Flightmare focuses on multi-drone simulations, Airsim natively supports hardware and software in co-simulation for rapid flight control and RL-trained solution rapid prototyping.

Simulators allow controlling an agent in the simulation by issuing commands in real-time. For this reason, the simulation time is synchronous to the "wall clock" time spent. Moreover, simulators can simulate physics faster than in real-time, provided that they run on adequate computing resources. However, photorealistic simulators rely on game engines for the rendering part, designed to maximize the number of rendered frames under the real-time bound.

A recent survey [8] identifies simulation environments that are photorealistic, accelerable and support the employment of RL algorithms. RaiSim [9] is based on the Unity game engine and allows for regulating the simulation speed. Isaac Gym [10] is a physics-accurate and photorealistic simulation tool developed by NVIDIA that supports automatic acceleration. However, at the time of the writing, Isaac Gym was a preview release, and NVIDIA plans to integrate it into the NVIDIA Omniverse Platform. Unity ML [11] is a plugin of the Unity game engine that provides the tools to set up virtual environments for RL. Unity ML allows to speed up the simulation by changing a time scale parameter. However, Unity simulates reality by showing a series of discrete simulation frames at variable time intervals that depend on rendering time. This implies that by increasing the time scale in a simulation,

the rendering time does not change. The analysis reported in the survey [8] focuses on RL simulators for generic robotic applications and does not consider AirSim among the possible valid alternatives. Not all general-purpose robotics simulators currently provide hardware support and software stack for Flight Control systems. Although they provide some UAV models, co-simulation may be decisive for adapting to real employment. Finally, AirSim from 2016 to 2020 is confirmed among these candidates as the most cited simulation environment [3]. The scenario at the moment makes us think of AirSim as one of the most suitable UAV simulators for RL.
In this regard, in the following sections, we will answer two research questions: RQ1: *Is it possible to accelerate RL training for UAVs in AirSim?* RQ2: *Which one is the implication in terms of accuracy of the simulated drone flight, interaction with the environment, and trained RL algorithm accuracy?*
Referring to the above-mentioned research questions, in this paper, we achieved the following contributions:
1) We discovered that the accuracy of trajectories degrades fast with the simulation time step reduction due to the latency incurring in the communication between the UAV agent and the RL algorithm.
2) We proposed a new method of controlling the agent in the simulator through asynchronous commands and time barriers (code available at [12]) In this way, on a pre-defined deterministic path, we obtained an effective speed-up of 62x with an error on the trajectories of 9% w.r.t. real-time simulation.
3) Compared to the results we obtained on a pre-defined deterministic path, the attainable acceleration speed-ups are significantly lower w.r.t. the real-time simulation. We investigated the issue, discovering that the rendering pipeline of the game engine introduces approximations and errors when the simulation is accelerated. To mitigate this problem, we added a valid check on the image provided by the camera API and re-issued the rendering if needed.

We performed the same experiment of an obstacle avoidance RL task in a lane of 150 m presented in [13]. In this, we evaluated the impact of the simulation acceleration with and without the proposed solution. With the default AirSim asynchronous commands, our results show that it is impossible to train an RL algorithm with accelerated simulation as the accelerated training fails over any acceleration factors. On the contrary, we obtain the same real-time training performance from a week of training to less than two days with the proposed synchronous command.

In Section 2, we describe the basic concepts of RL and the key characteristics of AirSim. A motivational example regarding acceleration issues, a possible solution to them and a validation strategy are explained in Section 3. In Section 4 the results of the tests carried out are shown. We conclude our work in Section 5.

II. BACKGROUND

A. Reinforcement Learning

Deep RL aims at solving complex robotic tasks by mimicking the human training behaviour with the use of the neural networks [1].

Thanks to the policy π, described by a non-linear universal function approximator called a neural network, the agent chooses an action a_t, modifying the environment. The environment sends to the agent the new visible information (called observation) s_t and the reward r_t that measures the goodness of the action [1].

In particular, a well-known algorithm is the Deep Q-Learning (DQN) [14]. The goal of this algorithm is to maximize the action-value function:

$$Q^{\pi}(s,a) \approx r + \gamma \max_{a'} Q^{\pi}(s',a') = Q^{\pi}_{tar}(s,a) \quad (1)$$

where $Q^{\pi}_{tar}(s,a)$ is the target action-value function and $Q^{\pi}(s',a')$ is produced by the neural network that is used for choosing the actions a in a state s. Since the duration of the task can be unlimited, the rewards are multiplied by a discount factor γ.

An RL algorithm is composed of two phases called training and inference. In the training phase, a policy is learned by the policy network using a loss defined as mean square error between $Q^{\pi}_{tar}(s,a)$ and $Q^{\pi}(s,a)$. In the inference, a trained network described by the parameters θ is used for acting according to the policy π. In the following, we refer to this network as a "neural network (π_{θ})".

B. AirSim

AirSim is an open-source simulator, developed by Microsoft, oriented to vehicle simulation and specifically for UAV [4]. It is built on Unreal Engine 4 and its target is the experimentation of RL for autonomous vehicles. Unreal Engine is in charge of updating the state of the UAV agent. The physical state of a UAV agent in AirSim comprises six measures: position, orientation, linear velocity, linear acceleration, angular velocity, and angular acceleration. In addition, AirSim implements sensors models such as Cameras and Lidars.

In the rest of the paper, we will refer to the "state of the UAV" in a broad sense, including both the physical state of AirSim and sensor outputs. Simulation settings of AirSim can be configured statically throughout a JSON file. Among the many parameters, this file allows to (i) enable/disable the scene rendering while keeping the rendering for the sensor's camera always active, and (ii) changes the ratio between simulation and the wall clock time (*ClockSpeed* setting). As an example $ClockSpeed = 1$ implies real-time simulation, while $ClockSpeed = 10$ implies an 10x acceleration factor. We will refer to it also as the AirSim accelerator factor and leverage it to speed-up RL training tasks.

Although external Flight Control Systems are supported, by default, AirSim provides its own, called *Simple Flight*. The peculiarity of the *Simple Flight* is using a stoppable clock to pause the simulation at any point. AirSim provides a set of APIs (Client APIs) to interact with this built-in autopilot. The Mission Computer algorithm uses these Client APIs to issue commands and observe the UAV state. We will refer to this in the next section as Mission Computer Application (MCA). According to the complexity of the MCA, following multiple UAV states could be needed to compute a single command.

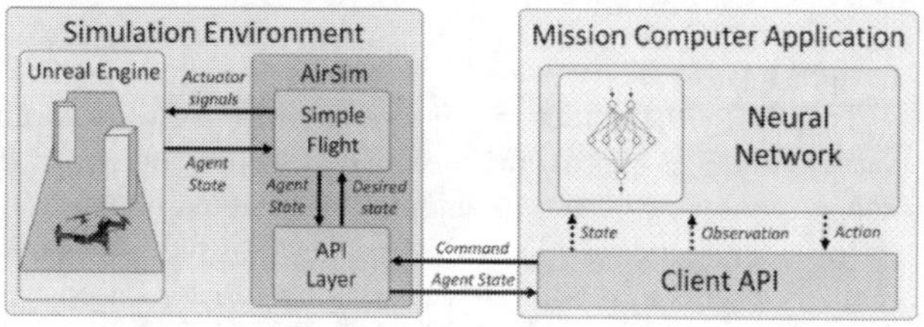

Fig. 1. The full pipeline of the RL setup. The blue box is the simulation environment. The yellow box represents the MSA in which the policy neural network (π_θ) is who chooses the agent's actions. The API provided by AirSim ables the communication between both components.

The Client API offers an asynchronous command allowing the MCA to set the desired UAV speed. The asynchronous command requires a set of input parameters: the velocity vector and the command duration. After this command is issued, the *Simple Flight* starts to execute it, and the MCA is free to continue with its program flow. Before launching another command, the MCA must wait for the previous command completion (using the *join()* method of the Client API); otherwise, the previous one will be overwritten - practically enforcing a synchronous control.

To know the UAV state, AirSim offers two data gathering methods: i) On-demand query via Client API; ii) Built-in periodic recording in a log file. The MCA can gather multiple UAV states during the command execution by issuing a concurrent thread that pauses the simulation at specific time intervals and gathers the UAV states. For this reason, additional input is required to specify the UAV state sampling time (T_{sample}). We refer to this control sequence as AirSim Default Synchronous Command (ADSC). In the following sections, we will study how the ADSC impairs the accuracy of the simulation when accelerated with the $ClockSpeed > 1$.

III. Methodology

A. Motivational Example

In the RL paradigm, no dataset is provided since the agent has to learn directly from his experience. Figure 1 depicts the communication flow between the MCA and the simulation environment. The policy neural network (π_θ) provides the chosen action to the environment. When the simulator executes the action, the environment evolves following its transition function; then, it sends the new state and a reward score to the agent. The reward score represents the goodness of the chosen action.

The simulated environment must replicate as faithfully as possible the real-world physics. Client API allows the RL algorithm to query the simulation environment to collect the current agent state and to send commands to the agent. The *Simple Flight* pilots the UAV agent according to the directives received by the neural network, which acts as a MCA.

To explain how *ClockSpeed* affects the simulation, we illustrate the callback timing of the synchronous commands and the velocity trend on different acceleration values. We use a path composed of three consecutive movements with ADSC along the same axis (two steps forward and one step back) in the standard environment provided by AirSim, disabling the rendering. The data relating to the agent's speed is collected every 0.05 s of simulation time using the record mode, while the timing of the callbacks is gathered by client API. In this example, the imposed movements act in the same axis at a velocity of 1 m/s for 1 s.

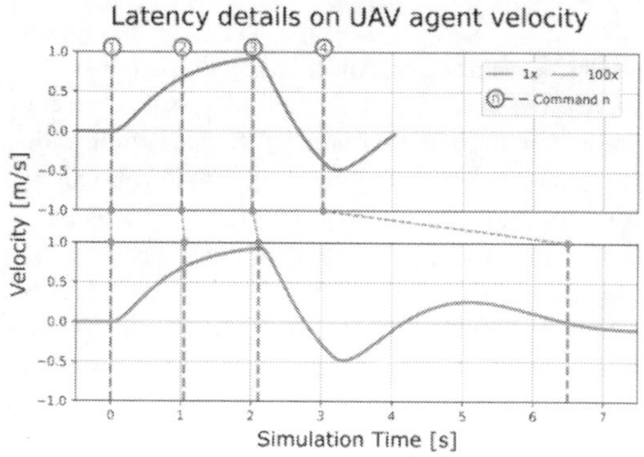

Fig. 2. Latency comparison between a real-time game (in the top) and a 100x accelerated game (in the bottom). The x-axis represents the simulation time in s, and the y-axis the agent velocity in m/s. Vertical lines indicate the time expired command.

Figure 2 shows on the x-axis the simulation time and on the y-axis the speed of the UAV agent. With dashed lines, the plot reports the time command expiration of the UAV agent action in a real-time simulation (the top plot) and a 100x accelerated simulation (the bottom plot). The figure shows that the accelerated simulation is subject to command delays as the dashed lines do not happen precisely on the instants in which the command was issued. We have identified the cause of the delays in: i) Latency between the simulator and the application during the data gathering; ii) Latency of the *Simple Flight* in communicating the move command to the UAV agent. These latencies are involved in ADSC as the MCA waits for the synchronous command completion.

The delay in the move command increases with the accelerator factor. Latencies also exist in real-time simulations (*ClockSpeed*=1) but become noticeable only when the acceleration increases. During the command delay, the simulator continues to evaluate the UAV.

Figure 3 shows the coordinates of the drone flights in real-time (blue line) and in 100x acceleration (green line). In the plot axes, the 3D Cartesian coordinates are reported. We can see the impact of the latencies on the agent's trajectory by accelerating the simulation in a single game.

Another issue related to the acceleration of the simulation is the quality of the images collected by the agent camera. Enabling the rendering in an accelerated game and visually inspecting the camera images, we noticed that some images are affected by salt-and-pepper noise and disturbances in brightness in very dark scenes. We also noted issues with the rendered colours of the objects in the scene. Unreal Engine renders the scene by following a pipeline in which processing is computed in multiple phases. Accelerated simulation reduces the rendering time and the time available for each stage, making some of them hard to be completed and perturbing the

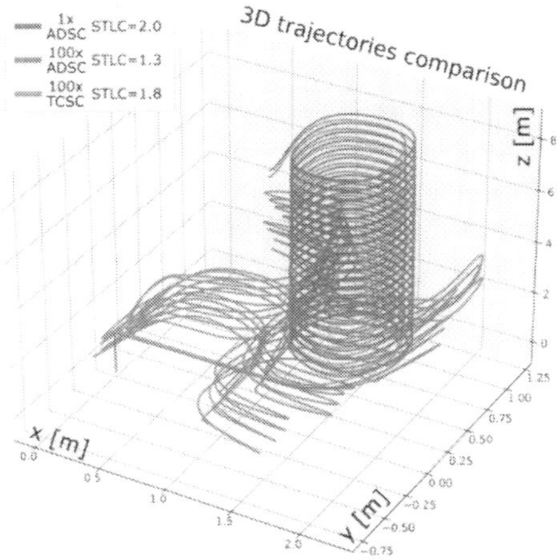

Fig. 3. Comparison of trajectories between a real-time game (in blue) and a 100x accelerated games. The axes x-y-z represents the 3D coordinates of the simulation environment.

returned images. This issue must be mitigated since the quality of camera images is essential for considered RL tasks.

B. Speed-Up Effects Mitigation

We demonstrated how communication latencies affect the accelerated simulation modifying the UAV agent trajectories. While the MCA waits for the end of the ADSC, the simulation continues at the selected *ClockSpeed*. The error in the accuracy of the trajectories exacerbates as the Airsim acceleration factor increases.

To overcome this issue, we propose a new command called Time-Controlled Simulation Command (TCSC) in this paper. The TCSC uses the stoppable clock of the *Simple Flight* to control the simulation until the command expires. This control is implemented by periodic stimulation interrupts interleaved with command expired-time checks.

Figure 4 details the trellis diagram of TCSC. The MCA issues the TCSC with the associated inputs: the velocity vector, the expected command duration (T_{move}), and the UAV state sampling time (T_{sample}), then:
1) TCSC measures the start time (T_start) and issues the asynchronous command in the Clint API with a command duration equal to T_{move}. 2) Internally the TCSC leverages the Client API of AirSim to continue the simulation until a predefined time ($T_{wakeup} = min T_{move}, T_{sample}$) is expired.
3) When this happens, the simulator is paused, and the TCSC uses the Client API to collect the current simulation time (T_{sim}). If T_{sim} is lower than the $T_{start} + T_{wakeup}$, the TCSC continues the simulation for the differences between the two times ($T_{wakeup} = T_{start} + T_{wakeup} - T_{sim}$). If this difference is below a minimum threshold (T_{th}), set as the Client API latency, than T_{sim} is considered larger than $T_{start} + T_{wakeup}$.
4) If T_{sim} is larger than the $T_{start} + T_{wakeup}$ the TCSC gathers the UAV state. At this point if $T_{sim} \geq T_{start} + T_{move}$ the TCSC ends, otherwise it sets $T_{move} = T_{move} - T_{sample}$, and returs to (2.).

To avoid interference between the AirSim acceleration factor and the camera images in the simulation, we disabled the

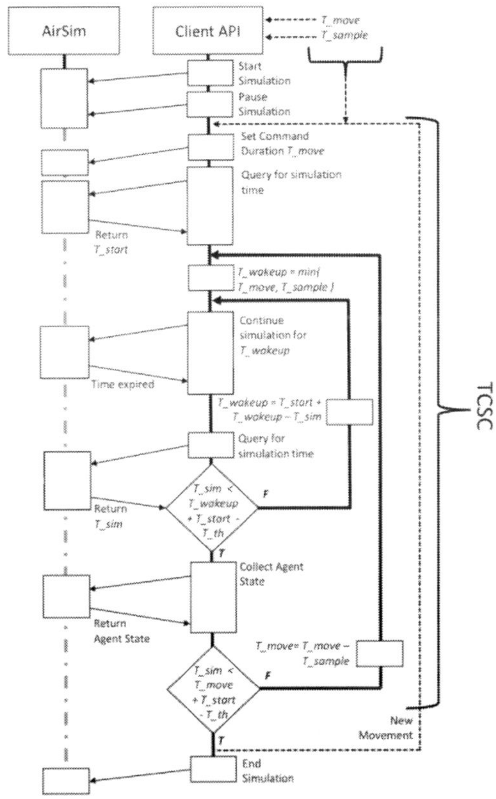

Fig. 4. This trellis diagram represents the TCSC. Inputs are the time duration command T_{move}, agent state sampling time T_{sample} and a velocity vector (not used in the graph).

camera auto exposure. Moreover, we implemented a simple method based on the average image brightness to solve the camera image perturbation. The assumption is that this parameter slowly changes across consecutive camera images. Suppose the average image brightness changed more than the 10% w.r.t previous camera image. In that case, the image is considered perturbed, and a new camera image is requested to the rendering engine through the Client API. In addition, the average image brightness is compared with a minimum threshold to ensure that the camera image is not too dark. During these checks, the simulation is paused; thus, the simulation accuracy is not impaired.

C. Characterization Methodology

Evaluating the impact of the simulation acceleration on RL tasks requires assessing different effects: (i) the trajectory accuracy; (ii) the visual perception accuracy; (iii) their impact on the agent performance trained in RL.

For this purpose, we defined the following methodology:

- Replicating a State-of-the-Art (SoA) UAV RL task [13], consisting of learning an obstacle avoidance policy based on images with AirSim.
- Defining two pre-defined deterministic control sequences (path) on which to assess the (i) accuracy of a trajectory and (ii) the visual perception accuracy.

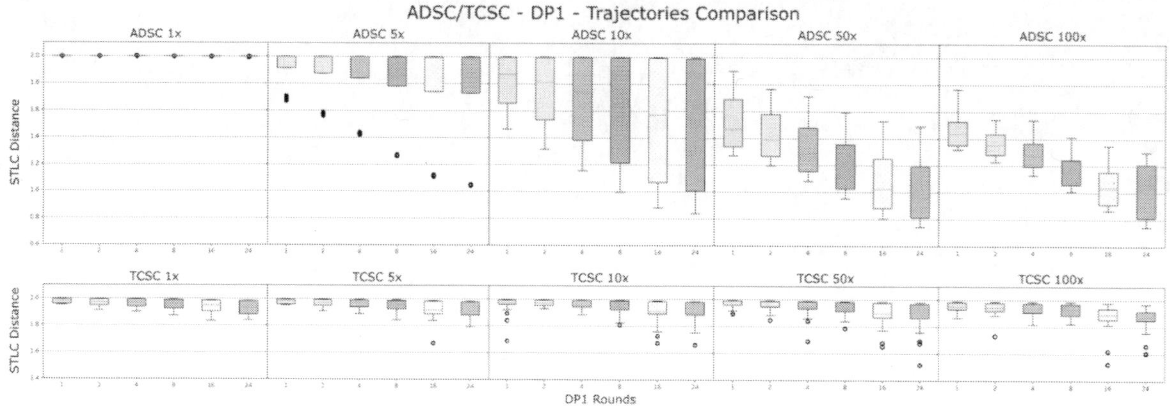

Fig. 5. The plot reports the STLC distance (y-axis) of the trajectories recorded, computed in averaging pair-wise, for each game replica combination performed in DP1. The references are the ADSC real-time games. In the sub-plots x-axis, the DP1 command length (DP1-1r to DP1-24r) is marked. Sub-plot rows identify the command used to perform the games (ADSC and TCSC). Sub-plots columns identify the AirSim accelerated factor. STLC distance has a score of 0 and 2, where 2 means trajectories completely overlapped.

- Comparing the accuracy of an agent trained in RL with different simulation acceleration.

1) Environment Setup: To improve how TCSC affects the simulation and the RL performance, we replicate the experiments performed in [13]. The task involves the avoidance of obstacles along a lane of 150 meters. We will refer to this simulated environment as the RL AirSim environment (AirSim-RLE). We mimic a Dynamic Vision Sensor (DVS) in which every pixel detects the variation of the log brightness. For this purpose we used the v2e [15] DVS model. If the variation exceeds a certain threshold, an event is created. An event is defined as a tuple of four elements: the coordinates of the pixel (x,y), the timestamp, and the polarity (which can be + or −). We simulated a UAV flying by steps of 1 s at a speed of 1 m/s and collecting three frames per command. For this reason we set $T_{move} = 1s$ and $T_{sample} = 0.33s$. Then a completed game requires more than two minutes.

In addition to the AirSim-RLE, we leverage an additional AirSim environment, the default AirSim one, Blocks, on which we perform the trajectory accuracy tests. We will refer to this environment as the AirSim default environment (AirSim-DE).

2) Performance Metrics:

a) Trajectory accuracy: To quantify the effect of the latency on the trajectories, we sampled the position of an agent in the AirSim-DE with rendering disabled. The test is performed for both commands, ADSC and TCSC. The paths are composed of a repetition of four movements designed to move on a square perimeter (Deterministic Path #1 - DP1). The UAV will move on the path for an increasing number of times per game: we considered the following number of rounds (1,2,4,8,16,24). We will later refer to these combinations as (DP1-1r, DP1-2r, ..., DP1-24r). The agent speed is 1 m/s while the command duration varies from 0.1 s to 1 s. We perform twenty games per path for each AirSim acceleration factor and command duration. The data collected are composed of a set of 3D coordinates with the corresponding simulator time with a sampling time of 0.05 s. We use the Spatiotemporal Linear Combine distance (STLC) [16] to compare the different trajectories. We use as a reference the real-time trajectory. For each AirSim acceleration factor, we compute an average STLC distance by averaging the pair-wise STLC distance computed for each game replica combination (resulting in a 20x20 matrix). This metric has a score of 0 and 2, where 2 is the maximum value indicating that the trajectories are entirely overlapped. As a reference, the trajectories reported in Figure 3 have an STLC distance with the trajectory A of 1.3 for the trajectory B and 1.86 for the trajectory C. We conclude that STLC distances above 1.8 means visually similar trajectories.

b) Visual perception accuracy: Assessing the visual perception accuracy of a UAV flight simulation is of primary interest if a camera input guides the drone control task. We thus need to assess if the AirSim acceleration factor introduces visual perception accuracy distortion on top of the UAV trajectory errors. We set the UAV to follow a pre-defined deterministic path which reaches the end of the AirSim-RLE (without obstacle collision). We will refer to this as the Deterministic Path #2 (DP2). We repeated this simulation one time for each AirSim acceleration factor considered. The UAV commands used is TCSC with $T_{move} = 1s$ and $T_{sample} = 0.33s$. For each UAV state gathered, we collected the camera image and the UAV coordinates. We then compute for each sample: (i) The Euclidean distance between the coordinates at which the camera image is taken in the accelerated simulation and real-time simulation; (ii) The difference in the total number of DVS pixels in each polarity between the camera image taken in the accelerated and real-time simulation. This difference is reported as a percentage of the total number of pixels in the camera images with a resolution of 256x144 pixels. We will refer to this metric as DVS Event Dissimilarity (DVS-ED). The introduced metrics allow us to understand how the quality of the images changes in relation to the difference in the UAV coordinates when the image is taken. For nearby acquisition points, we expect a slight difference in the images obtained concerning an accelerated simulation. Otherwise, we can conclude that the AirSim acceleration factor induces an additional perturbation in the gathered camera images.

3) RL agent performance: The strategy of validating RL algorithms on accelerated simulations involves training the

UAV agent in RL for the designated task (obstacle avoidance) at different AirSim acceleration factors. The RL training procedure performs 5 000 games on the previously described AirSim-RLE. This test is replicated using both the ADSC and the TCSC. During the training, we record the simulation, image processing (DVS computation), and the policy neural network (π_θ) inference times.

After the RL training ends, as described in Section II-A, a policy neural network (π_θ) is obtained. We evaluate the accuracy of the UAV's flight with the trained policy neural network, and we measure the number of times the UAV reaches the end of the environment without collisions over 100 games - later, we will refer to this metric as the UAV success ratio.

First, we compared the two commands, ADSC and TCSC, in real-time. Using a real-time simulation, we trained the policy neural network in RL using the proposed TCSC. Then we evaluated the UAV success ratio using both TCSC and ADSC in inference over 100 games. This test provides evidence of the interchangeability of commands when the simulation happens in real-time, where the effects of latencies are negligible.

Second, we compare the UAV success ratio computed in real-time for the policy neural network (π_θ) trained with different AirSim acceleration factors. UAV success ratios equivalent to those obtained in the real-time training (reference case) are considered valid AirSim acceleration factors. To check the wall-time gained with the simulation acceleration, we calculate the effective speed-up of training procedures with different AirSim acceleration factors compared to the ADSC real-time one.

IV. Results

A. Experimental Setup

In this section, we describe the results obtained from the characterization methodology described in Section III-C. The tests have been performed in a server equipped with a 24-GB RAM NVIDIA Quadro RTX 6000 GPU, Intel(R) Xeon(R) Gold 5220 CPU @ 2.20 GHz and 188 GiB of RAM. In this section we considered the following AirSim acceleration factors: 1x (Real-time - Baseline), 5x, 10x, 50x, 100x.

B. Trajectory accuracy and speed-up

The first characterization test focuses on evaluating the impact of the AirSim acceleration factors on the trajectory accuracy for both the ADSC and the proposed TCSC. This is done in the AirSim-DE with the UAV flying following the pre-defined deterministic path DP1.

Each command considered (ADSC/TCSC) has been simulated at each AirSim acceleration factors [1x, 5x, 10x, 50x, 100x] for different command durations (0.1 s, 0.2 s, 0.5 s, 1 s) for an increasing command length (DP1-1r to DP1-24r). Each simulation setting has been repeated for 20 times.

Figure 5 reports the distribution of the STLC distance for each setting computed against the ADSC real-time case (ADSC-1x), which we consider as the baseline. This means that for all ADSC-1x steps, the STLC distance reaches near maximum value, $STLC_d = 2$. Slight differences are due to the

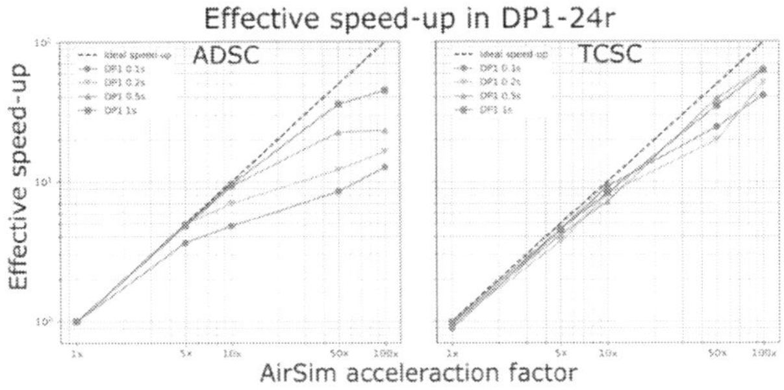

Fig. 6. Effective speed-up of the trajectories accuracy test on DP1-24r. Effective speed-ups (y-axis) are distinguished by the command duration. The x-axis identifies the set AirSim acceleration factor. The effective speed-up is computed for both commands, ADSC (on the left) and TCSC (on the right). The black line indicates the ideal curve.

non-determinism of the simulator, for which the trajectories vary between repetitions. In other tests, the variance of the STLC distance distributions increases as the AirSim acceleration factor increases. In the figure, we group the computed STLC distance based on the command length. The top plot refers to the ADSC case, while the bottom plot refers to the TSCS case. Different sub-plots refer to different AirSim accelerator factors, while the x-axis reports the command length on which the STLC distance has been computed.

For a given AirSim acceleration factor, the trajectory accuracy worsens with the command length, suggesting the error accumulates between consecutive commands. This is expected as the source of the trajectory error is the command latency. For the same reason, the proposed TCSC command significantly outperforms the ADSC trajectory accuracy.

Let us consider achieving an STLC distance higher than 1.8 in the median case (reported with a red line in the box plot). The proposed TCSC provides acceptable trajectory accuracy for all the AirSim acceleration factors while the default ADSC reaches it for acceleration lower than 5x.

To evaluate how an AirSim acceleration factor translates to simulation time reduction, we measured the time taken to perform the simulation in the above-tested settings and computed the effective speed-up against the real-time baseline. Figure 6 reports this value for the ADSC (left plot) and TCSC (right plot) for the different AirSim acceleration factors (x-axis). Different lines refer to different command durations. In the y-axis, we report the average effective speed-up computed against the real-time ADSC case, averaged among the repetitions and command lengths. With the dashed black line, we report the ideal effective speed-up curve.

From the plot, we can notice that, in general, the TCSC outperforms the ADSC showing an effective speed-up closer to the ideal curve. For the ADSC, the effective speed-up increases by increasing the command durations. This effect is more visible at high AirSim acceleration factors. This can be explained by the fact that for each command, the time spent in it is composed of the time of processing the command, the communication and callback latency, and the simulation time. The AirSim acceleration factor reduces only the simulation time. For shorter command durations, the simulation time is weightless on the total time; thus, the simulation acceleration

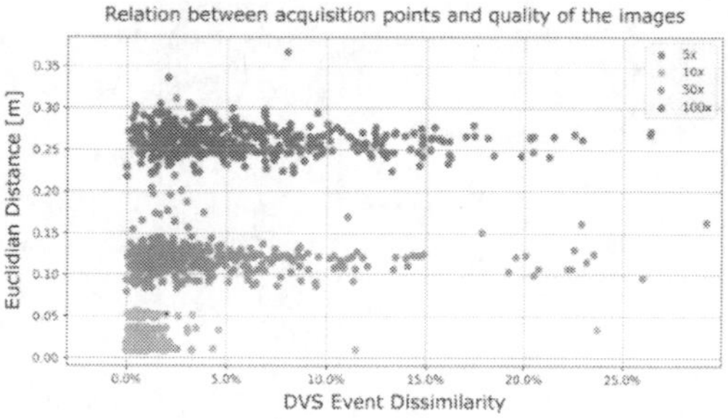

Fig. 7. Correlation between UAV position error measured and DVS-ED (x-axis) in DP2. Distance from positions is computed with euclidean distance (y-axis). Colors indicate the set Airsim acceleration factor.

benefits reduce. It is interesting to note that the proposed TCSC shows better scalability. This can be explained by the fact that the ADSC has an additional wait callback w.r.t. the TSCS, which is the source of a more significant amount of latency at high AirSim acceleration factors.

C. Visual perception accuracy

In this subsection, we evaluated the impact of the AirSim acceleration factor on the visual perception accuracy simulations. This is done by simulating the different AirSim acceleration factors of a UAV moving on the pre-defined deterministic path DP2 on the AirSim-RLE.

Figure 7 reports on the x-axis the DVS-ED and the y-axis the UAV position error measured as the euclidean distance. Both metrics are computed for each DVS camera image captured by the drone in the DP2 against the real-time AirSim acceleration factor one. Each point corresponds to a DVS camera image. Different colour refers to the different AirSim acceleration factors.

TABLE I
SUCCESS RATIO RELATING TO DIFFERENT AIRSIM ACCELERATION FACTORS TRAINING EVALUATED IN REAL-TIME INFERENCE. THE SUCCESS RATIO, COMPUTED IN AIRSIM-RLE IS PERFORMED WITH THE SAME TRAINING COMMAND (ADSC AND TCSC).

	AirSim Acceleration Factor				
	1x	5x	10x	50x	100x
ADSC	23	1	0	0	0
TCSC	21	30	23	14	13

As shown in Figure 7, the points relative to an AirSim acceleration factor of 5x are close to the origin: the euclidean distance is within 5 cm, the DVS-ED is below 3% from the DVS camera image obtained in real-time. This means that the simulation accelerated to 5x is almost identical to the real-time simulation. Increasing the AirSim acceleration factor to 10x slightly increases the DVS-ED to 5% while still maintaining the euclidean distance below the 5 cm. Also, there is not a big difference from the real-time simulation. It is interesting to notice that when the AirSim acceleration factor is increased to higher values (50x and 100x), the Euclidean distance increases but less than the DVS-ED. Moreover, at these AirSim acceleration factors, many points have similar euclidean distances but significantly different DVS-ED. This means that the difference in the images seen from the UAV's camera does not depend only on the position error induced by the simulation acceleration but that the latency in command can lead to a different camera orientation while the UAV is in a relatively similar position.

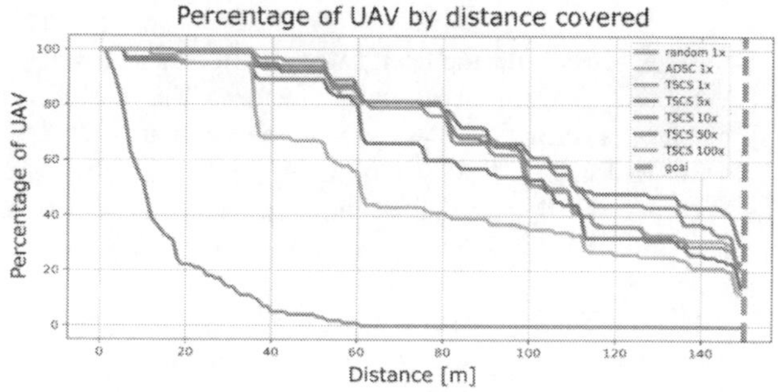

Fig. 8. Distance traveled in meters (x-axis) by the UAV agents during the 100 games inference (y-axis). The lines refer to the inference executed on different AirSim acceleration factors training. The red line represents the goal of the AirSim-RLE lane.

D. RL agent performance

This last section evaluates how the effects discussed impact the performance of an agent trained in RL in an accelerated simulation environment. As described in Section III-C3 we trained with RL a policy neural network (π_θ) to avoid obstacles based on the DVS camera input. In real-time with the ADSC (ADSC-1x), the training of 5000 games takes one week and 14 hours. The agent achieves a UAV success ratio of 23%.

Table I reports the UAV success ratio obtained when training the policy neural-network (π_θ) at different AirSim acceleration factors. All the UAV success ratios have been computed in real-time in the AirSim-RLE.

We can notice that the TCSC-1x has a similar performance to the baseline achieving the 21% of UAV success ratio. Moreover, the UAV success ratio is preserved till AirSim acceleration factors of 10x. For higher accelerations (50x and 100x), the score reduces to 62%. This indicates that the proposed command can preserve the RL training accuracy until a simulation acceleration of 10x. It is interesting to notice that the AirSim acceleration factors of 5x improve upon the ADSC-1x, suggesting that for this acceleration, the trajectory noise helps the trained model to generalize. In contrast, at higher acceleration factors, the loss in the DVS accuracy (DVS-ED) increases, jeopardizing the training accuracy.

Figure 8 reports on the x-axis the distance travelled in meters by the UAV agent in 100 trials (games) simulated in real-time using the policy neural network (π_θ) trained with accelerated simulations. For a given AirSim acceleration factor (reported in the plot with different colours), all the 100 trials have been simulated using the policy neural network weights (θ) obtained during the corresponding accelerated training. The y-axis reports the number of UAV agents sharing the same, which reached a given distance. In the plot, we report as well the reference cases performed in real-time with ADSC and TCSC are plotted. The lines have a similar trend with peaks corresponding with obstacle locations. The figure validates the TCSC experiment by demonstrating that simulation acceleration applied to RL algorithms does not alter

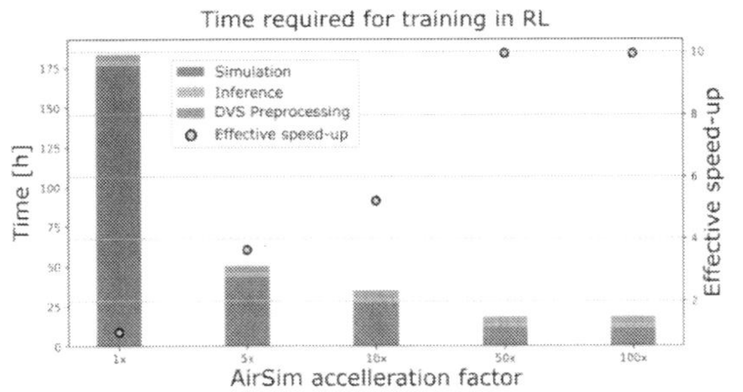

Fig. 9. Time in hours required for each training phase and effective speed-up of the training. The x-axis indicates the set AirSim acceleration factor. Y-axes indicate the hours required for the training separated by phases (on the left) and the effective training speed-up (on the right).

the simulation environment. By increasing the acceleration of the simulation, the trajectories and perception perturbations increase, impacting the performance of the RL.

Finally, Figure 9 reports on the left y-axis the simulation time required by the RL training for each AirSim acceleration factor (x-axis). On the right x-axis is reported the effective speed-up measured w.r.t. the real-time training time. With different colours, we account for the time spent in the RL training in performing the UAV agent in simulation, the policy neural network (π_θ) inference (choice of the following action), and image pre-processing to compute the DVS image. From it, we can notice that in real-time, the training time is dominated by the simulation time, which gets reduced by the AirSim acceleration factor. However, when comparing the effective speed-up with the one previously obtained with the rendering disabled (Figure 6) we can recognize a significant drop in the scalability. Indeed, with the rendering disabled, the effective speed-up for the TCSC was 50x. For a 100x AirSim acceleration factor (*ClockSpeed*) in the RL training (w. rendering enabled), we achieve for the same AirSim acceleration factor a 15.4x of effective speed-up. For the other AirSim acceleration factors, when considering only the simulation time, we obtain 4x speed-up with *ClockSpeed* set to 5x and 6.4x speed-up with 10x. At 50x *ClockSpeed* the achievable acceleration saturates to 14.8x of speed-up.

We can conclude that thanks to the proposed TCSC approach, the training time of one week has been reduced to two days (3.6x with $ClockSpeed = 5$) or one day and a half (5.2x with $ClockSpeed = 10$) without impairing the accuracy of the trained policy. In contrast, we empirically demonstrated that theefault ADSC does not allows performing an RL training with accelerated simulation. *ClockSpeed* values of 50x and 100x do not equal real-time but still achieve excellent results.

V. CONCLUSIONS

In this work, we described a method to speed-up the training of UAV agents trained in RL by reducing the simulation time. We refer to this method as a Time-Controlled Simulation Command (TCSC) in opposition to the AirSim Default Synchronous Command (ADSC). At the same time, we mitigate the issues related to the simulation acceleration. The proposed TCSC mitigates the error on the trajectories of UAV agents in accelerated simulation up to 65x diverging within 10 % compared to those computed in real-time. To validate the TCSC on RL algorithms, we replicated the work done by [13]. The designated task involves avoiding obstacles in a 150m lane through the use of camera images. The acceleration of the simulation generates perturbations in the camera images. We mitigated this noise by introducing a method based on image brightness. We performed accelerated training with TCSC and ADCS, comparing them in 100 games inferences on real-time simulations. Training with TCSC on accelerated simulation up to 6.4x has the same UAV success ratio of the inference with training performed in real-time. By accelerating the simulation to 4x in training, we have improved the UAV success ratio of the inference with training performed in real-time. Training with *ClockSpeed* of 50x and 100x achieved effective speed-up of 14.8x and 15.4x and replicated more than 62% of the UAV success ratio in real-time. Accelerated simulation training with ADSC failed to complete games in real-time inference. With TCSC, a training that in real-time simulation requires one week of simulations has been replicated in less than two days.

REFERENCES

[1] W. L. Keng and L. Graesser, "Slm lab," https://github.com/kengz/SLM-Lab, 2017.
[2] N. Salvatore *et al.*, "A neuro-inspired approach to intelligent collision avoidance and navigation," in *2020 AIAA/IEEE 39th Digital Avionics Systems Conference (DASC)*, 2020, pp. 1–9.
[3] J. Collins *et al.*, "A review of physics simulators for robotic applications," *IEEE Access*, vol. 9, pp. 51 416–51 431, 2021.
[4] S. Shah *et al.*, "Airsim: High-fidelity visual and physical simulation for autonomous vehicles," *CoRR*, vol. abs/1705.05065, 2017.
[5] Y. Song *et al.*, "Flightmare: A flexible quadrotor simulator," in *Proceedings of the 2020 Conference on Robot Learning*, 2021, pp. 1147–1157.
[6] N. Koenig and A. Howard, "Design and use paradigms for gazebo, an open-source multi-robot simulator," in *2004 IEEE/RSJ International Conference on Intelligent Robots and Systems (IROS) (IEEE Cat. No.04CH37566)*, vol. 3, 2004, pp. 2149–2154 vol.3.
[7] Webots, "http://www.cyberbotics.com," open-source Mobile Robot Simulation Software. [Online]. Available: http://www.cyberbotics.com
[8] T. Kim, M. Jang, and J. Kim, "A survey on simulation environments for reinforcement learning," in *2021 18th International Conference on Ubiquitous Robots (UR)*, 2021, pp. 63–67.
[9] J. Hwangbo, J. Lee, and M. Hutter, "Per-contact iteration method for solving contact dynamics," *IEEE Robotics and Automation Letters*, vol. 3, no. 2, pp. 895–902, 2018. [Online]. Available: www.raisim.com
[10] V. Makoviychuk *et al.*, "Isaac gym: High performance gpu-based physics simulation for robot learning," 2021. [Online]. Available: https://arxiv.org/abs/2108.10470
[11] A. Juliani *et al.*, "Unity: A general platform for intelligent agents," 2018. [Online]. Available: https://arxiv.org/abs/1809.02627
[12] L. Zanatta and A. Musa, "Ecs-lab / uav reinforcement learning with airsim · gitlab." [Online]. Available: https://gitlab.com/ecs-lab/uav-reinforcement-learning-with-airsim.git
[13] L. Zanatta *et al.*, "Artificial versus spiking neural networks for reinforcement learning in uav obstacle avoidance," in *Proceedings of the 19th ACM International Conference on Computing Frontiers*, ser. CF '22. New York, NY, USA: Association for Computing Machinery, 2022, p. 199–200. [Online]. Available: https://doi.org/10.1145/3528416.3530865
[14] V. Mnih *et al.*, "Playing atari with deep reinforcement learning," *arXiv preprint arXiv:1312.5602*, 2013.
[15] Y. Hu *et al.*, "v2e: From video frames to realistic dvs events," in *Proceedings of the IEEE/CVF Conference on Computer Vision and Pattern Recognition*, 2021, pp. 1312–1321.
[16] H. Su *et al.*, "A survey of trajectory distance measures and performance evaluation," *The VLDB Journal*, vol. 29, no. 1, pp. 3–32, oct 2019. [Online]. Available: https://doi.org/10.1007\%2Fs00778-019-00574-9

An Agent-Based Model for the Management of the Emergency Department During the COVID-19 Pandemic

[1,2,4]Ramona Galeano, [1]Dolores Rexachs, [1]Alvaro Wong, [5]Eva Bruballa,
[2]Cynthia Villalba, [3]Diego Galeano, [1]Emilio Luque

[1]*Computer Architecture and Operating Systems Department*
Universitat Autónoma de Barcelona (UAB)
Barcelona, Spain
e-mail: RamonaElizabeth.Galeano@autonoma.cat, Dolores.Rexachs@uab.cat
alvaro.wong@uab.es, eva.bruballa@eug.es, emilio.luque@uab.es
[2]*Facultad Politécnica*
[3]*Facultad de Ingeniería*
[4]*Facultad de Ciencias Médicas*
Universidad Nacional de Asunción
San Lorenzo, Paraguay
e-mail: cvillalba@pol.una.py, dgaleano@ing.una.py
[5]*Escuela Universitaria de Informática*
Escuela Universitaria Gimbernat

***Abstract*—The COVID-19 pandemic has caused significant mortality in healthcare worldwide. A challenge for hospitals is the management of overcrowding in emergency departments, which can be critical for patient survival and effective patient care. Modeling and simulation can provide a more accurate and effective method to test new management techniques without endangering patients. In this paper, we present an improvement/extension of a previous agent-based model proposal that allows imitating the operation of an emergency department to design a simulator that helps to plan and manage a pandemic situation. We have enhanced the model by adding the variables to patient and staff hospital agents participating in the transmission process; and separated emergency rooms for the infected and non infected to evaluate the effectiveness using different combinations such as laboratory tests, isolation, and other control policies. This modeling can help the configuration of the medical staff, nursing, beds, devices, and patient waiting time management. Furthermore, two health personnel levels (emergency intensivists (seniors) and personnel from different specialties (junior)) have been incorporated in the emergency department to treat COVID patients.**

Keywords: simulation, pandemic, COVID-19, agent-based model.

I. Introduction

A pandemic occurs when an infectious disease spreads and affects many people in more than one continent. Pandemics are caused by viruses that can be easily transmitted from person to person and spreads over a wide geographical area, usually, spreading in to many countries or attacking almost all individuals in a locality or region.

The unpredictability, uncertainty, fear, and restrictions related to the COVID-19 pandemic have represented particular challenges, mainly due to government's measures of quarantine, confinement, and social distancing, among others. The pandemic has also affected the economy worldwide, generating critical situations in companies around the world, unemployment, and economic difficulties for most families and individuals.

During the pandemic, management of hospital's emergency departments have played a key role for patient survival. Improving such services without knowing in advance how changes made can affect patient care cycle remains challenging. One of the critical points in managing the emergency department is improving its ability to contain the spread of contagious diseases. For instance, we could seek to understand how changes made to specific variables in the emergency management cycle could help reduce the spread of the virus.

The three main approaches used in the simulation of an emergency department are agent-based simulation, discrete event simulation, and system dynamics [1] [2]. The advantages of using simulation is to facilitate the automatic search for scenarios that can provide the best solutions given a set of constraints and future states. This automation of the search for improvements to an emergency department can significantly help managers who need answers to problems.

We have previously developed agent-based models for modeling the management in an emergency department [3]–[6]. Agent-based model is an approach to model systems in which individual agents interact. It offers ways to more easily model interactions of individuals and also how these interactions affect other agents in the system [7].

In this paper, we propose designing and developing an agent-based model that allows modeling the management of an emergency department during the COVID-19 pandemic. Our work presented here builds upon the work of Jaramillo et al. [6] that developed a simulator for planning and management of Methicillin-resistant Staphylococcus aureus (MRSA) spreads among hospitalized patients which has the advantage of having been verified and validated in several cycles or iterations, taking into account a wide variety of data and configurations, and with the participation of emergency department staff at the Hospital of Sabadell (Spain). Jaramillo's [6] work is a simulator with a design that allows the spread of infections by contact (MRSA). It does not work in a pandemic situation. The pandemic has emerged, and some requirements must be added to make it work in a pandemic situation.

We have modified the Jaramillo et al. [6] agent-based model to be useful for COVID-19 emergency rooms. First, we have incorporated COVID-related variables for each patient that includes their state of infection, symptoms, viral load, and Polymerase Chain Reaction (PCR) test result. And variables for each hospital staff that include acuity level, age, location, infected or not, symptomatic or not, vaccinated or not, viral load, and PCR test. Second, we have made the simulator more flexible to include: (i) the management of multiple emergency rooms within the same hospital; (ii) multiple PCR test results for each patient; and (iii) separate emergency rooms for the infected and non-infected.

Our emergency clinical staff has been modeled incorporating two possible levels of experience: juniors (with limited or low experience) and seniors (with experience). This is very important because during a significant part of the "Covid attack", in addition to emergency intensivists (seniors), some health personnel from different specialties (juniors compared with the intensivists) were incorporated into the emergency department.

A set of synthetic input data has been prepared for the simulation, which is why the distribution of arrival patients had to be generated. COVID and NO COVID with different levels of severity and the general distribution of simulated patient ages.

Our simulator describes the behavior of the emergency department during the COVID-19 pandemic and can assist doctors and administrators as a decision support system for emergency department management. Our simulator allows us to build virtual scenarios to understand the transmission phenomenon of COVID-19, and the potential impact of implementing different policies on the rates of viral spread.

The rest of the paper is organized as follows. In Section II, we explain state of the art. Section III presents the description of the emergency department model. Section IV describes the initial simulation. Section V presents the experiments and discussion, and Section VI presents the conclusions and the future work.

II. State of the Art

A problem stands out in the 21st century: the increase in microbial resistance and oncological diseases to the appearance of new infectious diseases, such as COVID-19. Some viruses have caused severe pandemics. According to World Health Organization (WHO) data, many emerging and re-emerging infectious diseases are of zoonotic origin. The coronavirus is a big family of viruses that can cause disease in animals and humans.

COVID-19, also called novel coronavirus disease, is caused by severe acute respiratory syndrome coronavirus 2. The high probability of infections in high population density places made the initial transmission faster and stronger. This pandemic put health systems in different parts of the world in uncertainty; they had few resources to face a pandemic of such magnitude.

COVID-19 is transmitted by direct contagion from person to person, by droplets of respiratory secretions emitted when breathing, speaking, yelling, coughing, sneezing, kissing, etc., from one to two meters away. The deposit of secretions generates droplet aerosols that remain in the air at greater distances.

The simulation topics most frequently found in the literature in the COVID-19 simulation area are studies for contact tracing with COVID-19, transmission models of healthy patients with infectious, affected tourist cities, spread in health systems [8], patient flow improvement [9], how simulation modeling can help reduce the impact of COVID-19 [10], among others.

Some simulation methods found that were used in the area of COVID-19 simulations are discrete events [9] [11] [12], artificial intelligence [13] and agent-based simulation [14]. Some countries used the simulation to predict scenarios, including the behavior of the Delta variant to know the number of deaths, infected, and vaccinated infected, others to see the evolution of COVID-19, others to establish the infected, quarantined, recovered, and dead, using the Susceptible Exposed Infected Asymptomatic Quarantined Recovered (SEIAQR) model [15].

The studies about the emergency department deal with the practice of protocols or objects for medical procedures. Another job in the emergency department talks about managing the resources in intensive care, intensive care beds and their devices, but there is not a similar work as ours at the time.

Some of our works in the emergency department area are: Create a simulator for the emergency department with the participation of the Sabadell Hospital emergency team [3]. Active agents, passive agents, and the environment are identified, and an initial simulation is created using NetLogo [3]. Another task is to optimize the emergency department's performance [4]. Extensive search optimization is used to find the optimal configuration of emergency department staff, a multi-dimensional, multi-objective problem [4]. An index is proposed to minimize the patient's length of stay in the emergency department. The results obtained using alternative Monte Carlo and Pipeline schemes are promising [4]. This paper presents a layer-based application framework for discovering knowledge of an emergency department system by simulating micro-level behaviors of its components [5]. This paper proposes the use of a simulation tool, the MRSA Simulator to design and conduct virtual clinical trials to study contact transmission of MRSA among hospitalized patients [6].

The difference between our job and the others is that this model of COVID-19 in the emergency department- simulator will allow the emergency department managers to analyze and evaluate potential solutions for the beds and devices. And also has been considered at two levels with experience and without experience (juniors and seniors); when reinforcing, the health personnel treating COVID have incorporated emergency intensivists (seniors) and health personnel from different specialties (juniors). And to evaluate the effectiveness of different combinations of scenarios. Many countries have been experiencing extreme stress with patients unable to access therapy beds, dying in emergency department corridors while waiting for beds to be released, and a lack of experienced doctors.

III. Description of the Emergency Department Model

This section presents a model for the emergency department during the COVID-19 pandemic. The general objective of this research is to propose a model that allows the functionality of the simulator to be extended to adapt it to changes in the operation of the emergency department when there are exceptional situations such as pandemics, in such a way that it helps in the planning and management of the service.

The first step of the work consists of making a conceptual model of the system's operation, from which the computational model that will allow the system to be simulated is elaborated. It is planned to use the simulation environment and a high-level platform.

One of the main properties of the agent-based model is its scope; that is, the domain in which it is capable of executing modeling and simulation scenarios. Agent-based models are increasingly used in several scientific areas, in the simulation of large-scale dynamic complex systems and the observation of emergent behaviors. Complex systems can be thought of simply as sets of interacting agents or entities [16].

The agents can be organizations, human beings, companies, institutions, and any other entity that intends to pursue a specific purpose. Agent-based models are mainly used in the case of complex modeling phenomena, where many active agents or entities interact with each other with specific inherent attributes to establish relationships, thus facilitating automated reasoning and problem-solving [16]. Agent-based models are rule-based systems.

Agent-based model simulation tools support researchers and practitioners in investigating how the macroscopic behavior of a system depends on micro-level properties, constraints, and rules. Agents as objects are typified by specific states and sets of attributes, properties, or functional rules; behaviors that can trigger particular actions through predefined parameters [16].

The ultimate goal is to build simulations of complex systems that evolve as a set of artifacts that interact between multiple decentralized modules. Individual objects or agents refer to the elements that live in the environment and have properties that can change over time; agents can manifest as different independent objects under a discrete or continuous configuration. The agents interact, and the system is constituted by the active interaction of entities or agents and conflict resolution [16].

A. Active agents:

The active agents are the individuals who act dynamically; they are all the human actors in the emergency department. They are:

Patient: They are the essential individuals in the system.

Admissions staff: The personnel to whom the patient goes to request an appointment, update their data and request the opening or search of their medical record.

Doctor: They interact with patients to diagnose and treat them.

The triage nurse: They are who calls the patient to carry out the pre-consultation.

Laboratory Staff: These are the persons who perform the tests and analyze the patient if necessary.

Nurse: They provide treatment to the patient, takes and sends test to laboratorys.

B. State variables

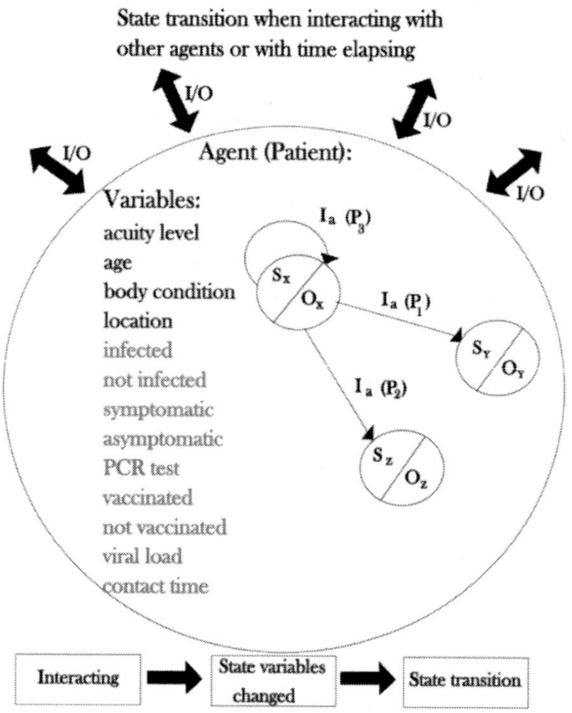

Fig. 1. State transition when interacting with other agents or with time elapsing

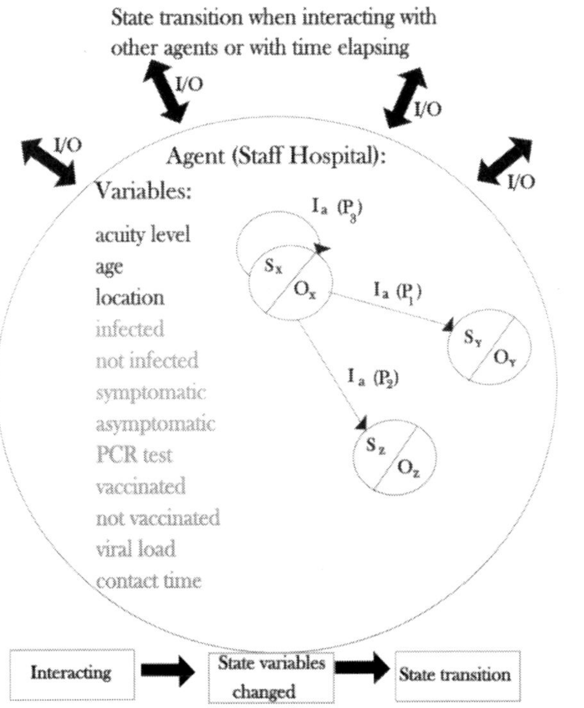

Fig. 2. State transition when interacting with other agents or with time elapsing

The agents move from one place to another by interacting with other agents. During this time, each agent changes its state as a result of the interactions. A state machine perfectly represents this behavior, so they have chosen a state machine to model all agents. Specifically, the agents are represented by a probabilistic Moore machine. An initial set of state variables defined through the round of physician interviews is based on the minimum amount of information needed to model each patient and staff. An initial set of state variables is shown in Figure 1 for the agent patient and Figure 2 for the hospital staff (admissions staff, doctor, the triage nurse, laboratory staff and nurse).

The input vector (I) contains a series of input values that includes many different values. The output (O) depends on the state. The transitions between states depend on the current state in time (ST). The agent patient variables are acuity level, age, body condition, location, infected or not, symptomatic or not, vaccinated or not, viral load, contact time and PCR test. The hospital staff (admissions staff, doctor, triage nurse, laboratory staff, nurse) the variables are acuity level, age, location, infected or not, symptomatic or not, vaccinated or not, viral load, and PCR test.

The agents are divided by their state variables and their behaviors. The values of the state variables of an agent at a given time t defines the situation of a said agent at that time t. The behavior of each agent depends on the category to which it belongs and is defined based on the rules previously assigned to each. To represent the different states of the agents during the attention process are used finite state machines.

These Finite State Machines (FSM) are commonly used to organize and represent a flow of execution. They can be graphically represented as a sequence of nodes and arrows, where nodes are states and arrows are transitions. Each state of the state machines is defined based on the value of the agent's state variables at a given time, considering that each has more than one possible value and a probability associated with each.

The agent's passage from one state to another will then be determined by (a) the current state and (b) by the input value it receives as a result of the interaction with another agent, always considering that this value will be granted based on a previously defined probability.

There is a single-state machine for all the different types of agents in the model, so some combinations of values don't make sense and would never occur during the model operation. Still, it is preferable to have one machine for all agents than different machines because there is the possibility of increasing the model to the point of reflecting the difference between patients with varying levels of knowledge.

C. Output

The agents are represented by Moore machines; each state can have a different output. The output of an agent-based simulator includes the status information (sensors) of the emergency department; some of the outputs are the length of stay (LOS), the length of waiting (LOW) for each stage (e.g., waiting time for service request: wtsr, time of admission: at, waiting time in admission: wta, waiting time in nursing: wtn, time nursing care: twnc, waiting time in doctor's treatment: wtd, doctor treatment care time: twmd and others), destination, age, acuity level, infected, symptomatic, PCR test, vaccinated, viral load. In this way, the simulator does not directly provide information about the simulated department's behavior. In contrast, cross-analysis through different simulation scenarios is how to obtain information.

IV. Initial Simulation

An initial simulation is created to verify the proposed model designed, using the NetLogo [17] agent-based simulation environment, a high-level platform especially suited for modeling complex systems that develop over time. NetLogo [17] allows visualizations of actions and agent interactions, an essential aspect considering that a primary use of the tool is gathering feedback from the emergency department.

The emergency department is divided into different zones in which different types of agents can act, maintaining interactions that can also be different. The input to our model is a group of patients arriving in the emergency department. After the arrival of the patient and the registration is completed by the admission staff, based on the seriousness of their situation in the triage, the patients are categorized, taking into account their acuity level. There are five different values, level 1 is for the most critical situation, and level 5 is not urgent [18]. There are different areas in emergency departments (Figure 3):

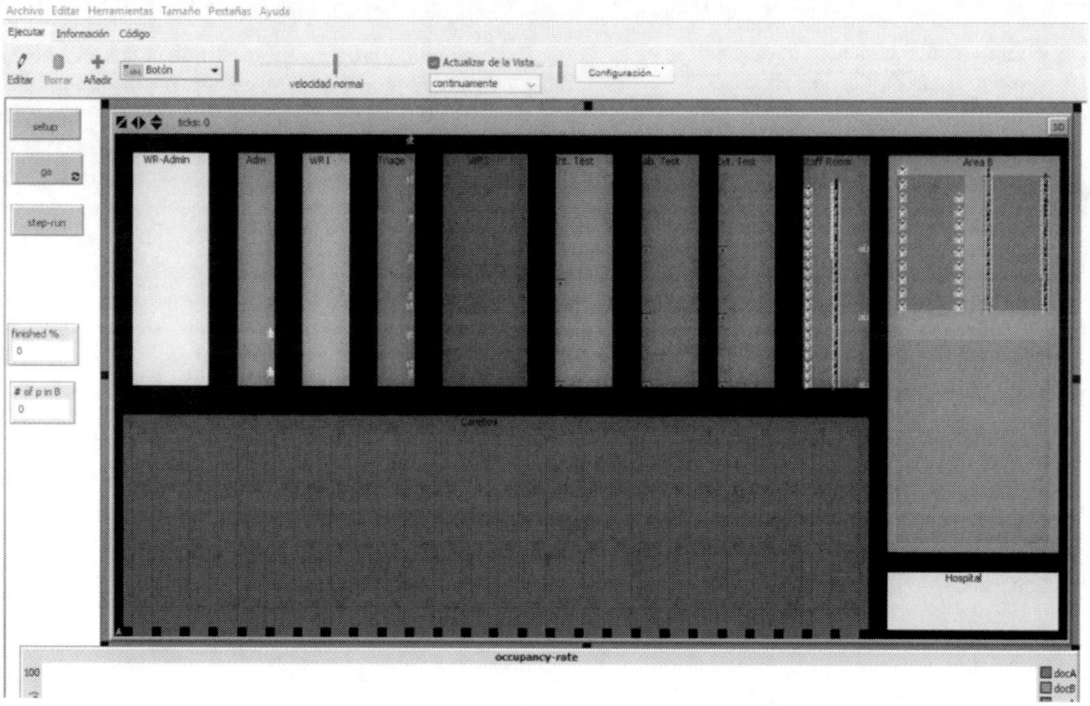

Fig. 3. Simulation display in Netlogo of the emergency department

admissions area, triage area, diagnosis-treatment area, waiting rooms, etc. After triage, patients with diagnosed acuity levels 1, 2, and 3 are treated separately and assigned to Area A, and patients 4 and 5 are treated in Area B.

$$n_{scenarios} = n_{admissions} * n_{timeadmissions} * n_{triagenursing}$$
$$*n_{timetriagenursing} * n_{nursing} * n_{timenursing}$$
$$*n_{doctor} * n_{timedoctor} \quad (1)$$

The scenario adopted for this initial stage is to simulate the patients who move through the emergency department. The areas and the different types of active agents represented in this simulation are patients, admission staff, triage nurses, nurses, doctors, auxiliary staff, laboratory tests, internal tests, external tests, ambulance, and care box. Each combination of values represents a different scenario simulation. Wide varieties of values make up the parameter space. The parameters can generate a large number of different scenarios (1).

In general, the time to compute a time interval of a simulation based on agents is the product of time it takes to simulate the actions of an agent within the world of simulation in this step. In the model described agents in the simulation are the hospital staff and patients. The simulator will be conducted by time. Time is divided into discrete, identical intervals and period each time step the agents operating system. Each time step are divided into two phases. Assuming that the simulator this at time t, the phases are: First, each agent processes the inputs of the last phase, (It-1) and according to that input and the state as it was during the last step (St -1) and changes to its new state St. Second, each agent emits its output to its current state, Ot. This output uses receivers to switch to the next state. In time each agent changes state. It may change to the same state it was previously, but there is a change nonetheless. The metrics that are to be used for each state input It and output Ot are: waiting time to request a service: twrs, Time for register a required service: trs, time admission: ta, waiting time in admission: twa, waiting time in nursing: twn, time nursing care: te, waiting time in doctor: Twmc, health care Time: tm. The machine simulation has been chosen as the basis for when the simulator is implemented because NetLogo [17] has all the features needed to implement a model of this type. NetLogo [17] is a simulation environment agent-based model and provides a basis for machine simulation agent based system.

The run time of a simulation step, in an agent based model simulation, is the product of the time it takes to simulate the actions of an agent and the number of agents in the simulation world in this step. In the model described, agents in the simulation are the hospital staff and patients. During simulation, the hospital staff is fixed, does not enter or exit the simulation. On the other hand, patients are constantly in and out of the simulation. This changes the load of each time slot simulation, base on the equation (2) that calculates the running time Ti in step i, with the number of hospital staff h, the number of patients in the simulation in step i and the runtime of a Tagente agent.

We assume that the runtime of an agent is a fixed value. In different simulations, the number of hospital staff can change, but during one simulation, the number of hospital staff is maintained. Concerning the number of patients, this can change from one simulation step to the other because there are patients in and out, but within each simulation step, this number is constant. For a simulation that takes n steps, equation (3) shows the formula.

$$Ti = (h + pi)Tagente \tag{2}$$

$$T = (hn + pk)Tagente \tag{3}$$

In order to generalize the process of all patients, the next status will be decided by probability distribution during simulation. The distribution model of the probability was based on the statistical data from the emergency department. Figure 4 indicates the general process during the patients stay in emergency department; P1(%), P2(%), P3(%) and Pn (%) represent the probability of the next state transition separately, equation (4), (5), (6), (7) show the formulae. All of the probabilities follow some probability distributions. The probability density function of the distribution is decided by several key parameters based on the statistical analysis of doctor's decision and patient's behavior, the value of these parameters are estimated by a tuning process from real historical data of the specified emergency department. The uniform forms of the density functions are:

$$Pi = f(LOS, age, level) \tag{4}$$

$$\sum_{i=1}^{n} P_i = 100\% \tag{5}$$

$$P' = f'(TOT, age, level) \tag{6}$$

$$\sum_{i=1}^{n} P'_i = 100\% \tag{7}$$

where LOS is the patient's length of stay and age is the age of the patient, which also has big influence to the probability of status transition. Level is the acuity level of the patient and TOT is the type of test service or diagnosis by doctor. The functions f and f' are the probability density function. These functions will be implemented by analyzing real historical data in tuning process. As the simulator is implementing the general model of the emergency departments, the tuning/calibration process must be carried out for each one of them, in order to adjust its simulation parameters to the specific characteristics of each department (e.g., experience of the specific department staff). Therefore, combined with (1) - (10), every patient will show different behavior during the execution of the model because of the probability distribution and their own differences in body condition. But the statistical property of agents will reflect their common behavior.

In the case of active agents for medical staff, two different levels of experience are considered (LOW, labeled as junior, and high, labeled as a senior). The less experienced user will need more time to carry out their part of the process than the most experienced. The time of the agents is fixed internally by the programmer. Still, the simulator user can easily define the number of each type of personnel and their level of experience using the configuration console. The less experienced will use more time to carry out their work because they have no experience; they could be a resident doctor who has just finished. The more experienced will take less time. They already know the process and treatment because they have a lot of experience and years of service. To make a preliminary demonstration of how a simulation can be reproduced using only a few parameters, a simplified set of patient attributes and patient flow is less complicated have been defined. The time of the doctor's attention change according to each patient and its severity level.

V. Experiments and Discussion

Preliminary results obtained with the Instituto de Previsión Social (IPS) Ingavi data are:

A. *Case Study: COVID-19 at the IPS Ingavi of Paraguay*

TABLE I
QUANTITATIVE REPRESENTATION OF THE SIMULATED EMERGENCY DEPARTMENT OF THE HOSPITAL IPS INGAVI

Value of the human resources configuration		
Label	***Interpretation***	***Number***
JA	Junior Admission staff	3
SA	Senior Admission staff	3
JTN	Junior Triage Nurse	5
STN	Senior Triage Nurse	5
JNA	Junior Nurse area A	5
SNA	Senior Nurse area A	5
JNB	Junior Nurse area B	5
SNB	Senior Nurse area B	5
JLE	Junior Outside Laboratory	3
SLI	Senior Internal Laboratory	3
JDA	Junior Doctor area A	10
SDA	Senior Doctor area A	10
JDB	Junior Doctor area B	10
SDB	Senior Doctor area B	10

[a]Value of the human resources configuration

The IPS Ingavi is a modern high-complexity hospital in Paraguay, offering medical care and emergency department to more than 2,000 insured persons per day, with approximately

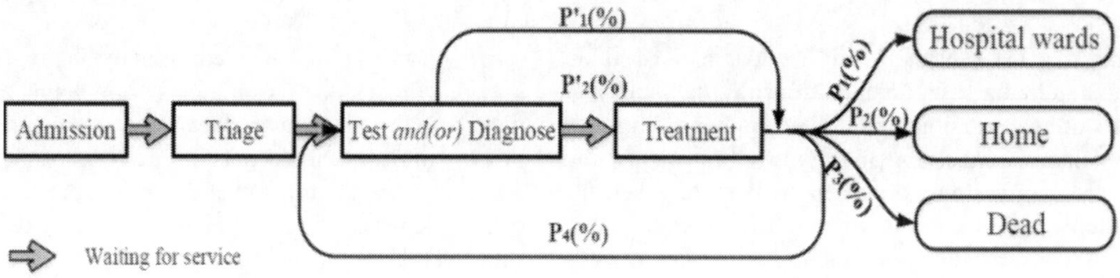

Fig. 4. Waiting for service

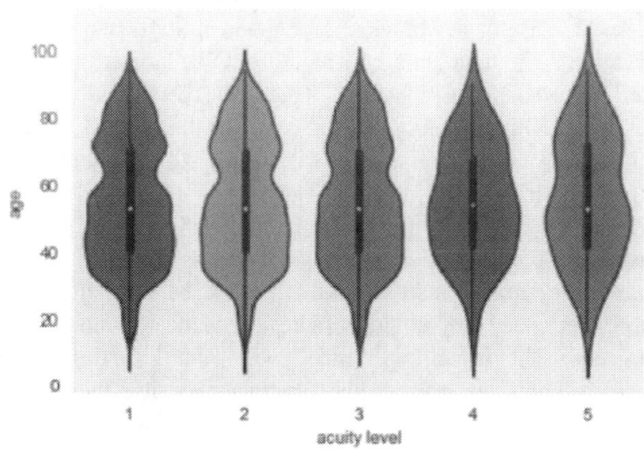

Fig. 5. Overall arrival acuity level and the patient's age distribution

1,500,000 insured persons. It is one of the reference hospitals for caring for patients with COVID-19 in the country.

From March 2020 to September 2021, the IPS Ingavi Hospital treated approximately 15,000 COVID-19 patients, of whom 1,500 died despite medical efforts. In the most critical period of the disease, up to 10 deceased patients were registered daily, and per month they had between 200 and 300 deaths. Table I shows the values of the human resources configuration of the parameters to represent the simulated emergency department.

Netlogo [17] stores information about everything that happens during the execution of the simulator and allows the creation of reports that can be exported and processed with statistics. We did an initial simulation with the data and got to analyze the simulator's behavior against the variables that influence the emergency department; several simulations have been carried out with different values to observe what results we could get.

The patient arrival model includes patients with severity L (acuity level). To do quantitative verification and validation, we built a patient arrival model according to the actual data from our cooperative Hospital.

A set of synthetic input data has been prepared for the simulation, which is why the distribution of arrival patients had to be generated. COVID and NO COVID with different levels of severity, the general distribution of simulated patient ages and the patient arrival rates distribution due to hours of the day.

Patient arrival is the emergency department simulator's input, directly influencing the system's behavior. A precision model to reflect patient arrival is necessary to simulate and predict the behavior of an emergency department; the patient arrival model includes arrival patients, in the Figure 7 shown the patient arrival rates distribution due to hours of the day in the hospital. This figure shows the arrival of patients at the hospital according to the time and day of the week, and it can be seen that the range of approximately 6 to 21 hours is the range where patients go to the hospital the most.

One of the simulator results is that the distribution of L (acuity) among arrival patients was obtained through statistical analysis of the actual data and the overall patient age distribution, as shown in Figure 5 and Figure 6. Levels 1,2,3 are the most serious, and 4,5 are milder symptoms. As can be seen in Figure 5 and Figure 6, at severity level 1,2,3,4,5, the age range that most visits the hospital in the emergency area is between 40 and 80 years old.

VI. Conclusion

As a result of our research, we present an improvement/extension of a previous agent-based model for managing the emergency department during COVID-19. Based on such an emergency department and after carefully analyzing the care process, we have enhanced the model by adding the variables to patient agents and hospital staff participating in the transmission process. We manage different scenarios to adapt the simulator to pandemic situations, for example, separate emergency rooms for the infected and non-infected, to evaluate the effectiveness using different combinations such as laboratory tests, isolation, and other control policies.

In addition, our emergency clinical staff has been modeled incorporating two possible levels of experience: juniors (with limited or low experience) and seniors (with experience). This is very important because during a significant part of the "Covid attack", in addition to emergency intensivists (seniors), some health personnel from different specialties (juniors compared with the intensivists) were incorporated into the emergency department.

A set of synthetic input data has been prepared for the simulation, which is why the distribution of arrival patients had to be generated. COVID and NO COVID with different levels of severity, the general distribution of simulated patient

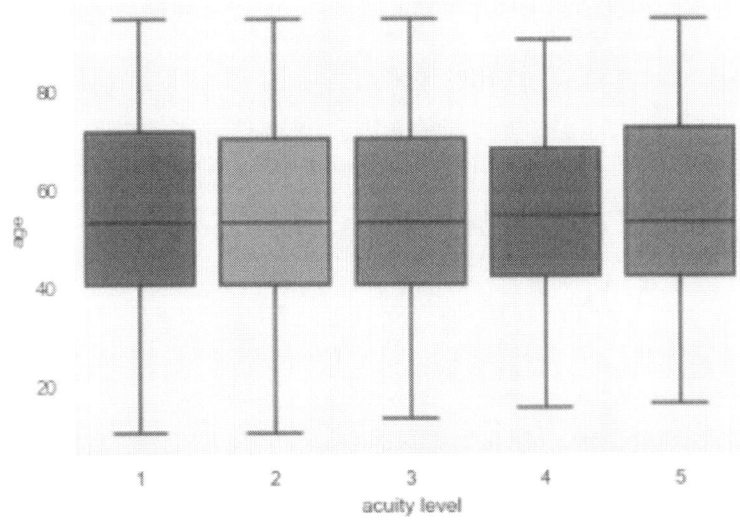

Fig. 6. Overall arrival acuity level and the patient's age distribution

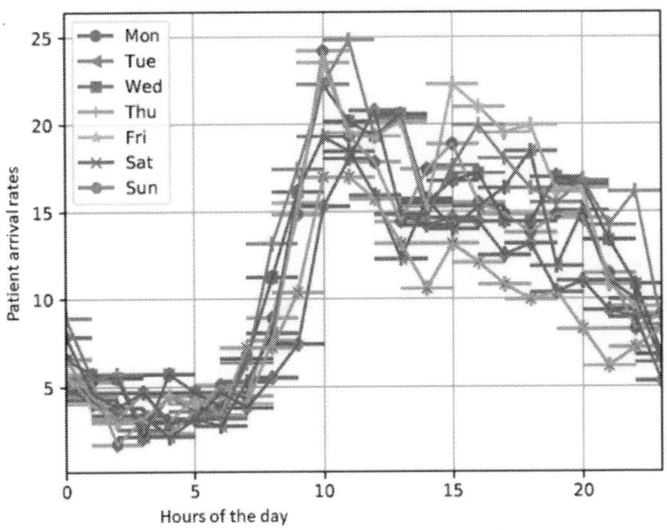

Fig. 7. Patient arrival rates distribution due to hour of day

ages and the patient arrival rates distribution due to hours of the day.

One of the significant differences between our job and the others is that this model/simulator of "COVID-19 in the emergency department" allows the emergency department managers to analyze and evaluate potential solutions for the clinical staff, boxes/beds, and devices.

Our future work is to make a digital twin of the Hospital, to validate and add more details to the agent-based simulator to make it as consistent and close as possible in a pandemic situation, and to build different scenarios for decision-making.

ACKNOWLEDGMENT

This research has been supported by the Agencia Estatal de Investigacion (AEI), Spain and the Fondo Europeo de Desarrollo Regional (FEDER) UE, under contract PID2020-112496GB-I00 and partially funded by the Fundacion Escuelas Universitarias Gimbernat (EUG).

This research has been funded through the scholarship by Carlos Antonio Lopez of Paraguay (Becal)

REFERENCES

[1] E. Bonabeau, "Agent-based modeling: Methods and techniques for simulating human systems," *Proceedings of the national academy of sciences*, vol. 99, no. suppl 3, pp. 7280–7287, 2002.

[2] P. Escudero-Marin and M. Pidd, "Using abms to simulate emergency departments," in *Proceedings of the 2011 Winter Simulation Conference (WSC)*, pp. 1239–1250, IEEE, 2011.

[3] M. Taboada, E. Cabrera, M. L. Iglesias, F. Epelde, and E. Luque, "An agent-based decision support system for hospitals emergency departments," *Procedia Computer Science*, vol. 4, pp. 1870–1879, 2011.

[4] E. Cabrera, E. Luque, M. Taboada, F. Epelde, and M. L. Iglesias, "Abms optimization for emergency departments," in *Proceedings of the 2012 winter simulation conference (WSC)*, pp. 1–12, IEEE, 2012.

[5] Z. Liu, D. Rexachs, E. Luque, F. Epelde, and E. Cabrera, "Simulating the micro-level behavior of emergency department for macro-level features prediction," in *2015 Winter Simulation Conference (WSC)*, pp. 171–182, IEEE, 2015.

[6] C. Jaramillo, D. Rexachs, F. Epelde, and E. Luque, "Virtual clinical trials: A tool for the study of transmission of nosocomial infections," *Procedia Computer Science*, vol. 108, pp. 109–118, 2017.

[7] C. Macal and M. North, "Introductory tutorial: Agent-based modeling and simulation," in *Proceedings of the winter simulation conference 2014*, pp. 6–20, IEEE, 2014.

[8] R. Moss et al., "Coronavirus disease model to inform transmission-reducing measures and health system preparedness, australia," *Emerging infectious diseases*, vol. 26, no. 12, p. 2844, 2020.

[9] M. Zeinalnezhad, A. G. Chofreh, F. A. Goni, J. J. Klemeš, and E. Sari, "Simulation and improvement of patients' workflow in heart clinics during covid-19 pandemic using timed coloured petri nets," *International journal of environmental research and public health*, vol. 17, no. 22, p. 8577, 2020.

[10] C. Currie et al., "How simulation modelling can help reduce the impact of covid-19," *Journal of Simulation*, vol. 14, no. 2, pp. 83–97, 2020.

[11] J. Le Lay et al., "Impact of covid-19 epidemics on bed requirements in a healthcare center using data-driven discrete-event simulation," in *2020 Winter Simulation Conference (WSC)*, pp. 771–781, IEEE, 2020.
[12] G. Fava, T. Giovannelli, M. Messedaglia, and M. Roma, "Effect of different patient peak arrivals on an emergency department via discrete event simulation: a case study," *Simulation*, p. 00375497211038756, 2021.
[13] V. Ahuja and L. V. Nair, "Artificial intelligence and technology in covid era: A narrative review," *Journal of Anaesthesiology, Clinical Pharmacology*, vol. 37, no. 1, p. 28, 2021.
[14] M. Laskowski, R. D. McLeod, M. R. Friesen, B. W. Podaima, and A. S. Alfa, "Models of emergency departments for reducing patient waiting times," *PloS one*, vol. 4, no. 7, p. e6127, 2009.
[15] Z. Chen, Z. Shu, X. Huang, K. Peng, and J. Pan, "Modelling analysis of covid-19 transmission and the state of emergency in japan," *International Journal of Environmental Research and Public Health*, vol. 18, no. 13, p. 6858, 2021.
[16] S. Abar, G. K. Theodoropoulos, P. Lemarinier, and G. M. P. O'Hare, "Agent Based Modelling and Simulation tools: A review of the state-of-art software," *Computer Science Review*, vol. 24, pp. 13–33, May 2017.
[17] U. Wilensky and W. Rand, *An introduction to agent-based modeling: modeling natural, social, and engineered complex systems with NetLogo*. Mit Press, 2015.
[18] E. Bruballa, A. Wong, D. Rexachs, E. Luque, and F. Epelde, "Evaluation of response capacity to patient attention demand in an emergency department," *Int. J. Adv. Syst. Meas*, vol. 10, no. 1-2, pp. 11–22, 2017.

A Case Study Concept for Supply Chain Resilience Analysis

Frank Schätter, Florian Haas, Frank Morelli
Pforzheim University
Business School
Tiefenbronner Str. 65, 75175 Pforzheim, Germany
frank.schaetter@hs-pforzheim.de, florian.haas@hs-pforzheim.de, frank.morelli@hs-pforzheim.de

Abstract — **In times of crisis, the strong characteristic of a supply chain to be resilient is an important success factor. However, logistics structures are complex, and it is difficult for companies to assess where the vulnerable and, thus, critical parts of the supply chain are located. To provide an applicable and easy-to-use method, a two-step approach of resilience analysis was developed. This paper introduces a case study illustrating the different steps of this approach and gives an outlook with a focus on process mining.**

Keywords - supply chain resilience; supply chain data modelling and simulation; key resilience areas; process mining.

I. Introduction

Supply chain resilience analysis is one of the most important success factors and trends of supply chain management in today's world, e.g., see [1]. Recent events, not least the Ukraine war, have shown like a burning glass how vulnerable supply chains are when hit by external crisis events. But the challenges for companies in dealing with such events are complex. Many companies felt the negative impacts in the form of disruptions to material flows throughout the supply chain. In many cases, the situation was even further exacerbated by an unexpected growth in the company's own business - as it was the case in the construction industry during the coronavirus pandemic.

One challenge that has arisen repeatedly in recent years is that logistics managers often know little about the state of resilience of their own supply chain. In this context, resilience can be defined by the so-called triangle, which highlights the ability of structures to cope with the maximum negative impact of a disruption and the duration of the disruption [2]. The triangle that emerges between these two dimensions characterizes the extent of the current state of resilience. Companies need to define measures to reduce the net negative impact of a disruption with respect to these two dimensions.

This is exactly where our research comes in. Due to the limited knowledge of logistics managers regarding the state of resilience, we propose an easy-to-use procedure to preventively increase the transparency in the network and to simulate possible management decisions to improve the state of resilience. We aim at positive impacts on the dimensions of the resilience triangle by limiting either the maximum loss or the time of disruption, e.g., by storing critical materials in warehouses or by applying a multi-sourcing strategy. In our earlier research, see [3,4], we concentrated on the process that a supply chain resilience analysis should go through. In this paper, we present a case study to illustrate our earlier thinking.

The methodology used to operationalize our approach is case study research for qualitative data collection. The objective of case study research is to adequately represent reality. Case studies are based on empirical investigations that analyze a currently relevant issue in a practical context. Holism, empiricism, interpretation, and empathy can be named as the central parameters for this method [5]. Their use proves to be particularly suitable when the boundary between observation and context is not clearly evident. Therefore, the framework conditions of the phenomenon to be observed must also be included. Related studies analyze relationships and processes and join different methods and data sources [6]. Moreover, the use of a well-defined theoretical basis is particularly important to ensure generalizability of results [7].

The remainder of this paper is organized as follows. In the next section, we briefly summarize our two-stage approach for supply chain resilience analysis, then we present a case study and show how the two stages can be translated into reality. This paper also provides insights into initial analytical results; the next step is to further detail, apply, and discuss the case study with practitioners and to move forward with a process mining application. Concrete initiatives in this regard are summarized in the concluding section.

II. Two-Stage Approach of Supply Chain Resilience Analysis

Supply chain resilience analysis should be data-driven by applying the data that is directly available to companies: transactional data, which represents the physical flows in the chain and can be easily captured by Enterprise Resource Planning (ERP) systems, and event logs, which can be used to understand the actual management processes. Based on these two data sets, we have developed an approach that provides a guideline for logistics managers to easily assess both the current state of strategic resilience of the supply chain and the potentials within the actual processes that led to this state [4].

The first stage of our approach relates to the *data-based modeling of material flows* in the supply chain. In this way, a company's network becomes transparent in terms of its incoming and outgoing material flows from internal and external suppliers to internal and external customers. It must be mentioned that a supply chain is actually a very complex structure when considering the entire value creation process. Inbound involves suppliers up to the provision of raw materials (tier 1-n); outbound involves customers' customers establishing their own relationships and forming large, interconnected networks. Rather than claiming to be able to model this entire network (which is a challenging, if not impossible, undertaking), we focus explicitly on the direct links in the supply chain from a company's perspective that can be influenced by its own decisions and collaboration initiatives. We have defined the relevant data sets (e.g., columns) to be included in a model sufficient to assess the strategic state of resilience in the enterprise [4]. These data roughly refer to delivery items highlighting the sender and receiver locations (e.g., cities, IDs) of a single material flow, the date and time of delivery, the quantity of material, and relevant metrics such as weight, volume, and landed cost.

We also introduced a set of eight so-called "Key Resilience Areas" (KRAs) that can be focused on to assess the current state of supply chain resilience, which can be derived from the data-based supply chain model [4]. These KRAs provide insights into critical parts of the supply chain. First, there are *vulnerable entities* due to the geographic distribution of included companies (KRA1), suppliers sourced from with a risky single-sourcing strategy (KRA2), the consolidation of different materials within shipments (KRA6), and factories and warehouses that could be critical for valuable materials due to high volumes (KRA8). Second, *vulnerable transport relations* can be revealed in terms of frequent transportation delays of certain relations between senders and receivers (KRA5) or relationships at risk due to long distances (KRA7). A third category of analyses refers to *vulnerable materials* in the sense of an analysis of materials that are currently (not) stored in warehouses (KRA3). In addition, the average storage duration of critical materials (KRA4) shows the total quantity of a stored material in relation to demand.

The use of KRAs can be understood as a strategic assessment of the current structure in terms of its vulnerability, which is an important first step in understanding the state of resilience. Although such transparency of vulnerability is indeed important when implementing long-term strategies to assess the benefits of resilience and efficiency in the supply chain, a deep understanding of the decisions and processes behind this state is essential. Therefore, we propose a second analytical stage that focuses on the actual management decisions related to the processes within the supply chain. *Process mining* has become an important approach in this regard.

One of the biggest challenges in using process mining is the overwhelming amount of event log data available in companies. This is exactly where our approach comes in. To ensure that the highly relevant event log data can be used to uncover real opportunities to improve the state of resilience of a supply chain, the first stage of strategic resilience analysis is used as a filter: the collected event log data should be analyzed with a particular focus on the identified vulnerable entities, transportation relations, and materials. The reason for this is that these parts within the supply chain are responsible for potentially weak resilience and should therefore be assessed and possibly changed.

III. Conception of a Case Study

In this section, we present the concept and initial analytical results of a case study to illustrate the application of the two stages of our approach. We focus on a manufacturing company whose production warehouse is in Hamburg, Germany. The resilience analysis should focus on the inbound material flows from the tier 1 suppliers. It is assumed that all incoming materials are brought to the production warehouse in Hamburg before being shipped to the actual production sites. The company follows a European strategy, which means that all suppliers are located in the European Economic Area, including the United Kingdom.

A. Stage 1: Strategic resilience analysis by using a data-based supply chain model

Stage 1 proposes to develop a data-based model of the supply chain to analyze and simulate vulnerabilities in the network. For the case study, this model represents all inbound material flows from suppliers to the warehouse. In the following, the relevant aspects in the creation of the model and the application of KRAs for strategic resilience analysis are presented and discussed.

Data-based supply chain model

Logistics managers are provided with a complete list of transaction datasets required for the inbound material flow modeling, see [4]. The case study therefore considers delivery items from the last 12 months obtained from the company's ERP system. Here, a delivery item is defined as a single material-specific flow from a supplier to the production warehouse in Hamburg. The data-based supply chain model, thus, comprises the following data sets:

- A sender ID as a unique identifier of the supplier; the ID is assigned in the ERP system, a total of 3,783 suppliers are considered in the case study (E1 to E3783).
- The receiver ID as a unique identifier of the recipient. In the case study, the production warehouse is defined by the receiver ID 'WH1'.
- The country and city where the supply chain entities are located. If they are not included in the transaction data, other location master data should be used. In total, the 3,783 suppliers are in 3,755 cities and 21 countries; WH1 is located in Hamburg, Germany.
- Sending date and receiving date as timestamps which shows the lead time of the delivery item directly; in the case study, we focus on historic shipments from 2021. In total, the data includes 256 dates of shipment and receipt. Furthermore, the defined to-be lead times are available within the data.

- A unique material number that defines the actual shipment; in the case study, we look at 5,865 material numbers (M1 to M5865).
- The quantity of material in the shipment; in the case study, all quantities are expressed as the number of individual parts (not packages).
- The corresponding total weight of the delivery item in the unit kg. If this is not included in the transaction data, it can be calculated simply by multiplying the weight of an individual part specified in the material master data by the quantity.
- Geographic information about the sender and the receiver such as latitude and longitude of all locations. If this information is not available in the company's location master data, it must be calculated; there are various open access tools for this purpose available. We have used the "Log-hub supply chain apps" for this purpose.

The data includes a total of 62,461 delivery items with a total weight of 8,550 tons delivered within 12 months. This corresponds to an average weight per delivery item of 136 kg. Fig. 1 illustrates the inbound supply chain, with each line referring to a specific transport link in the supply network.

Figure 1. Illustration of inbound material flows in the supply chain

We propose a series of KRAs to analyze the current state of strategic supply chain resilience. In the case study, we focus on inbound tier 1 material flows and, thus, on the strengths and weaknesses of the current sourcing structure chosen by the company. To gain a better understanding in this regard, the following KRAs are considered relevant to the case study: the geographic distribution of locations (KRA1), materials sourcing strategies (KRA2), lead time deviations (KRA5), and the transport distances and durations (KRA7).

<u>*State of resilience: KRA1 & KRA2*</u>

With respect to KRA2, 64.7% of the supplied weight [kg] and 75.6% of the material numbers [#] refer to a single-sourcing approach - or at least to a strategy where the incoming material flows were mainly ordered from only one supplier within the last 12 months. Table I provides an overview of the top 10 single-sourcing material IDs by total weight. We see that the corresponding suppliers (out of 2,195 suppliers) account for 21.6% of the total single-sourcing material flow. This is an important aspect of resilience because if one of these suppliers was to fail, there would be significant disruption to the company's production facilities.

TABLE I. TOP 10 SINGLE-SOURCING SUPPLIERS BY WEIGHT [KG]

Material ID	Sender ID	Sender City & Country	Weight [kg]	Avg. del. weight [kg]	Weight share [%]
M2537	E1646	Kojetin, CZ	381.016	809	6,89%
M2868	E2434	Opava, CZ	183.688	633	3,32%
M441	E3184	Steinfurt, DE	93.462	1.507	1,69%
M2250	E3429	Vaterstetten, DE	86.219	713	1,56%
M4723	E2273	Neratovice, CZ	79.114	977	1,43%
M3417	E878	Duchcov, CZ	66.762	514	1,21%
M985	E1002	Ettlingen, DE	62.622	963	1,13%
M930	E2666	Radebeul, DE	62.554	2.406	1,13%
M5097	E2677	Rakovnik, CZ	61.434	407	1,11%
M444	E1509	Idstein, DE	59.701	1.456	1,08%
M2126	E3184	Steinfurt, DE	58.996	1.054	1,07%

Based on the bills of materials of the company under consideration, an indicator was added to the material master to indicate whether a material ID should be considered as critical or not (e.g., referring to the ABC/XYZ classification per material ID). The inbound data shows that 822 single-sourcing suppliers (from 2,195) refer to a material ID that can be classified as critical. Table II provides an overview of the geographic clusters of these suppliers in relation to the top 5 countries, the number of critical suppliers in each country, and the weight.

TABLE II. CRITICAL SUPPLIERS PER COUNTRY (TOP 5)

Country	Suppliers [#]	Weight [kg]	Weight [%]
DE	281	132,903	23.47%
CZ	271	397,199	70.15%
SK	116	1,430	0.25%
FR	68	10,717	1.89%
IT	41	6,933	1.22%

It becomes clear that Germany and the Czech Republic represent a geographical cluster of single-sourcing suppliers for critical materials (KRA1). In particular, the Czech Republic appears to be a very important region, as 70.15% of incoming material flows by weight [kg] are shipped from there. Hence, although most of these suppliers are in Germany (282), the functioning of shipments from the Czech Republic is of great importance for a functioning supply chain. In addition, a comparison of the top ten individual suppliers of critical materials and the top ten individual suppliers overall (see Table I) shows an overlap of six suppliers (E1646, E2434, E3184, E2273, E878, E2666, E3184). Thereby, five of these suppliers are in the Czech Republic, which underlines the criticality of the region. Fig. 2 summarizes the findings from the KRA1 analysis in terms of the top 30 suppliers of critical materials by shipping weight [kg].

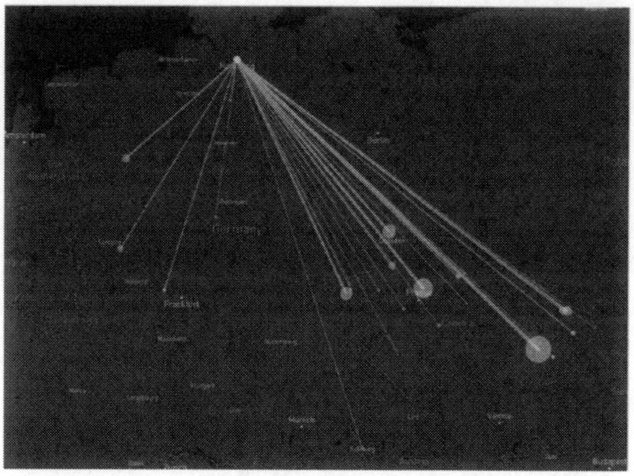

Figure 2. The top 30 single-sourcing suppliers of critical materials

State of resilience: KRA5 & KRA7

A deeper understanding of the resilience state of inbound material flows can be gained by examining the lead times experienced by suppliers in the past (here: 12 months). Second, the geographic locations of the suppliers provide direct insight into the actual transportation time and distance to the recipient - the longer this time and distance, the more susceptible the relation is to disruption (KRA7).

In the model, we can see target lead times of 7 days (Germany) and 20 days (e.g., Finland) defined by the companies. In addition, the actual lead time can be calculated based on the available sending and receiving time stamps. Since there are usually multiple shipments available per supplier within the considered time frame, we analyze the average lead time per supplier by comparing this time with the defined target lead time. The results show that in 2021, 371 suppliers (9.9%) had an average lead time deviation of more than 7 days. The corresponding shipping weight of these suppliers was relatively low (0.97%) and only 673 delivery items were affected.

While this suggests a relatively robust structure and, thus, resilience of the current network, there is still a risk that those suppliers could cause significant supply chain disruptions. This is particularly true for 151 suppliers that are in addition single-sourcing suppliers, and even more specifically for 20 of these single-sourcing suppliers who are delivering critical materials. It is imperative that decision makers should continue to monitor these suppliers, develop strategies to improve their delivery times, and avoid supply chain disruptions.

Finally, KRA7 refers to those suppliers characterized by long transport distances and/or times. In particular, single-sourcing suppliers identified in KRA5 that also supply critical materials face an increased risk of disruption if they are located at a great distance. The KRA analysis shows that 8 of these 20 suppliers are long-distance suppliers. Fig. 3 summarizes the results with respect to the 20 single-sourcing suppliers of critical materials; the 8 long-distance suppliers - which by definition are more than 1,200 km away from the warehouse - are highlighted in white.

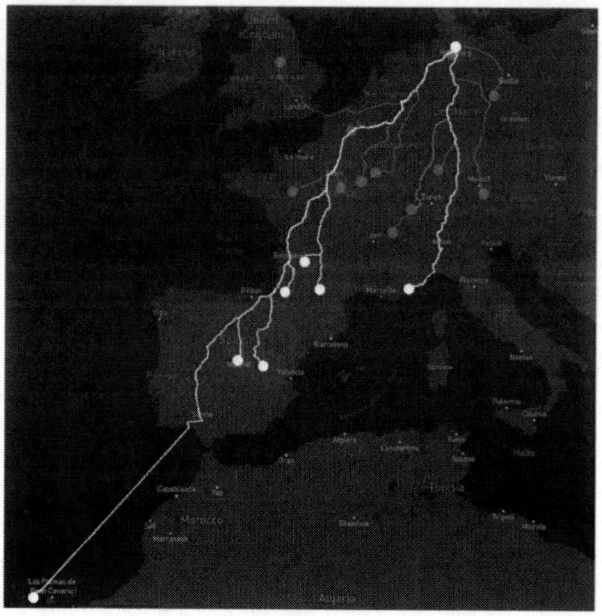

Figure 3. Critical single-sourcing suppliers regarding KRA5 & KRA7

B. *Stage 2: Process mining of procurement strategy*

In stage 2 of our approach, we suggest using process mining to precisely examine delivery items which are classified as critical in stage 1 in a more detailed analysis regarding root causes. Process mining offers the advantage of identifying the as-is process with its variants as it actually runs in the company. In this way, all foreseen and especially non-foreseen deviations become transparent.

Introduction to event-log based process mining

The process mining approach subsumes methods for analyzing business processes based on digital traces that instances leave in the system during their execution [8]. Process mining is based on various data sources that are collected based on events in an event log. On the one hand, the preparation of event logs must focus on the relevant data in the sense of simplicity according to Occam's razor; on the other hand, the loss of information must be minimized so that the event log is valid [9]. To conduct process mining, it is necessary to store additional data elements (e.g., attributes of resources) to leverage information about resources and organizational perspective. Process steps that were not previously recorded in terms of data can be considered as part of process mining. However, they must be added to the event log so that they can be considered within the current model. Since such manual processing usually proves to be time-consuming and uneconomical in operational practice, corresponding data has rarely been generated or used to date [10]. However, the event log must contain the relevant data for the considered process.

Process mining with focus on the procurement process

In the case study, we focus on the procurement process of the company under consideration. The application of process mining requires the execution of three steps. Step 1 is the collection of all events in an event log that include all relevant actions taken by the planner. The order line item should be used to uniquely identify the events. In step 2, the to-be process model is generated. All actions to reveal the standard procurement process are being plotted. Fig. 4 illustrates the process model regarding the procurement process as the result of step 2; the flashes show where the process can be interrupted.

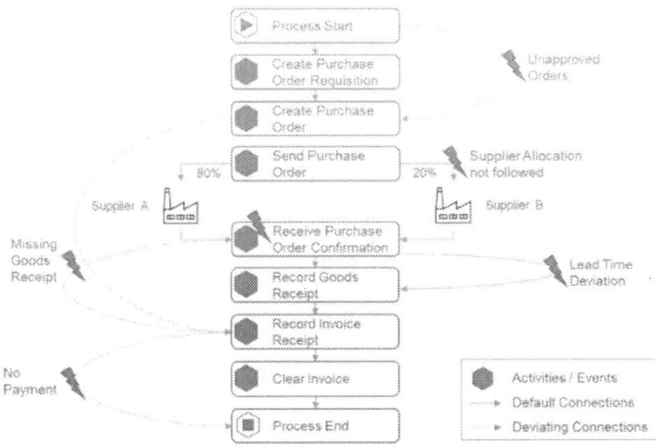

Figure 4. Generation of the process model using the example of a procurement process (step 2)

Step 3 finally focuses on the process analysis and improvements: the process starts with the creation of a purchase order requisition. If the first visible event is the created purchase order, it becomes transparent that an approval in the form of a purchase requisition is possibly missing. The next event that should be logged is that the purchase order has been sent to the supplier and confirmed. If the setting provides that orders should be allocated between more than one supplier, e.g., the setup follows a dual or even multiple procurement strategy, but the event log shows that purchase order confirmations are only received by one supplier. This immediately points to a possible shortfall in the process with an immediate negative impact on a company's state of resilience for this material. Also, if the event log shows that no purchase order confirmation has been received (although the supplier is maybe delivering), we can assume a lack in the process that negatively impacts the company's ability to act well in advance before a shortage becomes apparent because the material is actually missing.

Moreover, by the event goods receipt, a deviation in lead time from what has been agreed with the supplier can be detected. A permanently increased lead-time exposes the company to additional risks. Often forgotten is payment as the last step in the procurement process. The acceptance of an invoice for material that might not even been received is a financial risk. This - from a supply chain perspective more critical step - occurs if the invoice is properly cleared. Missing on-time payment can not only lead to a discontinued supply but also harm the company's reputation amongst its suppliers which negatively impacts the company's state in terms of preferred delivery in a bottleneck situation.

The provided examples underline the power of process mining. In fact, the purchasing process generally being followed becomes transparent as well as - even more important - unforeseen and unknown deviations from the standard. Now we are using the findings from stage 1 to focus our analysis in a targeted manner on precisely those materials and suppliers that were previously classified as critical. In this way, our approach allows us to reduce the extent of the order lines to be analyzed in a way that makes it manageable in practice. Immediate measures directly addressing the weaknesses identified by the event logs can be simulated and followed through.

Further advantages of the suggested two-step approach of a supply chain resilience analysis providing insights on the eight KRAs followed by implementation of measures derived from process mining in a very cost-effective way can be further illustrated using the procurement process. Decisions taken in the Source-to-Contract phase that expose the company to an increased supply risks can be identified by a combination of KRA2 (sourcing strategy of materials), KRA5 (transport delays), and KRA7 (transport distance). This allows to increase the resilience of a company's supply chain also from a strategic perspective, e.g., by increasing the number of suppliers, located at least domestically or even globally. Strategic decisions in terms of sourcing amongst others could also be to move supply from direct to indirect sources, to use bigger suppliers and to invest in long-term relationships.

Given the strategy has been adjusted to address weaknesses in the eight KRAs the second step assures that the strategy is also followed through the whole organization. Process mining relentlessly logs every operational decision as an event and, thus, every deviation becomes transparent and can be addressed by managerial action.

IV. CONCLUSION AND FUTURE WORK

Our research is based on real-world experience of past global crises which have shown that, first, a resilient supply chain design can be a success factor and, second, the current state of resilience is often not transparently available to logistics managers. Therefore, we developed a two-stage approach that sequentially uses data analytics and process mining to capture and improve the state of resilience within the supply chain. In this paper, we presented the concept of a case study focusing on the inbound material flows of a company whose warehouse is in Hamburg, Germany.

According to the first stage of our approach, we developed a data-based supply chain model that summarizes the shipments of materials from suppliers to warehouses. Using this model, we identified and analyzed elements in the supply chain that could be at risk, such as vulnerable locations or materials, via so-called KRAs. In the second stage of the approach, we showed how process mining of current procurement event logs can provide further insight into the decisions made by the company in the past and highlight measures to improve the current state of resilience. Thus, possible future configurations of the supply chain can be simulated and, thus, provide strategic decision support for logistics managers. It must be mentioned that this second stage is a work in progress concept which has not yet been verified with real data in the form of event logs. However, the case study illustrated the applicability of transaction data in terms of assessing the strategic state of resilience of a supply chain.

Hence, the next step required for the continuation of the approach presented is to choose a business case to gather the data elements. The following guiding principles, based on the "Process Mining Manifesto" are of particular importance here [11]. First, significant events need to be identified and evaluated. By looking at an example of a procurement process that follows a fixed procedure also for compliance reasons, we assume that the quality criteria as defined by Peters et al. can be met [10]. The next principle that needs to be considered for the continued research is the amount and condition of data that is being used. It proves to be purposeful to adjust the quantity and the quality of the data to one's own requirements. The level of detail or granularity of the selected attributes plays an important role for the event log data. Looking at a procurement process, it makes sense to be able to trace the document flow for individual purchase order items or lines (and not just purchase orders). For this, attributes such as the ID (identification number) of the purchase order items, the purchase order number or the material number are required [10]. Also, the question must be clarified which data should be analyzed to avoid "noise" in the sense of taking irrelevant data into account [11]. From our view, the presented case study results already show at this point that the two-step approach to supply chain resilience analysis with the KRAs concept is suitable for this purpose.

A limitation of contemporary process mining techniques can be seen in the fact that they tend to focus on distinct process instances and not on the multi-case setting of business process simulation. An event log with a unique and consistent case ID is available for this purpose. To utilize a multi-case context in supply chain resilience management, approaches, such as the multi-event-log and the execution management system from Celonis or the object-centered process mining of van der Aalst et al. can be applied [13,14,15]. Their goal is to provide multiple event logs that allow process correlations to be analyzed without having an overarching case ID. For the above-mentioned reasons, we intend to continue our research on the example of the procurement process. The KRA developed in stage 1 refer, however, also still to a whole set of other supply chain related processes of a company's operational performance. As things stand today, these must be analyzed individually by means of process mining, analogous to the procedure described for the example of the procurement process in stage 2. Here, a still more extensive linkage and recognition of the continuity would be desirable. We see the chance to even create an overarching case ID, for example, by linking the purchase order item with the transport order in the future. In the complex field of supply chain resilience management, this fact proves to be of central importance.

ACKNOWLEDGMENT

The supply chain visualizations in Fig. 1-3 were created using the Log-hub supply chain apps. Log-hub provided us with a free license for research purposes, for which we would like to express our sincere thanks.

REFERENCES

[1] Forbes, "2022 Global Supply Chains: Four trends that will shape the future," [Online], available from: https://www.forbes.com/sites/sap/2022/01/19/2022-global-supply-chains-four-trends-that-will-shape-the-future/?sh=23abf83d3ef4

[2] H. Carvalho, S.G. Azevedo, and V. Cruz-Machado, "Supply chain management resilience: a theory building approach," International Journal of Supply Chain and Operations Resilience, 1(1), pp. 3-27, 2014.

[3] F. Schätter and F. Morelli, "Business Process Simulation Focusing Supply Chain Risk Management Aspects," Special Track: Simulation and Modelling in Supply Chains, along with SIMUL 2021, pp. 38-43, 2021.

[4] F. Schätter, F. Morelli, and F. Haas, "Supply Chain Resilience Management Using Process Mining," European Council for Modelling and Simulation (Ed.), Communications of the ECMS Volume 36, Issue 1, June 2022, pp. 121-127, ECMS Digital Library, 2022.

[5] G. Gemmel, "Strategisches Informationsmanagement in Großprojekten der Industrie," [in English: „Information management in large-scale industrial projects"], Wiesbaden: Springer Verlag, 2014.

[6] G. Thomas, "How to do your case study," Los Angeles: SAGE Publications Limited, 2021.

[7] R.K. Yin, "Case study research and applications: Design and methods," Los Angeles, CA: SAGE Publications, Inc., 2018.

[8] R. Buck-Emden and F. Dahmann, "Analyse von Studienverläufen mit Process-Mining-Techniken," [in English: „Analysis of study progress with process mining techniques"], HMD Praxis der Wirtschaftsinformatik (55:4), pp. 846-865, doi: 10.1365/s40702-018-0410-1, 2018.

[9] S. Suriadi, R. Andrews, A.H.M. ter Hofstede, and M.T. Wynn, "Event log imperfection patterns for process mining: Towards a systematic approach to cleaning event logs," Information Systems (64), pp. 132–150 doi: 10.1016/j.is.2016.07.011, 2017.

[10] R. Peters and M. Nauroth, "Process-Mining," Wiesbaden: Springer-Gabler, 2019.

[11] W. van der Aalst, A. Adriansyah, A.K.A. de Medeiros, F. Arcieri, T. Baier, and T. Blickle, "Process Mining Manifesto," Business Process Management Workshops. BPM 2011 International Workshops, Clermont-Ferrand, France, August 29, 2011, F. Daniel, K. Barkaoui, S. Dustdar (Eds.), Springer, Berlin, pp. 169–194, 2012.

[12] N. Martin, B. Depaire, and A. Caris, "The Use of Process Mining in a Business Process Simulation Context: Overview and Challenges," IEEE Symposium on Computational Intelligence and Data Mining (CIDM), Orlando, FL (USA), pp. 1-8, 2014, ISBN: 978-1-4799-4518-4, 2014.

[13] W. van der Aalst and A. Berti, "Discovering Object-Centric Petri Nets," [Online], available from: http://arxiv.org/pdf/2010.02047v1, 2020.

[14] A.F. Ghahfarokhi, G. Park, A. Berti, and W. van der Aalst, "OCEL: A Standard for Object-Centric Event Logs," L. Bellatreche, M. Dumas, P. Karras, R. Matulevicius, A. Awad, M. Weidlich, M. Ivanoic, and O. Hartig (eds.), Communications in Computer and Information Science 1450, New Trends in Database and Information Systems, Springer-Verlag, pp. 169-175, 2021.

[15] W. van der Aalst, "Object-Centric Process Mining: Dealing with Divergence and Convergence in Event Data," P.C. Olveczky, G. Salaün (eds.), Software Engineering and Formal Methods, 17th International Conference, SEFM, Oslo, Norway, September 18-20, pp. 3-25, 2019.

Performance of Storage Strategies in a Highbay Warehouse

Frank Herrmann
Ostbayerische Technische Hochschule Regensburg - University of Applied Sciences Regensburg
Innovation and Competence Centre for Production Logistics and Factory Planning (IPF)
PO box 120327, 93025 Regensburg, Germany
E-Mail: Frank.Herrmann@OTH-Regensburg.de

Abstract— **Storage and retrieval times of goods in inventory processes determine the efficiency of highbay warehouses in companies. These times are highly dependent on the performance of rack feeders. Storage strategies have the greatest influence on this performance. This paper shows the impact of an efficient control of rack feeders through storage strategies. Storage strategies which are typically used in industrial inventory processes are analysed. For the analysis, a simulation system is implemented, so that the real process times are similar to the simulated ones. This results in recommendations for the use of storage strategies in companies.**

Keywords-Inventory processes, simulation of storages and retrievals of goods, storage strategies, highbay warehouse.

I. INTRODUCTION

In industrial production, huge warehouses, mostly in the form of a highbay warehouse, are used for the coordination of procurement processes, production processes and distribution processes within an enterprise and also between enterprises along the logistic process chain (see Figure 1 and [1][2][4]-[10][12]). In addition to this time bridging structure, inventory management becomes more and more important which realises an efficient order related picking [2][3][5]-[8][12]. Particularly, with an almost fully occupied automatic warehouse, the performance necessary for the handling of goods is not reached for picking in the warehouse.

Attempts are often made to improve the performance of warehouses by elaborate storage and handling measures [1][2][4][5][12]. In addition, in very highly automated companies, special approaches from research, as described in [14], can be used. An important performance criterion is the maximization of the handling of goods in the warehouse, i.e. the warehouse should be able to transfer to stock or to remove from stock as many storage units as possible within a given time span (e.g., an hour) [1][2][5]-[8][12][13].

Figure 1. View of a highbay warehouse – provided by Klug GmbH integrated systems.

The rest of the paper is structured as follows. Section II describes storage in large warehouses, Section III presents the key performance indicators, Section IV describes some storage strategies, followed by the testbed problem in Section V. Section VI presents the simulation study, with the results in Section VII. An analysis of the results is done in Section VIII and we conclude the work in Section IX.

II. STORAGE

With automatic warehouses, the product is stored in free-mounted racks. Figure 2 shows a model of a rack of the length L, height H and depth T (see [1][2][5]-[8]) and a Rack Feeder (RF). The RF is used to access the stored product.

The RF accesses the stored product usually stacked on palettes. A RF is an automated conveyor which simultaneously drives through a lane in a warehouse, heads for a certain rack shelf of height H about a lifting device and moves its load suspension device (LSD) into the rack shelves of depth T in order to pick or lay bins.

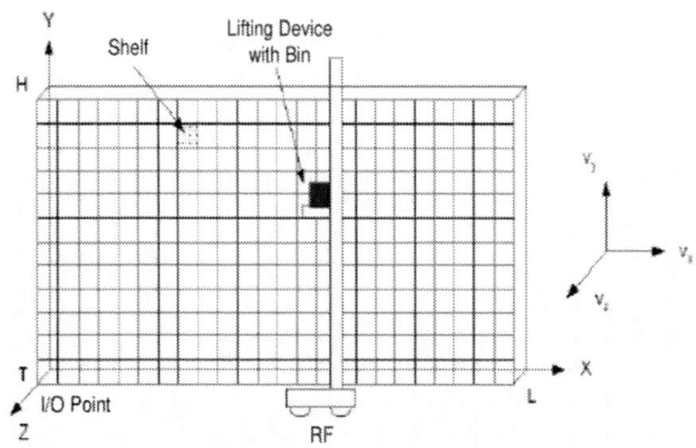

Figure 2. Model of a rack with rack feeder (RF) and entry (I) / exit (O) point (I/O point); speed (v) – see e.g. [8]

A rack feeder [1][2][4][8] can be used with single cycle or double cycle. With a single cycle, the rack feeder in the entry (I) / exit (O) point (I/O point) of the rack waits for a transport order. In the case of a transfer to stock, a bin is laid in the nearest free rack shelf. Afterwards, the rack feeder returns to the transfer point. In the case of a removal from stock, the needed rack shelf is headed and the bin is provided in the transfer point. With a double cycle, however, the rack feeder after an occurred storage (transfer to stock) can head immediately for another rack shelf from which a retrieval (remove from stock) should be affected.

III. KEY PERFORMANCE INDICATORS

The rack feeder operation has an effect on storage and retrieval times. These times are determined by the trajectory for the carriage and for the lift, because the number of goods which are transferred to stock or removed from stock are to be held steady during the analysis period. Such a trajectory is called working cycle, and the required time is called cycle time. The trajectory of the rack feeder consists of these phases: accelerating, driving at steady speed, braking, positioning at the destination. At the destination, a load suspension device cycle is carried out to take up or to deliver a bin. Such a cycle consists of extending the telescopic fork or table, lifting the lift truck, retracting the telescopic fork and lowering the lift truck – with a belt conveyor, there is no lifting and lowering.

Working cycles have variable driving times. The real speed is shown in Figure 3 (see also [1][2][5][7]). In most publications, times for accelerating, braking and positioning are not regarded. Instead, the well-known Tschebyscheff metric is applied on the constant speed in x and y directions.

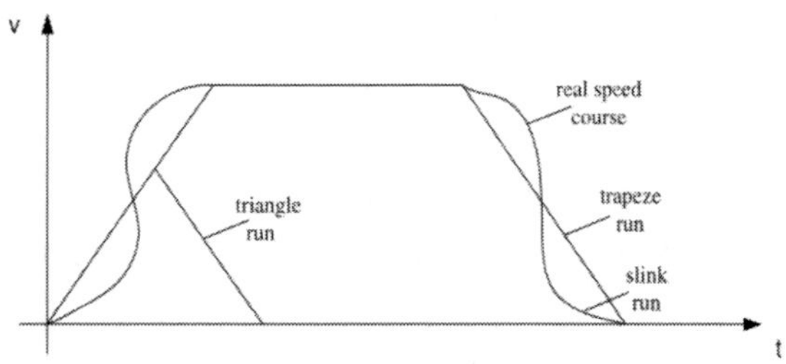

Figure 3. Real and simplified speed course (v).

Beside these variable driving times, a load suspension device cycle has constant times for positioning, for controlling that the correct shelf was reached and for switching as well as controlling operations. These times depend on specific technical data of a rack feeder. Altogether, this time is called “dead time“.

In [1] and [7], for each single time, a formula is deduced in detail. The used simulation system calculates the single times by these formulas and their sum is the (total) cycle time. For the test problem which is described below, cycle times were measured and compared to the calculated ones. In each case, the difference between these times was less than one second. Therefore, the simulation of storages and retrievals of goods in a warehouse by a rack feeder corresponds to reality.

IV. STORAGE STRATEGIES

In today's industrial warehouse processes, the following storage strategies are applied [1][2][5]-[7]:

1. Accidental (storage):
   By an accidental storage, any free shelf is selected for the bin to be stored. Only restrictions about the size of a shelf and the allowed weight are considered.
2. (Storage after) Zones:
   The shelves in the warehouse are divided into zones. Each item is stored in exactly one zone. Therefore, each product has a so-called zone flag. For storing a product with zone flag F, a free shelf near to the I/O point with zone flag F is chosen.
3. (Strategy of the) Fastest neighbour:
   With double cycles, a storage shelf A to a retrieval shelf B is selected so that A can be reached from B as quickly as possible. With single cycles, the shelf for storage is chosen so that it can be reached from the storage track as quickly as possible.
4. Channel (optimized storage):
   In a multiple-depth warehouse, the bins are stored in a channel from two consecutive shelves. A free channel is searched so that:
   - as many bins as possible of the load suspension device fit – different bin types are often excluded for channels – and
   - the beginning of the allocation of a channel is avoided.
5. Combination of different storage strategies: A strategy is the combination of the strategies zones and fastest neighbour. In the case of single cycles, the strategy after zones is used. With double cycles, the strategy of the fastest neighbour is applied. In addition, various combinations of the strategies zones and channel – with various channels – are regarded.
   In a multiple-deep warehouse, various combinations of the strategies zones and channel are investigated. Normally, bins are stored by strategy zones. Only in special cases a specific type of strategy channel is used. These are:
   - Combination of strategies zones and channel 1:
     If all bins on the Load Suspension Device (LSD) have the same zone flag and in this zone no channel with suitable depth is free, then a suitable channel in an adjacent zone is chosen.
   - Combination of strategies zones and channel 2:
     a channel with the zone Flag (F) of the bin at position 1 in the LSD is chosen. This ensures that at least one bin is in the correct zone z. If the zone z is occupied, then a free shelf nearby zone z is chosen.
   - Combination of strategies zones and channel 3:
     The normal procedure that the bins are stored by strategy zones is used if all bins on the LSD have the same zone flag. Otherwise, strategy channel is applied.
     If the suitable zone is occupied, then strategy channel is applied.

V. TEST PROBLEM

The problem is a modification of a small sized highbay warehouse at Leopold Fiebig GmbH in Karlsruhe, Germany. It consists of one aisle and two racks. Each rack has 10 fields in x direction (compare with Figure 2) and 32 fields in y direction. In z direction, there are two shelves, one behind the other. Each shelf can carry a bin. If both shelves are used and only the bin in the second shelf is taken, a stock transfer is necessary. Altogether, the warehouse has 1280 shelves. A rack is 4.5 m long, 8.5 m high and 1.30 m deep. The fields are started by a rack feeder which owns a load suspension device with two shelves. By a lifting bar construction of the rack feeder, high speeds in x and y direction are realized. Loading aids are stored twofold-depth or fourfold-depth. Such types of highbay warehouse are discussed in the literature under the name Commissioner (see, e.g. [4][9][10]).

VI. SIMULATION STUDY

For the simulation study, common commercially available simulation tools such as Plant Simulation from Siemens were first evaluated against a proprietary development. The tools allow extensive visualisations of the processes. However, they cannot significantly reduce the development effort required to control the handling of randomly arriving orders in and out of storage.

A tool is developed to simulate and analyse various highbay warehouses and storage strategies. It is implemented in C++. The tool uses an Oracle database for permanent data storage and to support the search for bays.

To validate the model, log files of the rack feeders in the highbay warehouse at Leopold Fiebig GmbH in Karlsruhe, Germany, were evaluated. These files were used to determine the driving time between the coordinates approached. With the help of a test module, the driving times of the rack feeders are calculated in the simulation for the same coordinates. Positioning times and grinding times are added to the calculated driving times and these are then compared with the real driving times. The differences in the driving times are less than one second. The simplifications mentioned above are likely to have a certain impact. This deviation is acceptable for the simulation. Thus, the simulation model and reality are identical if the simulation runs only slowly enough.

Due to the above-mentioned log files, accidental storages and retrievals appear – as typical in warehouses. In this case, they are normally distributed.

VII. NUMERICAL RESULTS

In industrial warehouses, the storage and retrieval of orders vary based on their importance described by an ABC indicator. For the simulations of an ABC indicator with the storage and retrieval orders 80% of A bin, 15% of B bin and 5% of C bin was chosen. With the single cycles or with the single and double cycles, 15 is the number of storages and retrievals per simulation experiment and 5 is the standard deviation. With pure double cycles, the standard deviation is put on 0 to receive the same number of storage and retrieval orders for every simulation experiment. The highbay warehouse in the test problem has three channels. Therefore, there are three combinations of the strategy zones and optimized channel, namely “combination of zone and channel 1”, “combination of zone and channel 2” as well as “combination of zone and channel 3”.

In the case of single cycles, Figure 4 shows the mean cycle times for the different storage strategies. These cycle times increase with the warehouse utilization. The increase is about 5 to 10% if the warehouse utilization rises from 50% to 99%. The strategy “channel” is mostly influenced by the warehouse utilization. With a warehouse utilization of 50% and 80%, the strategy “zone” delivers the maximum mean cycle times. With a warehouse utilization of 99%, the strategy “channel” has the worst value. The strategy “combination of zone and channel 3“ always delivers the minimum mean cycle times. The percental deviation of the best strategy to the worst strategy amounts with a warehouse utilization of 50% to 7.96%, with a warehouse utilization of 80% to 6.96 %, and with a warehouse utilization of 99% to 5.08%. So, the increase in output by the application of the best storage strategy with rising warehouse utilization becomes smaller.

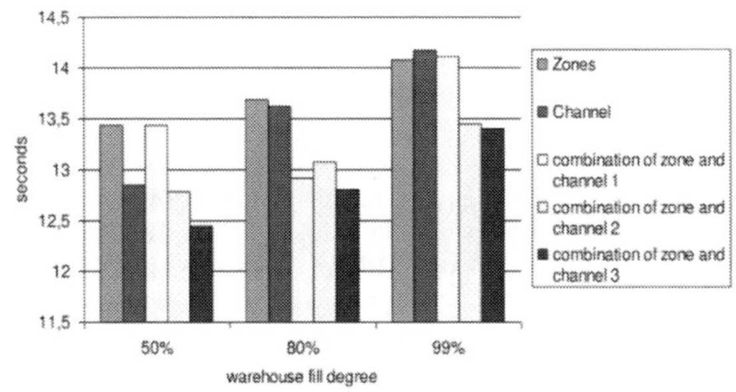

Figure 4. Mean cycle times with single cycles.

The use of the strategy “combination of zone and channel 3“ causes the least stock transfers, see Figure 5. The decrease of the number of stock transfers arises by accidental determination of the number of bins for retrievals – in this case, the number of bins for retrievals decreases. The probability of stock transfers is between 44% and 52%. The smallest values are reached for every warehouse filling degree by the strategy “combination of zone and channel 3“.

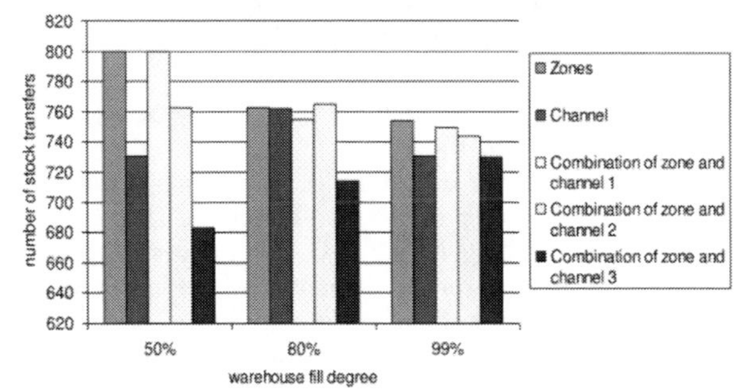

Figure 5. Number of stock transfers with single cycles.

Single cycles and double cycles give the same results structurally like with the single cycles; they are shown in

Figure 6. The percental deviation shows that the relative difference decreases between the best strategy and the worst strategy with rising warehouse filling degree and also the improvement in performance decreases by the use of the most favorable strategy. Also, in this case, the mean cycle time correlates with the warehouse filling degree.

Figure 6 shows the stock transfers to the single warehouse filling degrees for every storage strategy. The strategy "combination of zone and channel 3" has the smallest number of stock transfers at the warehouse filling degrees of 50% and 80%. With a warehouse filling degree of 99%, the strategy "channel" causes the smallest values.

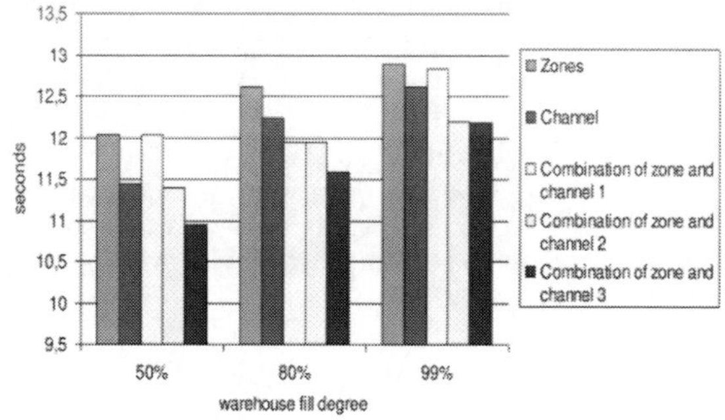

Figure 6. Mean cycle times with single and double cycles.

Comparing Figure 6 and Figure 7 shows that the strategy with the highest mean cycle times does not always have the most stock transfers and vice versa. Also, the strategies with the smallest mean cycle times do not always have the least stock transfers. Therefore, based on the number of stock transfers, one cannot make a statement about the quality of a strategy.

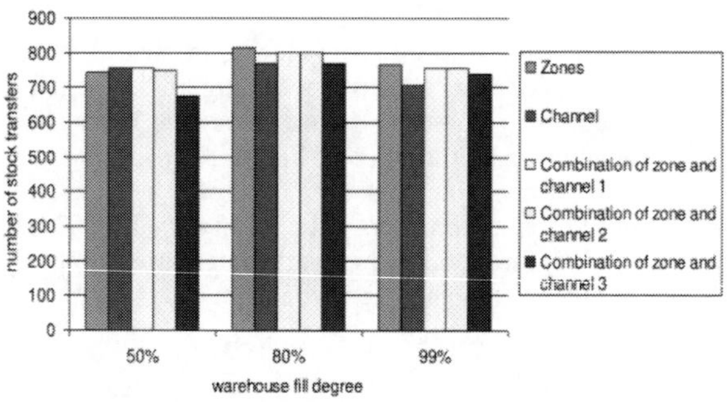

Figure 7. Number of stock transfers with single and double cycles.

The results for double cycles are essentially the same as the ones with single cycle and double cycle. They are shown in Figure 8 and Figure 9. Also, here, the strategies of type "combination of zone and channel" react most clearly to the increase of the warehouse filling degree. A comparison of these deviations with the deviations from both previous simulation runs shows that with double cycle the relative profit is the largest by the most favorable storage strategy. Indeed, the improvement in performance here also decreases with the warehouse filling degree.

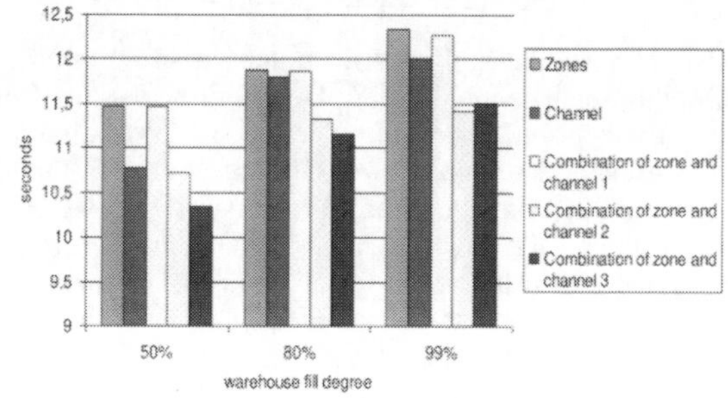

Figure 8. Mean cycle times with double cycles.

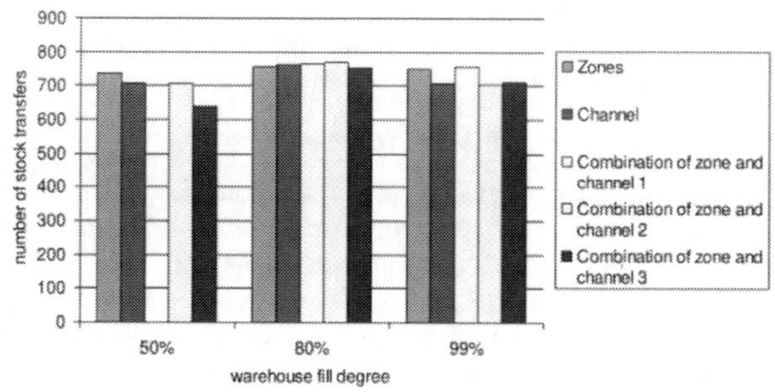

Figure 9. Number of stock transfers with double cycles.

There is no warehouse strategy that always generates the most or the least stock transfers. With a warehouse filling degree of 50%, there is a correlation between the number of stock transfers and the mean cycle time. Such a correlation does not exist with other warehouse filling degrees. Hence, the number of stock transfers cannot be inferred from the mean cycle time and vice versa.

VIII. IMPROVED ANALYSIS COMPARED TO LITERATURE

Lipplot and Blunck specify in [11] the increase of the handling of goods in warehouses with zones compared with warehouses without zones is between 15% and 20%. Gudehus says in [4] that the increase of the handling of goods by using zones is limited to 15%. The simulation shows that the mean cycle times by strategy zones is lower about 40% than by strategy channel in the case of a warehouse utilization of 50%. With increasing warehouse utilization the relative reduction is lower; in the case of a warehouse utilization of 99% the general proves that the improvement in performance depends on the ABC indicator of orders, the warehouse utilization as well as the sequence of storages and retrievals.

Seemüller regards in [7] the strategies chaotic storage, which fits with the strategy accidental (storage), storage close to retrieval, which is comparable to the strategy of the fastest neighbour, and multiple storage in which several bins are stored side by side. In his calculations, Seemüller regards a rack feeder with three load suspension devices (next to one another). In a single-deep warehouse, the performance of the strategy chaotic storage is independent of the warehouse utilization and significantly lower than using the other two strategies. This investigation exposes the same results. Seemüller approves a reduction in the mean cycle times by using double cycles which is approved by this investigation as well. But, this investigation in particular and a simulation in general, show concrete values.

There are no quantitative results published about the improvement in performance of multiple-deep warehouses by storage strategies. Nevertheless, investigations about storage strategies for multiple-deep warehouses were published.

Seemüller regards in [7] the strategies chaotic storage, storage close to retrieval and multiple storage for multiple-deep warehouses. So, the most effective strategy in this investigation is not investigated by Seemüller.

The probability of stock transfers is analyzed in [6]. The authors describe the run of the probabilities of stock transfers in a twice-deep warehouse as a function of the warehouse utilization by a curve. For a warehouse utilization of 50%, the probability of stock transfers is 32%, for a utilization of 80%, the probability for stock transfers is 45% and at a utilization of 100% the probability is 50%. The probabilities for stock transfers in this investigation are higher. With a warehouse utilization of 50%, the probability for stock transfers is already 44%. Furthermore, probabilities for stock transfers of more than 50% appear. The number of stock transfers is determined by the retrievals. The retrievals depend on the orders. Hence, a stochastic process is given which is not considered in the static curve in [6]. By allowing the beginning of the allocation of a channel even if this can be avoided, the probability for stock transfers should become smaller. This will be analyzed in further investigations at the IPF.

IX. CONCLUSION

The state of the art in the literature comprises non-quantitative statements. By the simulation introduced here, quantitative results for concrete enterprises and warehouses, respectively, are delivered. Compared with the published results, the investigation proves partly clearly higher performance in the handling of goods and probabilities of stock transfers.

For a specific small highbay warehouse, the one of Leopold Fiebig GmbH in Karlsruhe, Germany, actual driving times were used by simulation. The results differ significantly from those results published in the literature. Finally, such an effective and efficient implementation is a good basis for newer approaches, which are elaborated in [15], among others.

For the concrete storage strategies, it was proven that all together, a combination of the strategies zones and channel causes the best results.

Preliminary measurements suggest that similar results are observed in other warehouses. Further development of this into significant measurements and results is one of the tasks at the IPF.

Methodically quite demanding, but very interesting, is a generalization of these results for as many warehouse types as possible. The IPF will also continue to research this problem in the future.

REFERENCES

[1] D. Arnold, „Materialflusslehre [Material Flow Theory]". Vieweg Verlag, 2nd edition, 1998.

[2] D. Arnold, „Materialfluss in Logistiksystemen [Material flow in logistic systems]". Springer-Verlag, 2005.

[3] T. Gudehus, „Grundlagen der Kommissioniertechnik [Basics of picking technology]". Verlag W. Girardet, Essen, 1973.

[4] T. Gudehus and H. Kotzab, „Comprehensive Logistics". Springer-Verlag, 2012.

[5] M. Heindl and F. Herrmann, „Verkürzung von Ein- und Auslagerzeiten in Lagerprozessen [Shortening of storage and retrieval times in warehouse processes]", in: PPS Management, GITO Verlag, Berlin, November (4) 2007, p. 47 – 50.

[6] C.R. Lippolt and D. Arnold, „Hochregallager mit doppelttiefer Lagerung [Highbay warehouse with double-deep storage]", in: F + H Fördern und Heben, 2004.

[7] S. Seemüller, „Durchsatzberechnung automatischer Kleinteilelager im Umfeld des elektronischen Handels [Throughput calculation of automatic small parts warehouses in the field of electronic commerce]", Technische Universität München, Diss., 2005.

[8] J.A. Tompkins and J.D. Smith (Editors), „The Warehouse Management Handbook" Tompkins, Raleigh, 1998.

[9] G. Richards, „Warehouse Management: The Definitive Guide to Improving Efficiency and Minimizing Costs in the Modern Warehouse", Kogan Page, 2021.

[10] J.A. Tompkins, J.A. White, Y.A. Bozer, E.H. Frazelle, J.M.A. Tanchovo, and J. Trevino, „Facilities Planning". Wiley, New York, 2nd edition, 1996.

[11] C.R. Lippolt and S. Blunck, „Zonenbildung in Hochregallagern bei beliebiger Lage der Übergabestellen am Regalrand [Zone formation in high-bay warehouses with any position of the transfer points at the edge of the rack]", in Operations Research Proceedings, Springer-Verlag, 2000.

[12] J. Heizer, B. Render, and C. Munson, "Principles of Operations Management: Sustainability and Supply Chain Management". Pearson Education Limited, 2020.

[13] R.V.Subrahmanyam, M.K. Kumar, S. Nair, S. Warrier, and B.N. Prashanth, "Design and development of automatic warehouse sorting rover", in Materialstoday: Proceedings, vol. 46, Part 10, pp. 4497 – 4503, 2021.

[14] D. Roy, S. Nigam, R. de Koster, I. Adan, and J. Resing, "Robot-storage zone assignment strategies in mobile fulfillment systems", in Transportation Research Part E: Logistics and Transportation Review, vol. 122, pp. 119 - 142, 2019.

[15] N. Sundararajan and R. Terkar, "Improving productivity in fastener manufacturing through the application of Lean-Kaizen principles", Materials Today: Proceedings, vol. 62, Part 2, pp. 1169 - 1178, 2022.

The Process-Simulation.Center

Prototype of an Integrated Management System for Research, Lectures, and Practice

Carlo Simon, Stefan Haag and Lara Zakfeld

Hochschule Worms
Erenburgerstr. 19, 67549 Worms, Germany
Email: {simon, haag, zakfeld}@hs-worms.de

Abstract—**Sustainability and plurality continue to gain significance for society and companies. Thus, the consequences of management decisions on environment and people must be predicted and optimized. To this end, multiperspective simulations of various aspects of dynamic systems become more and more important. There is need for adequate tools, and for people to conduct this challenging modeling and simulation work. The Process-Simulation.Center is an Integrated Management System for company-wide documentation and simulation of (business) processes using Petri nets, process maps and organizational charts. It stores the models in a central database, the P-S.C Cloud, and allows all members of an organization to access the models according to an elaborated rights concept. To ensure regulatory requirements, the models run through an approval process. These aspects distinguishes the Process-Simulation.Center from other university projects to develop software for modeling and simulation, and enable new applications of the Petri net methodology. This article presents the current prototype and its application in research, lectures, and practice.**

Keywords—**Prototype; Petri Nets; Process Map; Organigram; Integrated Management System.**

I. INTRODUCTION

Business information systems are build on the base of process, data, and organizational models and an integration of these perspectives. Processes are typically modeled using BPMN, as EPC, and rarely as flowcharts [1]. Petri nets are semantically richer. They facilitate analyses, complex simulations, and hence deep integration of the previously mentioned views. Surprisingly they are used more rarely. Probably there is a need to automatically enrich given other models to make this method more popular.

Illustrative teaching on Petri nets requires the use of software for modeling, simulation, and analysis. However, an evaluation of 91 Petri net tools published in [2] shows that these tools, typically developed at universities, are outdated or nor longer maintained. In [1], deficits in (also commercial) process management software with regard to resource-dependent simulation were also pointed out.

The works [3] and [4] explain how to teach basic Petri net modeling techniques, but exclude how to embed such models in Integrated Management Systems (IMS) and how to collaborate within such tools. A low-threshold offer for the use of an Integrated Management System based on Petri nets is missing so far.

This situation led to the development of the Process-Simulation.Center (*P-S.C*, [5]. It may be used free of charge by academic users. Other users can get a free trial access for three months. The *P-S.C* is currently denoted as a prototype following the notion of a prototype's definition [6]. It is used to test essential elements and functions of Highly Integrated Management Systems (HIMS), in particular cross-model and resource-dependent simulations, impossible with existing systems. As proposed during the presentation of [7] at the SIMUL 2021 conference, a multilingual user interface is also implemented.

Models are stored in the *P-S.C Cloud*. Users in the same mandators can edit their models together. The following functionalities have been implemented in the prototype, and are presented in more detail in this article:

1) The *P-S.C* features several products which allow for defining mandators for different target groups such as academics or companies.
2) Users of a mandator may have different authorization.
3) An approval workflow uses these different authorization concepts, thus, and models possess a life cycle. Changes to the models are tracked in a history.
4) Users may be grouped together.
5) The access to the models is controlled with the aid of user and group rights.

With the implementation of these concepts, the *P-S.C* now fulfills important requirements of Integrated Management Systems. Through this, also new teaching and learning content can be made tangible. The concrete technical and didactical implementation will be addressed in the following sections, inviting colleagues to also use the *P-S.C* in teaching and in their own projects.

The following Section II explains the development steps as well as the current status of the *P-S.C*. Then, the new mandator concept and the possibilities to organize users and models within a mandator are presented in Section III. Section IV explains the novel authorization concepts and the approval process. How to use the *P-S.C* on a daily basis is presented in Section V and how to gain the respective visualization for a simulated process is presented in Section VI. The paper closes with a conclusion and an outlook in Section VII.

II. Development of the P-S.C

The *P-S.C* is a tool for modeling and simulation of the structural and process-oriented organization of companies. For several years, the prototype is already in use for research, teaching, and industry transfer projects at Worms University. The development process combines recommendations of the Design Science Research Guidelines [8] and evolutionary prototyping [9].

Figure 1 shows the development stages of the prototype over the years. The *P-S.C* is constantly being further developed. In the last 18 months, key functions have been introduced which are the core elements of Integrated Management Systems.

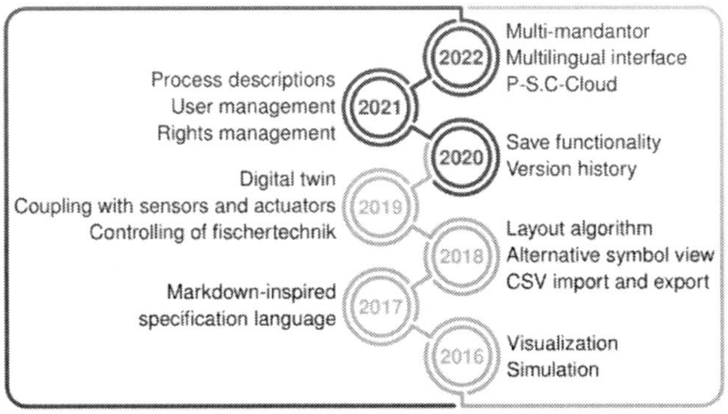

Figure 1. Milestones by Year.

The development of the *P-S.C* began in 2016 through the visualization of Petri nets in a web-based environment. In the first two years, the foundation for the later work was laid, in which Petri nets became simulatable and a markdown-inspired language for the specification of complex models was created. Meanwhile, the *P-S.C* is a tool for modeling and simulating simple and higher Petri nets with integration of swimlanes, for creating organizational charts, and for combining models using process maps (cf. [10]).

Since 2018, a layout algorithm accelerates the model development and makes it much faster compared to typical point-and-click UIs. Alternative symbols taken from the Font-awesome font set can be used to illustrate the models, and a CSV interface makes it easy to import data and export simulation results (cf. [11]).

Installed locally on a Raspberry Pi, the *P-S.C* has been able to access the GPIO interface of the Raspi since 2019. This way it may interact with external devices such as fischertechnik and can be used for plant control (cf. [12]) and as a digital twin. In addition to these techniques, case studies that explain how to create enterprise-wide process models, how to identify bottlenecks according to the Theory of Constraints, and how to simulate push and pull strategies in production processes have been integrated in the tool's internal tutorial.

Ever since the beginning of the development, this (internal) tutorial is constantly maintained and further developed. More than 80 examples explain how to use the tool, model with Petri nets, and solve challenging problems of dynamic systems with the aid of simulation.

The newly introduced *P-S.C Cloud* provides a simple way to store users' own models. In combination with the mandator concept, an authorization concept and an approval process have been implemented. Both are used extensively in teaching. Classes of students can be separated into groups. Exercises are assigned exclusively to the groups, and feedback is given using the approval process. Exercises, solutions, and feedback can be layouted with HTML5. Hence, techniques typically known from IMS are used to support learning processes.

In the meantime, more than 300 students have learned and worked using their own *P-S.C*-account. Their experiences and those gained through transfer projects with companies have been valuable sources for new requirements for the prototype.

The *P-S.C* has facilitated the development of new modeling and simulation techniques that have been presented on several international conferences. Especially at the SIMUL 2021, there was a request for a multilingual User Interface which has been fulfilled as of now. In addition to German, an English version of the *P-S.C* is available with the systems in place to support more.

To increase the visibility of this research work, the Group for Applied Process Simulation (GAPS) was founded at Worms University [13].

The most recently implemented milestones will be explained next in more detail in the course of this paper, and an outlook on the next steps will be given.

III. Mandators, Roles, Groups

The *P-S.C Cloud* is set up to serve different mandators simultaneously. As requested for a multi-mandator-capable system in [14], in the *P-S.C* the users of the different mandators can work without mutual insight into other peoples' data as if the environment were exclusively available to them.

The *P-S.C* supports various types of mandators for academic and professional purposes that account for different product categories. A first special (internal) mandator is *Tutorial*. A second special mandator is *Public*. It allows users to experience the possibilities of the *P-S.C* regarding modeling and simulation. Guests receive an account which is valid for three months and offers a limited number of own models separated from other users. They also have full access to the tutorial.

In all other mandators, several users can work together. Distinguished users with special roles can assign rights and duties and have the possibility to administrate their mandator as explained for mandator *Academic* next:

Mandator *Academic* establishes the roles *Admin*, *Lecturer* and *Student*: *Admin* users can add other users and define their roles. *Lecturer* users define learning groups and assign (other) users to them. They also create models or assign new modeling tasks in the descriptions of models that are assigned to the different groups. *Lecturer* users can also codify the user and group rights of models and, thus, their visibility within the mandator. Finally, they play a decisive role in the approval process. *Student* users have full access to the tutorial, work together in their groups, can submit solutions by requesting approval for their models, or take on specific responsibilities as process owners within their group.

The processes around enrollment and organization of learning groups are shown in Figure 2, where the *places* represent the information that arises, and the *transitions* represent the activities conducted according to the *swimlanes*: new users that register with the system initially receive a *Guest* role. If the registration mail address is related to an Academic mandate, an *Admin* user can enroll *Guest* users in the corresponding mandator and assign *Lecturer* or *Student* roles. *Lecturer* users then can define groups and assign *Student* users to them.

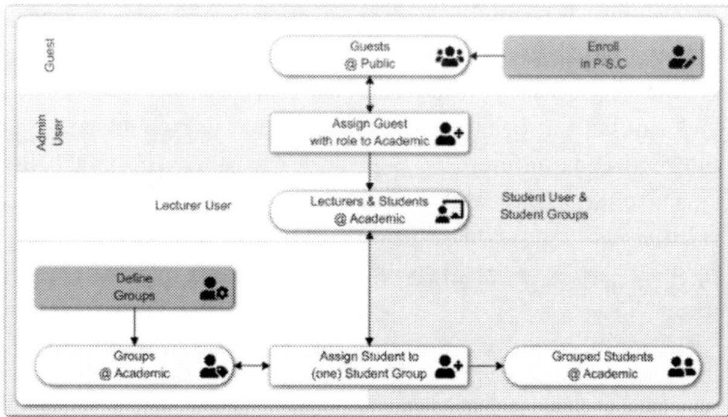

Figure 2. Petri Net Model: Enroll in Mandators and Organize Learning Groups (P-S.C export)

IV. Models, Rights, and Approval Process

Within a mandator, rights control which users may access which models. The following access modes are distinguished:

1) View a model without its specification.
2) Comment on a model.
3) See a model including its specification.
4) Simulate a model.
5) Change the working version of a model.
6) Ask for approval of a model.

In the current prototype, models cannot yet be commented.

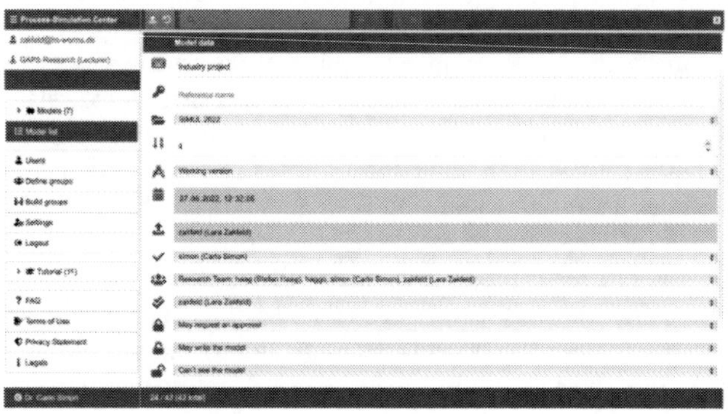

Figure 3. Rights Management of a Model (P-S.C Screenshot)

The *P-S.C*-screenshot in Figure 3 shows the possible settings per model. The rights can be defined separately for the process owner (🔒), users of the group (🔒) and all other users (🔓) where the opening of the lock symbolizes the extension of the numbers of users that might have access. The *P-S.C* adopts the most general right of a user that holds with respect to a specific model.

For all kinds of the aforementioned users, the different six rights are simply codified with the aid of drop-down menus. Also, other settings for each model can be made here.

Lecturer users can create new models, assign them to other users and groups, obligate a process owner, and also give permission to other interested members.

Models are initially created as *Working version*. When students have solved their modeling task, they release it for approval which is expressed by the state *Approval requested*. *Lecturer* users and the *Student* users can revoke the request for their own models, but *Lecturer* users also may accept the request and the model state changes to *Approved*. If a further working version is created for the model and the approval process is executed another time, formerly approved versions change their state to *Archived*. These models can still be read from the history log.

V. The Process-Simulation.Center Our Simulation Lab

The following insights in how the working group GAPS uses the tool might give a better comprehension of its possibilities. The tool is used for research, teaching and in first industrial projects. To separate these concerns from each other, each work focus has its own mandator. Currently, GAPS uses four active *P-S.C* mandators in parallel:

- The *GAPS* research mandator.
- *Academic* mandators for two different student groups.
- A mandator *Consulting* for an industry project.

Figure 4 shows a screenshot of the *P-S.C* with the (foldable) menu on the left side. The entire user interface and the settings are now available in German and English. Further languages can be added easily if required.

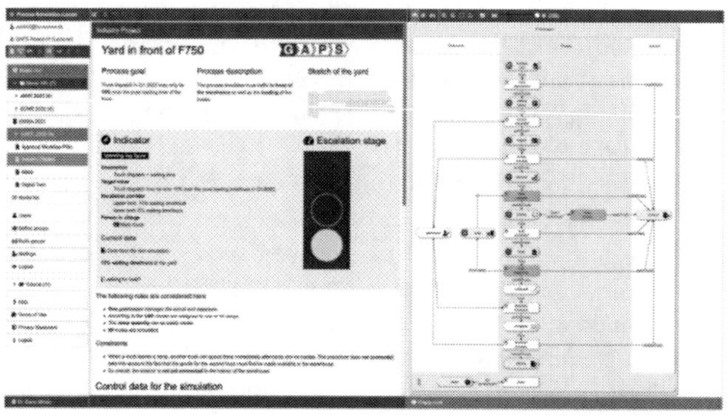

Figure 4. English user interface of the *P-S.C* (P-S.C Screenshot)

For each model, there are three views (from left to right):

- A model description.
- The model as a graph.

- The model specification codified in a special markdown language (not shown here).

This operating concept that differs from usual point-and-click interfaces, facilitates a rapid development of complex scenarios with a consistent visual appearance because of the implemented layout algorithms.

VI. From Model to Visualization

Modeling processes, running simulations, and presenting results in an appealing and helpful visualization outlines the entire journey along the simulation pipeline [15]. Due to the last development steps, this is fully possible in the *P-S.C*. Important functional elements of *P-S.C* coalesce. The CSV interface enables the use of externally provided simulation input data, tracking of the Petri net firing sequences, and an export of the markings of specific places. This data can then be visualized in external BI tools. One medium-term goal is a lively, automatically generated visualization based on the real data within the tool itself.

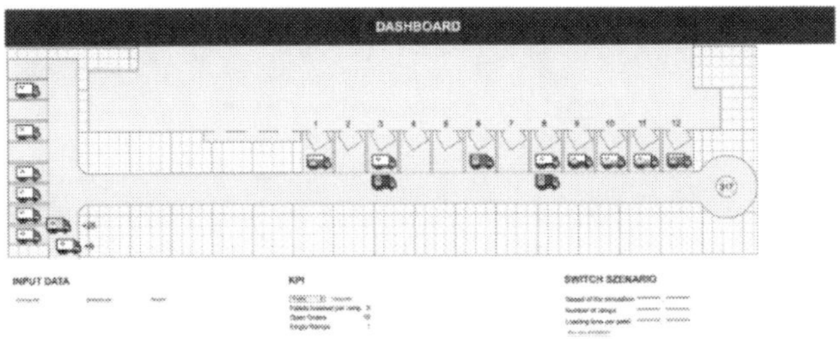

Figure 5. Dashboard Visualization of a Warehouse Front Yard

As an example, Figure 5 illustrates how to derive a visualization from a simulation model with a dashboard - in this case the yard of a warehouse (the model depicted in Figure 4). This approach enables people to see and understand data [16], offers a visual uniform representation and gives an active assistance to decision makers on the basis of current data [10].

What is represented here is the simplification of a real world example. A logistics provider simulates possible scenarios of an upcoming warehouse with the *P-S.C*. The Petri net of Figure 4 simulates all movements of trucks and protocols them on place *Protocol* at the right border. These series of numbers are exported and then translated into an animated dashboard where all truck movements can be observed. Due to the general nature of Petri nets, application to any other industries and processes are also possible.

An appealing visualization quickly awakens new ideas and user needs such as an interactive dashboard where input into the dashboard is looped back into the simulation. Likely, this will be a future requirement for the *P-S.C*. A short-term requirement for the tool that can be seen as a preparatory step is: having interactive elements for the description, for example a monitor for the current filling of a specific place.

VII. Conclusion

The development phases show a constantly evolving prototype. New features are evaluated in terms of their cost-benefit ratio in terms of new opportunities for users. Good examples are the multilingual user interface or the *P-S.C Cloud*, which facilitate the use of the tool for each group.

Such new features also enable students to use the *P-S.C* for intra-corporate theses. Some of the scenarios they have to model in their companies are also challenging from a research perspective, especially if they face multiperspective considerations and problems how to increase sustainability.

The working group observes that formerly separated activities merge and that in a next step this multidisciplinarity opens new fields of applications also for other industries.

References

[1] C. Simon, S. Haag, and L. Zakfeld, "Requirements for Highly Integrated Management Systems - Simulation Expands Past-oriented Documentation to Future-oriented Optimization," in *Proceedings of The Thirteenth International Conference on Advances in System Simulation (SIMUL)*. Barcelona, Spain: IARIA, 2021, pp. 58–64.

[2] C. Simon, "Web-Based Simulation Of Production Schedules With High-Level Petri Nets," in *ECMS 2018: 32rd International ECMS Conference on Modelling and Simulation*, L. Nolle, A. Burger, C. Tholena, J. Werner, and J. Wellhausen, Eds. Wilhelmshaven, Germany: SCS Europe, 2018, pp. 275–281.

[3] J. F. i Jové, A. Guasch, P. F. i Casas, and J. Casanovas, "Teaching system modelling and simulation through Petri Nets and Arena," *Proceedings of the Winter Simulation Conference 2014*, pp. 3662–3673, 2014.

[4] D. Gasevic and V. Devedzic, "Teaching petri nets using p3." *Educational Technology and Society*, vol. 7, pp. 153–166, 2004.

[5] C. Simon, "The Process-Simulation.Center," https://process-simulation.center/ (last accessed 12.09.2022), 2022, PSC.

[6] R. Budde, K. Kautz, K. Kuhlenkamp, and H. Züllighoven, *Prototyping*. Berlin, Heidelberg, Germany: Springer, 1992.

[7] C. Simon, L. Zakfeld, C. E. Jensen, D. Klietsch, and M. Montag, "Can simulation prevent companies from the bullwhip trap? New approaches to model the bullwhip effect with the aid of Excel and high-level Petri nets," in *Proceedings of The Thirteenth International Conference on Advances in System Simulation (SIMUL)*. Barcelona, Spain: IARIA, 2021, pp. 31–37.

[8] A. R. Hevner, S. T. March, J. Park, and S. Ram, "Design Science in Information Systems Research," *MIS Q.*, vol. 28, no. 1, pp. 75–105, Mar 2004.

[9] C. Floyd, "A Systematic Look at Prototyping," in *Approaches to Prototyping*. Berlin, Heidelberg: Springer, 1984, pp. 1–18.

[10] C. Simon, S. Haag, and L. Zakfeld, "Stratification of Timed Petri-nets at the Example of a Production Process," in *ECMS 2022: 36th International ECMS Conference on Modelling and Simulation*, 2022, pp. 128–134.

[11] C. Simon and S. Haag, "Simulatable Reference Models To Transform Enterprises For The Digital Age – A Case Study," in *European Conference on Modeling and Simulation (Wildau, DEU)*. Saarbrücken, Germany: Pirrot, 2020, pp. 294–300.

[12] C. Simon and S. Haag, "Digitale Zwillinge modellieren und verstehen - Eine Fallstudie zum problembasierten und forschenden Lernen," in *Modellierung: Modellierung in der Hochschullehre (Wien, AUT)*. Aachen, Germany: CEUR-WS, 2020, pp. 101–112, In English: *Model and understand digital twins*.

[13] C. Simon, S. Haag, and L. Zakfeld, "GAPS," https://www.hs-worms.de/en/gaps/ (last accessed 12.09.22), 2022, GAPS.

[14] H. R. Hansen, J. Mendling, and G. Neumann, *Wirtschaftsinformatik*, 12th ed. Berlin: De Gruyter - Oldenbourg, 2019, In English: *Business Information Systems*.

[15] C. Simon, S. Haag, and L. Zakfeld, "Research-Agenda for Process Simulation Dashboards," in *European Conference on Modeling and Simulation (Kuwait, KWT)*. Saarbrücken, Germany: Pirrot, 2021, pp. 243–249.

[16] S. Few, *Information Dashboard Design: Displaying Data for At-A-Glance Monitoring*, 1st ed. CA: Analytics Press, 2013.

International Academy, Research, and Industry Association (IARIA)
412 Derby Way
Wilmington, DE 19810

ISBN 978-1-7138-6970-2

CURRAN ASSOCIATES INC.
proceedings.com

109th Annual Meeting of the South Dakota Academy of Science

Proceedings of the South Dakota Academy of Science
Volume 103

Aberdeen, South Dakota, USA
19-20 April 2024

South Dakota Academy of Science